AL-SANŪSĪ

GREAT MEDIEVAL THINKERS

Series Editor
Brian Davies
Fordham University

DUNS SCOTUS
Richard Cross

BERNARD OF CLAIRVAUX
G. R. Evans

JOHN SCOTTUS ERIUGENA
Deirdre Carabine

ROBERT GROSSETESTE
James McEvoy

BOETHIUS
John Marenbon

PETER LOMBARD
Philipp W. Rosemann

ABELARD AND HELOISE
Constant J. Mews

BONAVENTURE
Christopher M. Cullen

AL-KINDĪ
Peter Adamson

ANSELM
Sandra Visser and Thomas Williams

JOHN WYCLIF
Stephen Edmund Lahey

JOHN BURIDAN
Gyula Klima

HUGH OF SAINT VICTOR
Paul Rorem

AVICENNA
Jon McGinnis

ROBERT HOLCOT
John T. Slotemaker and Jeffrey C. Witt

ROBERT KILWARDBY
José Filipe Silva

AL-RĀZĪ
Peter Adamson

AL-SANŪSĪ
Khaled El-Rouayheb

AL-SANŪSĪ

KHALED EL-ROUAYHEB

OXFORD
UNIVERSITY PRESS

OXFORD
UNIVERSITY PRESS

Oxford University Press is a department of the University of Oxford. It furthers the University's objective of excellence in research, scholarship, and education by publishing worldwide. Oxford is a registered trade mark of Oxford University Press in the UK and in certain other countries.

Published in the United States of America by Oxford University Press
198 Madison Avenue, New York, NY 10016, United States of America.

Library of Congress Cataloging-in-Publication Data
Names: El-Rouayheb, Khaled author
Title: Al-Sanūsī / Khaled El-Rouayheb.
Description: New York, NY : Oxford University Press, [2026] |
Series: Great medieval thinkers | Includes bibliographical references and index. |
Identifiers: LCCN 2025044154 (print) | LCCN 2025044155 (ebook) |
ISBN 9780197835647 paperback | ISBN 9780197835630 hardback |
ISBN 9780197835678 | ISBN 9780197835654 epub
Subjects: LCSH: Sanūsī, Muḥammad ibn Yūsuf, approximately 1427–approximately 1490
Classification: LCC B753.S264 E47 2025 (print) | LCC B753.S264 (ebook)
LC record available at https://lccn.loc.gov/2025044154
LC ebook record available at https://lccn.loc.gov/2025044155

DOI: 10.1093/oso/9780197835630.001.0001

Paperback printed by Integrated Books International, United States of America
Hardback printed by by Lightning Source, Inc., United States of America

MIX
Paper
FSC FSC® C183721

The manufacturer's authorized representative in the EU for product safety is Oxford University Press España S.A. of Parque Empresarial San Fernando de Henares, Avenida de Castilla, 2 – 28830 Madrid (www.oup.es/en or product.safety@oup.com).
OUP España S.A. also acts as importer into Spain of products made by the manufacturer.

Contents

Series Foreword ix
Acknowledgments xiii
Transliteration Conventions xv
Abbreviations of Frequently Cited Works xvii

1. Introduction 1

2. Life, Works, and Intellectual Milieu 6
   1 Tlemcen 6
   2 Sanūsī: Student and scholar 8
   3 Sanūsī the saint 11
   4 Works 14
   5 Ash'arism in North Africa 17
   6 Ash'arism: East and West 26

3. The Condemnation of Imitation 31
   1 Imitation in the Ash'ari tradition 32
   2 Sanūsī's condemnation of imitation 40
   3 Did Sanūsī moderate his position in later works? 49
   4 "Fossilized Conservatism"? 53

4. What Every Believer Should Know 57
   1 What is necessarily and impossibly true of God 58
   2 Different types of divine attribute 59
   3 Proof of God's existence 61
   4 Proofs of God's attributes of negation 64
   5 Proofs of God's entitative attributes 67
   6 What is contingently true of God 69
   7 What is necessarily and impossibly true of God's prophets 72
   8 What is contingently true of the prophets 75
   9 The two professions 77
   10 Is the average believer expected to be a philosopher? 79

5. Logic 84
1 Background 86
2 *The Epitome of Logic*: An overview 89
3 The *Commentary on the Epitome*: A closer look 96
4 Sanūsī's impact 112

6. Proofs for the Existence of God 114
1 Background 115
2 First proof 118
3 Sanūsī's first proof and the question of natural causation 125
4 Second proof 128
5 Sanūsī's proofs and "the Avicennian turn" 138

7. The Divine Attributes 141
1 Per se attributes 141
2 Negative attributes 143
3 Entitative attributes 149
4 The Aristotelian–Neoplatonist philosophers on the attributes 155
5 The seven core attributes 159
6 The eternality and immutability of the divine attributes 163
7 Sanūsī and his sources 166

8. Occasionalism 169
1 Power and Will: Their attachments 170
2 The proof of God's oneness 176
3 The creation of human acts 179
4 Sanūsī and Juwaynī compared 188
5 Sanūsī on medicine 189

9. Some Older Theological Controversies 195
1 God's Speech 196
2 Are good and bad known by natural reason? 206
3 Must God tell us the truth? 213

10. From Knowledge to Works 220
1 Occasionalist ethics 221
2 Occasionalism and the benefits of litanies and invocations 236
3 *The Tried and Tested Means* 241

Series Foreword

Many people would be surprised to be told that there *were* any great medieval thinkers. If a *great* thinker is one from whom we can learn today, and if 'medieval' serves as an adjective for describing anything which existed from (roughly) the years 600 to 1500 AD, then, so it is often supposed, medieval thinkers cannot be called 'great'.

Why not? One answer often given appeals to ways in which medieval authors with a taste for argument and speculation tend to invoke 'authorities', especially religious ones. Such subservience to authority is not the stuff of which great thought is made—so it is often said. It is also frequently said that greatness is not to be found in the thinking of those who lived before the rise of modern science, not to mention that of modern philosophy and theology. Students of science are nowadays hardly ever referred to literature earlier than the seventeenth century.

Students of philosophy are often taught nothing about the history of ideas between Aristotle (384–322 BC.) and Descartes (1596–1650). Contemporary students of theology are often encouraged to believe that significant theological thinking is largely a product of the nineteenth century.

Yet the origins of modern science lie in the conviction that the world is open to rational investigation and is orderly rather than chaotic—a conviction which came fully to birth, and was systematically explored and developed, during the middle ages. And it is in medieval authors that we find some of the most sophisticated and rigorous discussions ever offered in the areas of philosophy and theology—not surprisingly, perhaps, if we note that medieval philosophers and theologians, like their contemporary counterparts, were often university teachers (or something like that) who participated in an ongoing world-wide debate and were not (like many seventeenth, eighteenth, and even nineteenth century philosophers and theologians), working in relative isolation from a large community of teachers and students with whom they were regularly involved. As for the question of appeal to authority: it is certainly true that many medieval thinkers believed in authority (especially religious authority) as a serious court of appeal. But as contemporary philosophers are increasingly reminding us, authority is as much an ingredient in our thinking as it was for medieval authors. For most of what we take ourselves to know derives from the trust we have reposed in our various teachers, colleagues, friends, and acquaintances. When it comes to reliance on authority, the main difference between us and medieval thinkers lies in the fact that their reliance on authority (in so far as they display it) was often more focused and explicitly acknowledged than it is by us. It does not lie in the fact that it was uncritical and naive in a way that our reliance on authority is not.

In recent years, such truths have come to be recognized at what we might call the 'academic' level. No longer disposed to think of the middle ages as 'dark' (meaning 'lacking in intellectual richness'), many university departments (and many publishers of books and journals) now devote a lot of their energy to the study of medieval authors. And they do so not simply on the assumption that medieval writers are historically significant but also in the light of the increasingly developing insight that they have things to say from which we might learn.

Following an extended period in which medieval thinking was thought to be of only antiquarian interest, we are now witnessing its revival as a contemporary voice—one with which to converse.

The *Great Medieval Thinkers* series reflects and is part of this exciting revival. Written by a distinguished team of experts, it aims to provide substantial introductions to a range of medieval authors. And it does so on the assumption that they are as worth reading today as they were when they wrote. Students of medieval 'literature' (e.g., the writings of Chaucer) are currently well supplied (if not over-supplied) with secondary works to aid them when reading the objects of their concern. But those with an interest in medieval philosophy and theology are by no means so fortunate when it comes to reliable and accessible volumes. The *Great Medieval Thinkers* series aspires to remedy that deficiency by concentrating on medieval philosophers and theologians, and by offering solid overviews of their lives and thought coupled with contemporary reflection on what they had to say. Taken individually, volumes in the series provide valuable treatments of single thinkers, many of whom are not currently covered by any comparable volumes. Taken together, they will constitute a rich and distinguished history and discussion of medieval philosophy and theology considered as a whole. With an eye on college and university students, and with an eye on the general reader, authors of volumes in the series strive to write in a clear and accessible manner so that each of the thinkers they write on can be learned about by those who have no previous knowledge about them. But each contributor to the series also intends to inform, engage, and generally entertain even those with specialist knowledge in the area of medieval thinking. So, as well as surveying and introducing, volumes in the series seek to advance the state of medieval studies both at the historical and the speculative level.

The subject of the present one is the North African Muḥammad ibn Yūsūf al-Sanūsī (d.1490), who wrote a series of works on natural theology and logic that were widely studied and commented upon until the end of the nineteenth century, especially in Islamic Africa but also beyond. Sanūsī has been long neglected even by specialists in medieval Islamic philosophy and theology. Yet his writings deserve to be recognized as containing major contributions to the Islamic theological tradition and are strikingly original in certain respects. This book is the first monograph in any Western language devoted to Sanūsī, and it fills a major gap in our understanding of him.

Brian Davies

Acknowledgments

I thank Brian Davies for agreeing to consider my book proposal for the Great Medieval Thinkers series, and the anonymous reviewers for Oxford University Press for their encouragement and suggestions for improvement. My thinking on a number of issues relevant to Sanūsī has benefited from discussions with Peter Adamson, Michael Cook, Jon McGinnis, Abdurrahman Mihirig, Caitlyn Olsen, Jan Thiele, and Rob Wisnovsky, though they are in no way responsible for any remaining idiosyncrasies, inaccuracies, and infelicities.

The greater part of the book was written during a sabbatical leave from Harvard University in 2024–2025. I am grateful for Harvard's generous leave policy, without which this book would have been delayed substantially, if written at all.

Last but not least, my loving family gave me the space and time to ponder, read, and write, and put up with the chronic absentmindedness of an academic immersed in a project.

Transliteration Conventions

All translations from the Arabic are my own, unless otherwise indicated. Quotations from the Quran follow Alan Jones, *The Qur'ān* (Gibb Memorial Trust, 2007). For transliterations from the Arabic, I follow the system of the *Journal of Islamic Studies*. For readers unfamiliar with such transliterations: the ā, ī, and ū indicate that the vowels are long (so Sanūsī is pronounced "Sanuusii"), and the ḍ, ḥ, ṣ, ṭ, and ẓ stand for Arabic consonants whose closest approximations in English are emphatic or guttural d, h, s, t, and z. The ʾ (e.g., in al-Jazāʾirī) is a glottal stop. The ʿ (e.g., in the proper name ʿAlī) is a voiced pharyngeal consonant that is often elided in pronunciation by non-Arabs or marked by a more guttural pronunciation of the ensuing vowel.

When giving the attributives of medieval Islamic scholars, I usually retain the definite article *al-* on first mention but not thereafter. So, for example, I have "al-Ghazālī (d.1111)" on first mention in a chapter, and "Ghazālī" thereafter. The exceptions are cases in which the definite article is part of a genitive construction (e.g., "Ibn al-Tilimsānī") or when leaving it out may lead to confusion (e.g., "al-Ashʿarī" for the eponymous founder of a school of theology and "Ashʿari" for the school itself).

Abbreviations of Frequently Cited Works

By Sanūsī

K	*Sharḥ al-ʿAqīda al-Kubrá*. Edited by Anas Muḥammad ʿAdnān al-Sharfāwī. Damascus: Dār al-Taqwá, 2019.
W	*Sharḥ al-ʿAqīda al-Wusṭá*. Edited by Anas Muḥammad ʿAdnān al-Sharfāwī. Damascus: Dār al-Taqwá, 2019.
S	*Sharḥ al-ʿAqīda al-Ṣughrá*. Edited by Anas Muḥammad ʿAdnān al-Sharfāwī. Damascus: Dār al-Taqwá, 2019.
SS	*Sharḥ Ṣughrá l-Ṣughrá*. Edited by Anas Muḥammad ʿAdnān al-Sharfāwī. Damascus: Dār al-Taqwá, 2019.
M	*Sharḥ al-Muqaddimāt*. Edited by Anas Muḥammad ʿAdnān al-Sharfāwī. Damascus: Dār al-Taqwá, 2019.
MS	*al-Manhaj al-sadīd fī sharḥ Kifāyat al-murīd*. Edited by Muṣṭafá Marzūqī. ʿAyn Malīla: Dār al-Hudá, 1994.
MM	*Sharḥ Mukhtaṣar al-manṭiq*. Cairo: No publisher indicated, 1292/1875.

By Mallālī

MQ	*al-Mawāhib al-quddūsiyya fī l-manāqib al-Sanūsiyya*. Edited by ʿAllāl Būrbīq. Algiers: Dār Kardāda, 2011.

1
Introduction

The North African scholar Muḥammad ibn Yūsuf al-Sanūsī (1436–1490), from Tlemcen in what is today Algeria, is one of the most influential theologians and logicians in the Islamic tradition. Very few contributors to those two fields were as widely read for so many centuries over so great an area of the Islamic world. And if one focuses on theologians and logicians from Islamic Africa, Sanūsī is undoubtedly *the* most impactful figure. As late as the second half of the nineteenth century, his works were still standard handbooks at the prestigious al-Azhar college in Cairo, being printed on several occasions by the scholarly printing presses there, often with the commentaries and glosses of prominent Egyptian religious scholars such as Ibrāhīm al-Bājūrī (d.1860) and Muḥammad 'Illaysh (d.1882).[1] Especially his *Short Creed* must be reckoned one of the most popular creedal works in Islamic history. It was studied for centuries throughout Islamic Africa, in adjacent regions of the Levant and western Arabia, as well as in the Malay Archipelago. The sheer number of its commentaries, glosses, annotations, and versifications is testimony to its influence. It was also translated or adapted into Berber, Fulfulde, Turkish, Javanese, and Malay.[2]

Given this impact, the reader may expect Sanūsī to be a relatively well-researched figure. But modern Western scholarship has been conspicuously sparse. The present book is in fact the first monograph on Sanūsī in English or any other European language. The stark mismatch between powerful historical impact and modest modern scholarly interest is related to an influential account of Islamic history that took shape in the second half of the nineteenth century and the early decades of the twentieth among both Western

Al-Sanūsī. Khaled El-Rouayheb, Oxford University Press.
 DOI: 10.1093/oso/9780197835630.003.0001

orientalists and many Muslim thinkers. According to that account, Islamic civilization enjoyed its golden age during the Abbasid Caliphate (750–1258) and subsequently underwent a long period of stagnation or decline that only came to an end in the modern period with the onset of sustained European influence and the efforts of so-called revivers and reformers from the Muslim world. From this perspective, one might concede that Sanūsī was very influential in large parts of the Islamic world until the nineteenth century, and yet still dismiss his work as representative of an intellectually impoverished era that will not repay careful study.

This basic presumption of late-medieval stagnation or decline has colored numerous histories of Islamic theology and logic. A widespread tendency, discernable already in Duncan Black Macdonald's *Development of Muslim Theology, Jurisprudence and Constitutional Theory* (1903) and A.S. Tritton's *Muslim Theology* (1947), was to focus on Islamic rational theology in the early, formative centuries, then—after al-Ghazālī (d.1111)—shift the focus toward later mystics as well as purist critics of rational theology such as Ibn Taymiyya (d.1328), and then jump many centuries ahead to the modern Islamic reform movements.[3] The later premodern tradition of Islamic rational theology was obviously assumed to have been moribund and unworthy of detailed discussion. This assumption was spelled out in very influential surveys from the middle decades of the twentieth century. In Louis Gardet and George Anawati's *Introduction à la théologie musulmane* (1948), Sanūsī is described as a representative of "fossilized conservatism" (*conservatisme figé*).[4] In W. Montgomery Watt's *Islamic Philosophy and Theology* (1962), the period between 1250 and 1900 is termed "The Age of Darkness," and Sanūsī is mentioned briefly in a very short chapter titled "The Sclerosis of Philosophical Theology."[5] The same disparagement of the period after the thirteenth century is explicit in Nicholas Rescher's *The Development of Arabic Logic* (1964). Rescher briefly mentioned Sanūsī and his works, albeit as a representative of the later "ossified" tradition of "schoolmasters" who continued to teach logic but without making any substantial contributions to the field.[6]

Yet, such damning assessments do not stand up to scrutiny. Rescher clearly did not study the later Arabic works on logic that he so sweepingly dismissed. He simply inferred that they were derivative and uninspired from the fact that they regularly took the form of commentaries and glosses on condensed madrasa handbooks, the underlying presumption—now largely discredited—being that such literary forms are necessarily pedantic and unoriginal. As I will show in Chapter 5, Sanūsī, though not iconoclastic, discussed advanced topics in logic, reflected critically on received doctrine, and adjudicated earlier controversies. His widely studied *Epitome of Logic* is also distinctive in significant ways—much more formally oriented—when compared to standard handbooks in the Turco-Persianate world.

In their assessment of Sanūsī as a theologian, Gardet, Anawati, and Watt only consulted his shorter theological writings addressed to beginning students or non-scholars. As I will try to show throughout this book, his longer, more advanced theological works, largely ignored in twentieth-century scholarship, deserve to be recognized as substantial contributions to a long-standing, sophisticated tradition. Even the significance of Sanūsī's shorter, more popular creeds is missed entirely if they are written off as stale reiterations or vulgarizations of the doctrines of earlier, more vigorous centuries. They rather reflected Sanūsī's conviction, for which he argued at length in his major theological works, that it is the individual duty of all believers to go beyond unthinking conformism in creedal matters. An individual who is nominally a Muslim but cannot justify his or her creedal beliefs rationally is, according to Sanūsī, either a sinner who is neglecting a religious duty or not truly a believer at all and will suffer accordingly on Judgment Day. Far from being fossilized conservatism, this was a radical and controversial view that was fervently resisted by many of Sanūsī's contemporaries, as will be detailed in Chapter 3 below.

The conviction that Islamic thought stagnated or declined after the fall of Baghdad to the Mongols in 1258, so dominant for much of the twentieth century, has been undone in recent decades. Scholars of Islamic philosophy, theology, law, science, Sufism, and belles-lettres have begun to recover some of the unjustly neglected intellectual and literary traditions of later centuries. The shift has been dramatic and is perhaps comparable to the successful effort by Western medievalists in the late nineteenth and early twentieth centuries to overturn the inherited image of a European "dark age" between classical antiquity and the Renaissance. At least when it comes to Islamic philosophy and theology, much of the recent research on later, so-called "postclassical" centuries—roughly from 1200 to 1800—has focused on thinkers from the Islamic East. It is important to redress the balance by giving due attention to figures from Islamic Africa. Sanūsī's works are foundational for the later African-Islamic theological and logical traditions, and this is surely sufficient justification for a book on him. I have tried to write it so that it can be read profitably even without prior knowledge of Islamic theology and philosophy, and have done my best to introduce background information when needed. I also hope the book, treating as it does a little-studied figure and regional tradition, will be of interest to more advanced readers in my field.

The extant writings of Sanūsī span a wide range of subjects besides theology and logic, including the science of hadith (the sayings and doings of the Prophet Muhammad), the astrolabe, and the mathematically demanding Islamic laws of inheritance. Trying to do justice to his contributions to all these disciplines would have come at the expense of depth. In what follows, I focus on his theological and logical writings that were, uncontroversially, the most impactful for later centuries.[7] In Chapter 2, I survey his life, writings, and intellectual milieu. In Chapter 3, I present his attack on imitation or conformism when it comes to creedal commitment and his insistence that every adult and sane believer should learn both the core articles of faith and their rational groundings.

In Chapter 4, I discuss his shorter creedal works, which give a sense of what he wanted all believers to know. Chapter 5 is devoted to Sanūsī's logical writings, especially the influential *Epitome of Logic*. Thereafter, I turn to his proofs for the existence of God (Chapter 6), his discussion of God's attributes (Chapter 7), his defense of occasionalism—the view that only God has causal power (Chapter 8), his intervention in two older theological controversies: the nature of God's Speech and whether there are objective values known by natural reason independently of revelation (Chapter 9), and his Sufi-inflected views on the practical-ethical consequences of the foregoing creedal commitments (Chapter 10). A concluding chapter will outline the reception of his works down to the modern period.

Sanūsī's theological works are tightly argued and often polemical. I have sought to be charitable throughout my exposition, but did not think it feasible or helpful to present his arguments and counterarguments while bracketing entirely my own sense of their strength or weakness. After all, it would be curious to place on a pedestal a thinker who so passionately emphasized the importance of thinking things through, as opposed to uncritically following the lead of others.

2

Life, Works, and Intellectual Milieu

The Andalusian scholar Aḥmad al-Balawī (d.1532) was in Tlemcen, in what is now western Algeria, in the years 1489–1491, hoping to study with leading scholars of the town and obtain prestigious certificates from them. He was mostly successful, though not in the case of the celebrated theologian Muḥammad ibn Yūsuf al-Sanūsī. He went to the small mosque where Sanūsī held forth (now known as the Mosque of Sidi Sanūsī) and was struck by the number of people in attendance, including not only students but also commoners. Students took turns reading in front of Sanūsī, with one of them holding an hourglass to make sure that time was fairly allotted. Balawī dearly wanted an individual reading session but did not press the matter, thinking there was time. And then Sanūsī passed away, in his mid-fifties, on May 9, 1490. Balawī noted that the funeral the next day was attended by throngs of people, "from the Sultan and down."[1] Sanūsī was buried in the cemetery between the city wall and the extramural suburb of ʿUbbād that grew around the shrine of the city's patron saint Abū Madyan (d.1198). The tomb itself later became enclosed by a mausoleum (*qubba*) that has survived until the present day. A French tourist guide from 1921 described it as the most venerated shrine in the cemetery.[2]

1 Tlemcen

Balawī's studies in Tlemcen were part of an established pattern. In the fourteenth and fifteenth centuries, the town was, with Tunis and Fes, the most important Islamic center of learning west of

Al-Sanūsī. Khaled El-Rouayheb, Oxford University Press.
 DOI: 10.1093/oso/9780197835630.003.0002

Cairo. As such, it attracted students from the wider region, for example, from Islamic Spain and the North African towns of Melilla, Oran, Oujda, Algiers, and Béjaïa. A thriving metropolis of an estimated 80,000 people, Tlemcen was in this period an important link in the trans-Saharan trade and maintained strong commercial ties to Granada, Aragon, and the Italian city-states.[3] Since the mid-thirteenth century, it had been the capital of the Zayyānid—also called the ʿAbd al-Wādid—dynasty that held effective power over the central Maghreb, between Morocco (ruled by the Marinid and later the Saʿdid dynasties) and Tunisia (ruled by the Ḥafṣids), though at various times they acknowledged the suzerainty of their western or eastern neighbors. The life of Sanūsī would overlap with the relatively stable and prosperous rule of two sultans: Abū ʿAbbās Aḥmad I (r.1431–1462) and Abū ʿAbdallah Muḥammad IV (r.1468–1504). The latter was the Sultan who, according to Balawī, attended Sanūsī's funeral.

Leo Africanus, writing in the early decades of the sixteenth century, described "the great city of Telensin" which he estimated was home to around "sixteen thousand families." He wrote (in passing betraying his partiality for his birth town Fes):

> Here each trade and occupation hath a peculiar place, after the manner of Fez, saving that the buildings of Fez are somewhat more stately. Here are also many and beautiful temples [*sic*], having their Mahumetan priests and preachers. Likewise here are five colleges most sumptuously built, some by the king of Telensin, and some by the king of Fez. Here also are store of goodly baths and hothouses, albeit they have not such plenty of water as is at Fez. Also here are very many inns built after the manner of Africa: unto two of which inns the merchants of Genoa and Venice do usually resort [. . .] The city-wall is very high and impregnable, having five great gates upon it, at every one of which there is placed a guard of soldiers, and certain receivers of the king's custom [. . .] The south part of the city is

> inhabited by Jews, lawyers, and notaries: here are also very many students, and professors of diverse arts, which have maintenance allowed them out of the five forenamed colleges.[4]

It was only over the course of the Ottoman period that Tlemcen would be overshadowed by other towns in the central Maghreb, especially Algiers. When the French occupied the town in 1842, it was a shadow of its former self, with a population of around 20,000 people.[5]

2 Sanūsī: Student and scholar

Almost all biographical information about Sanūsī can be traced back to a lengthy hagiography composed two years after his death by his student Muḥammad b. ʿUmar al-Mallālī. Sanūsī told Mallālī, one or two years before he died in 1490, that he was fifty-five years old (by the Islamic Hijri calendar), corroborating Balawī's statement that Sanūsī was fifty-six (Hijri years old) when he died and implying that he was born in 1436.[6] The attributive "Sanūsī" derives from the Snous tribe that occupied the highlands southwest of Tlemcen. The tribe was Berber-speaking until at least the early twentieth century, speaking a dialect closer to the Berbers of northeastern Morocco (Riff and Iznasen) than to the Kabyle Berbers east of Algiers.[7] Sanūsī's family, however, claimed to be Sharīfs, that is, descendants of the Prophet Muḥammad. His paternal grandmother was reportedly a descendant of al-Ḥasan, the Prophet's grandson.[8] The rank of a Sharīf was not just prestigious but also entailed legal and fiscal privileges. There had been an intense debate in the fourteenth and early fifteenth centuries in the Maghreb on whether descent from the Prophet from a maternal ancestor conferred true Sharīfian status.[9] By Sanūsī's time, the view that it did confer such status had become prevalent, and Sanūsī routinely added the epithet "al-Ḥasanī" after his name, as did Mallālī and later authors.

The first chapter of Mallālī's hagiography is devoted to Sanūsī's teachers (MQ 43–91). Medieval biographical sources sometimes lump together all teachers, without regard to the intensity and length of the interaction. Mallālī's account is more fine-grained, and an interesting pattern emerges. Sanūsī studied with—and alongside—his older maternal half-brother ʿAlī al-Tālūtī al-Anṣārī, with whom he appears to have been close. Tālūtī died just a few months before Sanūsī, and the two were buried next to each other (MQ 55–65). Sanūsī also studied Arabic grammar with a certain Naṣr al-Zawāwī, mathematics and inheritance laws with a certain Muḥammad b. Qāsim al-Ṣanhājī, and Quran recitation from a certain Yūsuf b. Aḥmad al-Sharīf. It is clear from Mallālī's account that Sanūsī was close to these teachers, studied with them for several years, reminisced vividly about them, and regularly visited their graves after their deaths.[10] Yet, it is striking that they were all obscure scholars. In later sources, all that is known of them is what Mallālī wrote in his hagiography.[11] Similarly, in the field for which Sanūsī would gain most renown, that of rational or natural theology (*kalām*), Mallālī wrote that Sanūsī had studied it with the otherwise unknown Abū l-Qāsim al-Kunbāshī (or al-Kunābushī), apparently a scholar from Béjaïa who stayed in Tlemcen for a short spell and taught Sanūsī and Sanūsī's older half-brother.[12] So, in a range of core disciplines, Sanūsī's teachers were relatively unknown scholars, remembered in the subsequent biographical tradition simply through their connection to Sanūsī.

Mallālī did, to be sure, mention some more eminent scholars of whom we have independent information. These included people whom Sanūsī met on trips to neighboring towns, such as the well-known Quran exegete ʿAbd al-Raḥmān al-Thaʿālibī (d.1471) from Algiers, as well as Ibrāhīm al-Tāzī (d.1462) from Oran who initiated Sanūsī into Sufism (MQ 71–90). The Andalusian mathematician ʿAlī al-Qalṣādī (d.1486) also issued Sanūsī a certificate, probably when Qalṣādī spent some months in Tlemcen and Oran on his way back to Granada from the pilgrimage to Mecca in 1450–1451.[13]

Of more well-known scholars from Tlemcen who reportedly taught Sanūsī, Mallālī mentioned the astronomer Muḥammad al-Ḥabbāk (d.1462), the jurist Muḥammad al-Jallāb (d.1470), and the polymath Ibn ʿAbbās al-ʿUbbādī (d.1467). But what he wrote in connection with the latter two scholars is curious. He had heard that Sanūsī studied one work on law with Jallāb but was not sure, and he remarked that Sanūsī reportedly only attended Ibn ʿAbbās al-ʿUbbādī's class on an advanced work on logic for three days, after which the teacher asked Sanūsī to stop attending (MQ 54–5). Balawī, who seems to have known Mallālī and derived biographical information on Sanūsī from him, also noted that Sanūsī attended Ibn ʿAbbās's classes but added "and he did not study a lot with him."[14] Such qualifications of the student–teacher relation are very unusual. Later accounts that are based on Mallālī do not retain the hesitation and qualification, simply adding Jallāb and Ibn ʿAbbās to a list of around a dozen scholars with whom Sanūsī studied. But Mallālī's original and vivid account, if accurate, suggests that Sanūsī was very much an outsider who studied most intensely with relatively obscure scholars in Tlemcen and had little interaction with the most eminent luminaries of the town.

This is supported by evidence from the travel account of a Cairene scholar who visited Tlemcen in 1464–1466. The visitor attended the classes of the most eminent scholars of the town. Apart from the aforementioned Ibn ʿAbbās al-ʿUbbādī, this included the Chief Judge Muḥammad al-ʿUqbānī (d.1467), the Imam of the Grand Mosque of Tlemcen Ibrāhīm al-ʿUqbānī (d.1475), and the Mufti of Tlemcen Ibn Zakrī (d.1494).[15] It is perhaps unsurprising that the Cairene scholar took no notice of Sanūsī who was not yet thirty then. But it is remarkable that none of the mentioned scholars are listed by Mallālī as teachers of Sanūsī, with the mentioned quasi-exception of Ibn ʿAbbās al-ʿUbbādī. In fact, there is reason to believe that Sanūsī's relationship with them was tense or hostile. His rivalry with Ibn Zakrī—who was older by around ten years and who appears to have been the favorite student of Ibn ʿAbbās al-ʿUbbādī—is well attested in biographical sources.[16] Additionally, when Sanūsī in one work passionately denounced some scholars for giving themselves airs and wallowing in the empty jargon of the heretical philosophers, some later glossators identified the target as "al-ʿUqbānī from among his contemporaries."[17]

Sanūsī's later scholarly reputation was acquired without the benefit of a position as a madrasa teacher, judge, or jurisconsult (mufti). As noted by Balawī in his aforementioned account of Sanūsī's last days, Sanūsī had numerous students, but these would attend his lessons in a small mosque close to his home in the Msoufa district in northeastern Tlemcen. He was not one of the "professors of diverse arts," mentioned by Leo Africanus, "which have maintenance allowed them out of the five forenamed colleges." His teaching harked back to the days before the madrasa institution spread in the Islamic world from the eleventh century, when men of independent means would sit in a mosque and teach anyone who was interested, free of charge, rather than receive a stipend from a madrasa endowment.

3 Sanūsī the saint

The second and third chapters of Mallālī's hagiography are devoted to Sanūsī's saintly qualities (MQ 95–128, 131–340). Though there is mention of the so-called *karāmāt* and *mukāshafāt* (extrasensory powers of action and mind-reading) expected of holy men, the bulk of the chapters are devoted to saintly character traits. These include what Mallālī called Sanūsī's knowledge (*ʿilm*), asceticism (*zuhd*), preaching (*waʿẓ*), God-fearingness (*waraʿ*), high-mindedness (*rafʿ al-himma*), forbearance (*ḥilm*), and patience (*ṣabr*). It is clear that Mallālī was writing with a certain cultural script of sainthood in mind. He regularly quoted earlier hagiographies of saints, especially those by Ibn al-Zayyāt al-Tādilī (d.1230) and Ibn ʿAṭāʾullāh al-Iskandarī (d.1309), as well as classic pietistic works such as the great *Revival of Religious Sciences* by al-Ghazālī (d.1111). It is therefore not always easy to tell what, in Mallālī's account, is the imparting of biographical fact and what is merely a commonplace of the hagiographical literature. The picture of Sanūsī that emerges does, in part, conform to a general expectation of a medieval North African saint: the nights spent in supererogatory prayer, the ever-present fear of God's judgment, the near-constant, under-the-breath invocations (*dhikr*) of God, the modest eating and sleeping, the refusal of gifts and positions offered by the ruler, the generosity to the poor. But some details seem to offer a more individualized portrait. Sanūsī was, wrote Mallālī, kind and amiable but was never fully present with those around him. He enjoyed solitude and visiting the ruins of al-Manṣūra—the abandoned town that the Marinids had built next to Tlemcen in the hope that it would supplant a city that they had difficulty conquering. He walked softly and avoided stepping on insects on the ground. He cried over a wolf when he saw it being hunted down and maimed by a pack of dogs and then killed by the dogs' owner. He was averse to being praised and having to listen to poetic panegyrics addressed to him. He disliked public teaching sessions—the kind of sessions that Balawī witnessed—partly because he had difficulty telling students or even commoners who attended to be quiet, and consequently a lot of time would be lost with naive or pointless questions and remarks. He opposed harshness in dealing with young boys in the primary schools. Unlike most scholars of his age, he found it almost impossible to compose anything in verse. He dressed conventionally and inconspicuously, so that someone who did not know him would think he was one of the ordinary inhabitants of the town. He had difficulty rejecting any request from people to act as an intercessor with the authorities, though toward the end of his life he became much more retiring.

Some less felicitous character traits also emerge, inadvertently, from Mallālī's account. A few anecdotes suggest that Sanūsī—like scholars more generally, past and present—was not immune to intellectual vanity. He once told Mallālī that someone he knew had an acquaintance who studied a creed in Tlemcen that was not by Sanūsī. The acquaintance died and appeared in a dream to Sanūsī's friend and related that the angels of death had berated him for studying other creedal works, rather than *The Short Creed* of Sanūsī. Mallālī then quoted Sanūsī as saying of his own work, "There is no doubt that this creed has no equal among works that I know. The one who studies it exclusively will have no need for other creeds and even lengthy tomes" (MQ 348). In another anecdote, Sanūsī told Mallālī that he wrote a commentary on an unusually difficult handbook from the Islamic East and ordered one of his students to show it, without mentioning the name of the commentator, to an eminent teacher in Tlemcen and ask him to explain the text. The unnamed teacher supposedly looked at the commentary and replied to the student that it could only be understood by its author, perhaps not unambiguous praise but taken by Mallālī, and apparently by Sanūsī himself, as evidence for Sanūsī's superior intellect (MQ 367).

A strain of stridency and intolerance is also apparent in Sanūsī's works. This colored even his references to other Muslim sects: The Khārijites were referred to as the "firewood of Hell," the Muʿtazilis were derided as dualist "Magians," and fideist opponents of logic and natural theology were said to be "idiots" who wallowed in their own ignorance. As for Aristotelian/Neoplatonist philosophers, Christians, and Jews, Sanūsī was even more scathing, often writing "may God curse them" or "may God destroy them" after mentioning them. As so often in the history of the three monotheist religions, saintliness toward one's own religious community went hand in hand with fierce hostility toward other sects and religions.

4 Works

The fourth chapter of Mallālī's hagiography is devoted to listing and briefly describing Sanūsī's writings (MQ 343–74). Rather than reproducing all titles, I will here mention those that can be considered major works. These include:

(i) *The Long Creed* and a commentary on it, the earliest and lengthiest of Sanūsī's creedal works.
(ii) *The Middle Creed*, a slightly abridged version of *The Long Creed* and a commentary on it.
(iii) The popular *Short Creed* and a commentary on it. This came to be known as "The Sanūsī Creed" (*al-Sanūsiyya*), "The Mother of Proofs" (*Umm al-barāhīn*), "Creeds" (*Kabbe*) in West Africa, and "The Twenty Attributes of God" (*Sifat Dua Puluh*) in the Malay Archipelago.
(iv) The *Shortened Short Creed*. Mallālī related that Sanūsī wrote this abridgment for the benefit of Mallālī's father who found the *Short Creed* too long to memorize. Sanūsī wrote a commentary on this as well.
(v) *The Preliminaries*, which introduces some of the basic concepts of theology. Sanūsī again wrote a commentary on this.

All these works were to become staple handbooks of theology throughout Islamic Africa down to the modern period.[18]

In the same discipline, Sanūsī also wrote:

(vi) A commentary on a didactic poem (of 355 lines) on Ash'ari creed and Sufi ethics by his older contemporary, the Algiers-based scholar Aḥmad al-Zawāwī al-Jazā'irī (d.1479).

(vii) A commentary on another, significantly shorter creedal poem (of 144 lines) by his contemporary from Tlemcen Muḥammad al-Ḥawḍī (d.1510).

Logic was another field in which Sanūsī had a powerful influence on the later North African tradition. Sanūsī wrote three works, all of which survive in numerous manuscript copies.

(viii) Most popular was his *Epitome* of logic, for which he wrote a commentary. This work elicited numerous commentaries, glosses, and versifications in later centuries. It will be discussed in greater detail in Chapter 5.

(ix) Sanūsī also wrote a commentary on the *Introduction*, written by the Persian scholar al-Abharī (d.1265) but reaching Sanūsī in a slightly reworked version by the Syrian-born, Cairo-based scholar al-Biqāʿī (d.1480).

(x) His longest and most detailed treatment of logic is his commentary on the *Epitome* of the Tunisian scholar Ibn ʿArafa (d.1401), a notoriously dense work in which Ibn ʿArafa had mentioned numerous disagreements and controversies among previous logicians. Sanūsī told Mallālī that Ibn ʿArafa's "discourse is difficult, especially in this *Epitome*. I had great difficulty disentangling it and could only do so when alone" (MQ 361). Sanūsī's commentary covered approximately two-thirds of Ibn ʿArafa's work, breaking off shortly after the beginning of the final and most abstruse section on hypothetical syllogisms.

Aside from his writings on theology and logic, Sanūsī's perhaps most widely studied scholarly work was:

(xi) A commentary on the esteemed collection by Muslim ibn al-Ḥajjāj (d.875) of canonical hadith—the reported sayings and doings of the Prophet Muhammad. Sanūsī explained in his introduction that his commentary was based on the earlier commentary by the Tunisian scholar Muḥammad al-Ubbī (d.1427), though Sanūsī abridged sections of that commentary and expanded others.

Of Sanūsī's other works that are complete but remain unpublished, two appear to have been widely copied:

(xii) A commentary on a handbook on the mathematically demanding Islamic laws of inheritance (*farāʾiḍ*) by Aḥmad al-Ḥawfī (d.1184). According to Mallālī, this was Sanūsī's first work, written when he was eighteen or nineteen years old (MQ 343).

(xiii) A commentary on a didactic poem on the astrolabe by his aforementioned teacher Muḥammad al-Ḥabbāk. This survives in several manuscript copies.[19]

Mallālī further listed numerous works that Sanūsī did not complete. These include a Quran commentary that Sanūsī began writing toward the end of his life. In his hagiography, Mallālī reproduced the unfinished work, covering only the first chapter of the Quran and the first verses of the second (MQ 377–450). One suspects that had he not done so, the fragment would have been lost. That fate seems to have befallen other commentaries that Sanūsī left in a fragmentary state when he died, for example (i) a commentary on *The Sentences* on logic by al-Khūnajī (d.1248), a standard handbook in North Africa in the period; (ii) a commentary on Avicenna's didactic poem on medicine, also popular in North Africa; and (iii) a commentary on a compendium on metaphysics and theology by the Persian scholar al-Ījī (d.1355). There are no traces of these works, and no quotations or paraphrases from them in later sources. It is likely that Sanūsī did not write much beyond the very early parts of the commentaries.

Given Sanūsī's reputation, it is unlikely that any of his completed or near-completed works were allowed to be lost by the subsequent tradition. The problem seems rather to have been that some later works were falsely attributed to him. One such popular work is a collection of invocations and supplications with otherworldly or worldly effects. It circulated under a title that roughly translates as "The Tried and Tested Means of Sanūsī" (*Mujarrabāt al-Sanūsī*). The fact that Mallālī does not mention this work is a reason to be cautious, and the further fact that there seem to be no extant manuscripts that are earlier than the seventeenth century only adds to the suspicion. Another popular work of doubtful authenticity is a commentary on a supposed hadith of the Prophet Muhammad (though it is not in any of the canonical collections) that says, "The stomach is the home of disease, diet is the chief remedy, and the origin of every disease is indigestion." Again, the work is not mentioned by Mallālī, and some manuscripts attribute the work to another scholar. These two works of questionable authenticity will be discussed in Chapters 8 and 9.

Another work that is attributed to Sanūsī and survives in numerous manuscript copies is a sharp, even abusive, polemic against a religious jurist from Meknes who had attacked as unlawful innovation (*bidʿa*) certain popular Sufi practices. It is striking that it is not mentioned by Mallālī or other medieval biographical sources.[20] There are also some internal anomalies that should arouse suspicion.[21] A thorough study of the contents and extant manuscripts would be helpful before coming to firm conclusions about authenticity.

5 Ashʿarism in North Africa

A brief account of Sanūsī's intellectual context requires some preliminary overview of the development of Ashʿarism in North Africa. First, it may be helpful to introduce the discipline of *kalām*, for Ashʿarism is a school of thought within that discipline. Some modern specialists have rendered *kalām* as "speculative theology," others as "dialectical theology," and yet others as "rational theology." None of these suggestions are entirely satisfactory, and some therefore prefer to leave the term untranslated. It should be pointed out, however, that practitioners of the discipline discussed issues that are often categorized as "natural theology" in the sense of "any attempt to reason about the existence and nature of God without dependence on purportedly divine revelation" or "the practice of philosophically reflecting on the existence and nature of God independently of real or apparent divine revelation or scripture."[22] To be sure, kalam scholars also discussed other issues that might be classified as "revealed theology," "political theory," or "philosophy." But though the term "natural theology" does not cover everything that practitioners of kalam discussed, it undoubtedly captures a core part.

The discipline of kalam emerged over the course of the eighth and ninth centuries, often spurred on by early questions such as: Does a sinner act in accordance with divine will? Are infidels predestined to hellfire? Should apparently anthropomorphic descriptions of God in the Quran be interpreted literally or figuratively? Is the Quran pre-eternal or was it created? There is also evidence that early caliphs of the Abbasid dynasty (750–1258) sponsored religious debates between representatives of the many religious groups within their far-flung empire (Muslims, Christians, Jews, Buddhists, Brahmins, Mandaeans, Zoroastrians) and that the Muslim representatives in such debates came to be known as *mutakallimūn*, i.e., those who practiced kalam.[23] In the ninth and tenth centuries, one can broadly discern three groups of Islamic thinkers in relation to this discipline.

First, the early practitioners of kalam themselves, most of whom—at this formative stage—tended to agree on certain substantive views, for example, that humans have the ability to choose and do otherwise than what they actually do, that God does not will evil or sin, that apparently anthropomorphic descriptions of God in the Quran should be interpreted figuratively, and that the Quran is created. This group came to be known by their opponents as Muʿtazilīs ("Schismatics"); they tended to refer to themselves with the more flattering designation "the people of justice and monotheism."[24] The term "justice" (*ʿadl*) indicated the view that reason can determine at least some things to be good or bad independently of revelation, and that such determinations apply to what God can or cannot do. For example, it would be rationally abhorrent for God to predetermine certain people to be infidels or sinners and yet punish them for this, to create the world and yet not create rational beings, to create human beings but not send forth prophets to guide them, or to cause pain in innocent infants without some sort of recompense in this life or the next. The term "monotheism" (*tawḥīd*) indicated the view that the Quran or God's Speech is not co-eternal with God, and more generally that God does not have multiple, co-eternal attributes that are distinct from—and cannot be reduced to—God's Self. Muʿtazilism slowly died out within mainstream Sunni Islam, though as late as the thirteenth century, there were still Sunni Muʿtazilīs (of the Ḥanafī school of law) in Central Asia. Many of their theses survived in later centuries within Shi'i Islam.

A second group consisted of religious thinkers who rejected what they saw as the illegitimate, newfangled discipline of kalam. This included the followers of Ibn Ḥanbal (d.855), later referred to as Ḥanbalīs.[25] Such thinkers had creedal commitments, and these were most often opposed to those of the Muʿtazilīs: the Quran is uncreated; human beings cannot do otherwise than they actually do; anything that comes to pass, including unbelief and sin, does so in accordance with God's will; anthropomorphic descriptions of God in the Quran must be accepted without question, and unaided human reason cannot ascertain objective standards of right and wrong that God's decrees and actions must respect. But more fundamentally, Islamic religious thinkers in this camp strove to ground their creedal commitments in revelation, especially in the hadith, i.e., later reports about the sayings and doings of the Prophet Muhammad, rather than natural reason. Modern Salafis also tend to have this view.

A third group tended to have creedal commitments that were close to those of the second group but were willing to use kalam-style reasoning to defend them. In other words, they thought it possible to establish mainstream creedal commitments through natural reason, as opposed to relying simply on hadith or passages from the Quran. Two early and particularly influential representatives of this trend were al-Ashʿarī (d.935) in Baghdad and al-Māturīdī (d.944) in Samarqand.[26] The followers of al-Ashʿarī became prevalent in the Levant and Islamic Africa, and also in Persia before the Safavid dynasty came to power there in the early sixteenth century and imposed Shiism on their subjects. The followers of al-Māturīdī became prevalent in Central Asia, in the Turkish-speaking areas of the Ottoman Empire, and among the Muslims of South Asia. Despite some initial friction, these two schools of thought—the Ashʿarīs and the Māturīdīs—came to recognize each other as orthodox, though differing on some issues. Their relationship with the second, fideist camp was historically more volatile. In general, Ashʿarīs and Māturīdīs professed respect for Ibn Ḥanbal himself and were often willing to recognize the Ḥanbalīs as orthodox. But there were times and places in which there was outright hostility and even violence, especially when some later Ḥanbalīs were confident or combative enough to declare all schools of kalam heretical, prompting Ashʿarīs and Māturīdīs to dismiss them as crass anthropomorphists and literalists.[27] For most of the premodern period, Ashʿarism and Māturīdism prevailed within mainstream, Sunni Islam, though their dominance has been challenged in modern times by the rise of Salafism, as well as by more modernist-liberal Muslim thinkers who often have greater sympathy with the supposedly more "rationalist" Muʿtazilīs.

Though there were differences among Ashʿarī scholars on some points of detail, there was broad agreement on the following core principles:[28]

- Natural theology is a legitimate discipline. It is praiseworthy for Muslims—especially the learned among them—not to accept their faith by naïve "imitation" (*taqlīd*) of elders and peers, but to exercise their reason and ascertain the rational foundations for belief in God, God's attributes, and Muḥammad's prophecy.
- God has numerous, distinct core attributes: Knowledge, Power, Life, Will, Speech, Sight, and Hearing. These are positive and eternal attributes that cannot be reduced to each other or to God's self. They are, in other words, "additional" (*zāʾida*) to the divine self. The opposing view, held by the Muʿtazilī theologians and the Islamic Aristotelian-Neoplatonist philosophers, is that such a plurality of distinct, irreducible attributes would entail an unacceptable compositeness in God.
- God's uncreated attribute of Speech does not consist of sounds and letters. The Arabic Quran is a created expression of God's eternal, uncreated Speech. Ashʿaris thus reject both the position of the Ḥanbalī school which insists that the Arabic Quran with its sounds and letters is uncreated, and the Muʿtazilī view that there is no eternal attribute of Speech and that God simply created the Arabic Quran.
- Passages in the Quran and hadith that suggest anthropomorphism must either be accepted agnostically, without attributing a body (*jism*), physical quality (*kayf*) or direction (*jiha*) to God, or interpreted figuratively.
- God is the only being with causal powers. Ordinary "causes" are merely occasions for God's direct creation of all substances and all attributes.

- In line with the previous principle, Ash'arīs tend to hold that humans have no causal powers and cannot bring about their own actions. Their intentions and abilities are merely occasions for God's creation of their actions.
- There are no objective values independent of God's command, and God is not bound by human notions of right and wrong. Ash'arīs thus take one side in Plato's "Euthyphro dilemma": acts are good because God commands them; God does not command them because they are good independently of divine command.

All of these principles will be discussed in greater detail in subsequent chapters.

The school's eponym al-Ash'arī had been active in Baghdad, and the early eminent representatives of the school in the tenth and eleventh centuries were primarily active in that city or in Nishapur in what is today northeastern Iran. From the eleventh century, the school started making significant inroads in North Africa.[29] Its successful spread may be due, at least in part, to two factors.

First, the Ash'ari school's creedal position fitted relatively well with preexisting Sunni sentiment in the region as expressed, for example, in the opening creedal segment of the influential *Epistle* of Ibn Abī Zayd al-Qayrawānī (d.996).[30] Qayrawānī's creed begins by emphasizing that God is one and unique; that He has a range of eternal attributes and names; that the Quran is God's uncreated speech; that nothing transpires in the world that is not in accordance with God's decree; that nothing other than God can bring anything into existence; and that God has predestined some people for salvation and others for damnation. There are, to be sure, some details in the creed that differ from standard Ash'arism. It seems unworried about "imitation," and it makes some assertions that might suggest anthropomorphism and that later Ash'ari commentators had to qualify or explain away, for example, that God is "above" the throne and that God will "come" on Judgment Day. Qayrawānī also defined belief (*īmān*) as including pious actions, whereas standard Ashʿarism defined belief as mental assent and considered actions an extrinsic consequence of belief. Nevertheless, the differences between Qayrawānī's creedal beliefs and mainstream Ashʿarism are relatively minor, especially when compared to the differences with Muʿtazilism. Bespeaking the continuities, Qayrawānī's work continued to be studied and commented even after the region had become overwhelmingly and explicitly Ashʿari. The school was widely seen—rightly or wrongly—as simply systematizing, rationally defending, and perhaps refining those creedal positions that the Sunni community already accepted.

Second, the Almohad rulers of the Maghreb (1147–1269) advocated a theology that in many ways overlapped with Ashʿarism. This fact has been missed by some modern historians, in part due to an overreliance for information on Almohad doctrine on hostile and ill-informed witnesses, and in part due to a superficial understanding of Ashʿarism. For example, the creedal writings of the movement's founder Ibn Tūmart (d.1130) show a marked hostility toward anthropomorphism (*tajsīm*), and this has sometimes been thought to be closer to the Muʿtazilis than to the Ashʿaris who supposedly accepted all anthropomorphic passages in the Quran and hadith "without asking how."[31] But this is to overlook the fact that the major Ashʿari theologians of the eleventh and twelfth centuries, for example, Ghazālī and his teacher al-Juwaynī (d.1085), explicitly adopted an anti-anthropomorphic stance and advocated the figurative interpretation of passages in the Quran and hadith that mention God's eyes, hands, and feet, and God sitting on a throne.[32]

A closer look at Ibn Tūmart's creedal writings confirm their closeness to Ashʿarism. In his most extensive creedal pronouncement, Ibn Tūmart began by emphasizing the importance of knowledge of monotheism without which acts of piety are to no avail.[33] He then distinguished between necessity, possibility, and impossibility—prefiguring the way in which Sanūsī tended to begin his shorter creeds. He then asserted that all humans know that they are created and that they therefore must have a creator. Similarly, the heavens and the Earth are created and must have a creator. This creator must be radically different from creation. His existence must be unqualified by time and space and physical quality (*kayf*). Scriptural passages that suggest anthropomorphism must be accepted while also affirming that God transcends the physical realm and space. The Creator must be alive, knowledgeable, powerful, willing, hearing, seeing, and speaking—to suppose otherwise is to attribute imperfection to the Creator. But these attributes must be understood to be without physical modality. All creation comes about in accordance with divine decree and predestination (*qaḍāʾ wa qadar*). God has predestined some for heaven and others for hellfire. God guides and misguides as He pleases, and yet this is justice, for there are no constraints on what God may do with His creation. The beatific vision of God in the afterlife must be affirmed, though again without attributing a physical modality to God. Finally, miracles are the proof of prophecy, and the Prophet Muḥammad performed miracles, first and foremost the Quran.

As the great North African historian Ibn Khaldūn (d.1406) pointed out, there is nothing in such Almohad creeds that would be rejected by Ashʿaris.[34] Indeed, what is most striking are the continuities with Sanūsī's short creeds. These typically also begin by emphasizing the importance of knowing the creed and then introduce the distinction between necessity, possibility, and impossibility. The mode of argumentation is also very similar, both authors often using indirect proof, for example: God must have attribute X because if this were not the case then it would follow that Y, but Y is false.

One noticeable difference between Ibn Tūmart's creeds and mainstream Ashʿarism is that the former tended not to take an explicit stand on the question of whether the divine attributes are additional (*zāʾida*) to the divine Self. This has been taken as an endorsement of the Muʿtazili position that God does not have multiple, irreducible divine attributes. But this need not be so, and the argument from silence is especially problematic in this case. The short and simple creeds written by Ibn Tūmart were meant to be taught by popular preachers to the common run of believers. His avoidance of a topic may simply be because he thought it sufficient for common believers to affirm God's being knowledgeable, powerful, willing, etc. without inquiring further into the ontological status of these attributes. There is, on the other hand, some evidence from the biographical literature to suggest that the earliest Almohads were opposed to the idea that the attributes are additional, but that this position was abandoned by Ibn Tūmart's successor ʿAbd al-Muʾmin (d.1163).[35] If such reports are true, this means that the Almohads had accepted the Ashʿari view of the divine attributes by the time they extended their rule throughout North Africa. All in all, though Ashʿaris may have wondered at some omissions in Ibn Tūmart's creedal writings, they would not have disagreed with anything actually mentioned there. As with Ibn Abī Zayd al-Qayrawānī's older *Epistle*, Ibn Tūmart's shortest creed *The Guide* was frequently commented on by Ashʿaris in later centuries, and Sanūsī himself is reported to have written one of these commentaries.[36]

Regardless of what Ibn Tūmart's own position may have been, it is clear that Ashʿarism went from strength to strength under Almohad rule. An early and influential exponent was Abū Bakr Ibn al-ʿArabī (d.1148)—not to be confused with the later mystic Muḥyī al-Dīn Ibn ʿArabī (d.1240). He wrote an Ashʿari creedal work entitled *The Intermediate in Creed* which Sanūsī cited and which clearly influenced him, as will be shown later.[37] Another influential exponent of Ashʿarism in twelfth-century North Africa was ʿUthmān al-Salāljī (d.1178) whose short handbook of Ashʿari theology, known as *The Demonstrative*, was widely studied in the region and elicited numerous commentaries.[38] Also widely studied in the centuries leading up to Sanūsī was *The Guidance*, a classic exposition of Ashʿarism by Juwaynī, the teacher of the famous Ghazālī in Nishapur. This is the work that Sanūsī and his half-brother reportedly studied with Kunbāshī—the aforementioned obscure scholar from Béjaïa who visited Tlemcen. Commentaries on *The Guidance* were written by Abū Bakr Ibn al-ʿArabī's student Ibn Maymūn al-ʿAbdarī (d.1172), the Andalusian scholar Ibn Dihāq al-Mālaqī (d.1214), and the Tunisian scholar Ibn Bazīza (d.1264). Another commentary, frequently cited by Sanūsī, was by the Egyptian scholar Taqī al-Dīn Muẓaffar al-Azdī, better known as al-Muqtaraḥ (d.1216). This al-Muqtaraḥ and his students Ibn al-Tilimsānī al-Fihrī (d.1260) and Abū Yaḥyā al-Sharīf al-Sabtī (fl.1231), though little known now, had a powerful influence on the later North African Ashʿarī tradition. Sanūsī regularly cited their writings, especially the following three works: (i) al-Muqtaraḥ's just-mentioned commentary on Juwaynī's *The Guidance*, (ii) Abū Yaḥyá al-Sharīf's commentary on al-Muqtaraḥ's *The Secrets of Reason*, and (iii) Ibn al-Tilimsānī's commentary on *Landmarks of the Principles of Religion* by the Eastern Ashʿarī theologian Fakhr al-Dīn al-Rāzī (d.1210).[39] Though Sanūsī's creedal writings are close in tone and style to his North African predecessors—Abū Bakr Ibn al-ʿArabī, Salāljī, and Ibn Tūmart—he assimilated, especially in his longer works, the more advanced content and more rigorous argumentation derived from al-Muqtaraḥ and his circle.

6 Ashʿarism: East and West

As mentioned in the previous section, Ashʿarism had spread to North Africa from the more eastern parts of the Islamic world—Baghdad and Nishapur. Yet, starting from the thirteenth century, the eastern and western Ashʿari traditions tended to develop in distinct directions. On the one hand, the major influences on Sanūsī mentioned in the previous section were not familiar in the Turco-Persianate world in later centuries—the reception of the works of Abū Bakr Ibn al-ʿArabī, Salāljī, Ibn Dihāq, al-Muqtaraḥ, Ibn al-Tilimsānī, and Abū Yaḥyā al-Sharīf was almost exclusively confined to North Africa. On the other hand, Eastern Ashʿaris, including Fakhr al-Dīn al-Rāzī and later scholars influenced by him, began to preface their theological writings with extensive overviews of the metaphysics and physics of the Aristotelian-Neoplatonic philosophers. In widely studied Eastern handbooks such as *The Dawning of Lights* by al-Bayḍāwī (d.1291) and *The Stations* by al-Ījī (d.1355), more than half the space is allocated to discussions of logical or epistemological preliminaries, "general metaphysics," i.e., existence, essence, and causation, and "substances and attributes," i.e., the ten Aristotelian categories. Traditional theological topics, such as proofs for the existence of God, the divine attributes, the creation of human acts, the nature of the Quran, prophecy, miracles, and the Imamate all tended to be confined to the last third of these works, marked off as natural theology (*ilāhiyyāt*) and revealed theology (*samʿiyyāt*).[40]

At the level of content, too, later Eastern Ashʿarīs often absorbed elements of Aristotelian-Neoplatonic philosophy. Ghazālī had famously attacked the Aristotelian-Neoplatonic philosophers—the *falāsifa*—on a number of points, including three that he believed took them outside the pale of Islam altogether: their belief in the pre-eternity of the world, their denial of God's knowledge of particulars in the sublunar world, and their denial of bodily resurrection. However, as some modern historians have noted, it is as if Ghazālī's identification of these three points provided a license for later theologians to take an agnostic view toward—and sometimes even to adopt—other positions characteristic of the *falāsifa*, for example hylomorphism, the four Aristotelian causes, the immateriality of the soul, the distinction between essence and existence, that quiddities are not "made" (*majʿūla*) and that it is merely the existence of quiddities that is caused, that knowledge is the form of an entity in the mind, and even the idea of an Active Intellect.[41]

North African Ashʿaris were—with some exceptions—skeptical of this philosophical turn.[42] Their creedal works tended to retain the traditional focus of earlier Ash'ari theologians such as Juwaynī. The one theological work of Fakhr al-Dīn al-Rāzī that was widely studied in North Africa was *Landmarks of the Principles of Religion*. This short handbook devoted a chapter (the second out of ten) to general metaphysics. In his standard commentary, Ibn al-Tilimsānī—the aforementioned star-pupil of al-Muqtaraḥ in Cairo—covered the chapter with characteristic incisiveness and lucidity, though without relish, noting that these kinds of issues are abstruse (*fīhā ghumūḍ*).[43] When commenting on the later, theological parts of the handbook, Ibn al-Tilimsānī not infrequently protested Rāzī's idiosyncrasies and compromises with the *falāsifa*. At one point, in the chapter dealing with the human soul, Ibn al-Tilimsānī refused to quote the last two sections of Rāzī's chapter in which he had outlined a hierarchy of human souls and their essentially distinct subtypes, each ruled by a talismanic spirit. What Rāzī wrote was, according to Ibn al-Tilimsānī, based on the Aristotelian–Neoplatonist philosophers' belief in intermediary heavenly intellects, the denial of bodily resurrection, and prophecy being acquired naturalistically through communion with talismanic spirits. "These three issues are pure unbelief and do not admit of any charitable interpretation," wrote Ibn al-Tilimsānī, "and I would that I knew what need there was to mention these without pointing out that they are corrupt views that deviate from the position of the people of truth!"[44]

Sanūsī, too, rejected the tendency of some later Eastern Ash'aris to delve into the theories of the *falāsifa*. He wrote:

> Let the beginner take utmost care not to take the principles of his religion from books that are filled with the discourse of the *falāsifa* and whose authors are enamored of reproducing their folly and what is explicit infidelity among their beliefs and whose impurity they have concealed by means of terms and expressions that are unclear to many and are mostly names without reference. This is like the books of Fakhr al-Dīn [al-Rāzī] in theology and

> the *Dawning* of al-Bayḍāwī and those who follow in their path. (S 137)

To be sure, Sanūsī here specifically condemned beginning students being exposed to this kind of philosophically inflected literature. This leaves open the possibility that he thought such literature to be appropriate for more advanced stages. He himself cited the works of Rāzī and Bayḍāwī in his more advanced writings and, if Mallālī was correct, planned to write a commentary on Ījī's *The Jewels of Kalam*, which is very much in the same tradition.[45] But it is nevertheless revealing that even Sanūsī's most advanced work—his *Long Creed* and its commentary—avoids delving into metaphysical and natural-philosophical preliminaries and in-depth discussions of the Aristotelian categories. The vehemence of his denunciations of the philosophers throughout his theological works is unmistakable.

A stark contrast to Sanūsī's attitude is provided by his contemporary Jalāl al-Dīn al-Dawānī (d.1502), who was active in Persia just before the Shi'i Safavids took power there. Dawānī identified as an Ashʿarī and retained a commitment to its core tenets, especially the creation of the world ex nihilo, bodily resurrection, occasionalism, and divine-command ethics.[46] But he engaged extensively and respectfully with the writings of the *falāsifa*, especially Avicenna (d.1037) and al-Suhrawardī (d.1191). Indeed, Dawānī's esteem for Avicenna was such that both premodern Islamic and modern Western authors have noted his penchant for establishing a philosophical position by simply finding the right quotation from Avicenna's works.[47] His disagreements with the *falāsifa* are expressed in a much less acerbic tone, and on a number of points, he was willing to adopt their positions. He rejected, for example, the mainstream Ashʿari view that the divine attributes are additional to the divine self.[48] He also went out of his way to argue that the philosophers were falsely accused of denying God's knowledge of particulars.[49] He also accepted Avicenna's view that the essence/existence distinction does not apply to God, and that

God's essence is identical to God's existence. Perhaps reflecting his sympathy for the mystic Ibn ʿArabī (d.1240), Dawānī even took this position further and equated God with existence as such, in other words embracing the controversial mystical and panentheist theory of "the oneness of existence" (*waḥdat al-wujūd*).[50] All this is far from the stricter Ashʿarism of Sanūsī. Dawānī's writings would come to be widely studied in later centuries in the Sunni regions of the Turco-Persianate world: the Turkish- and Kurdish-speaking parts of the Ottoman Empire, Uzbek Central Asia, and Mughal India. There is no evidence that Sanūsī read them. Had he done so, it is reasonable to suppose that he would have been repelled by their deviations from Ashʿari orthodoxy and their compromises with the "confusion, folly and infidelity" of the *falāsifa*.

3

The Condemnation of Imitation

In their seminal *Introduction à la théologie musulmane* (1948), Louis Gardet and George Anawati suggested that whereas theology in medieval Christianity was an instrument to understand and deepen faith in the "mysteries" of the creed, the Islamic discipline of *kalām* was an apologetic and defensive discipline whose task was merely to defend a creed already established by revelation against heretics and infidels. This basic and widely accepted thesis has led to a number of subsidiary claims. One such is that the method of *kalām* was "dialectical": it sought to demolish the positions of heretics and infidels rather than engage in more constructive reflection or theological system building. The supposed dialectical and apologetic nature of *kalām* also led scholars to ponder why the tradition survived in later periods when the need for apologia and polemic was believed to be less pressing. By the thirteenth century, mainstream Sunni thought had emerged victorious in its struggle against both the Muʿtazilī school and the adherents of Aristotelian–Neoplatonic philosophy, and non-Muslims had become an unthreatening minority in the Middle East. As *kalām* works continued to be written for centuries after that date, Gardet and Anawati inferred that this later literature must have constituted a "fossilized conservatism" (*conservatisme figé*): the old arguments were still reiterated but against long-vanquished foes who were no longer in a position to offer any resistance.[1]

The interpretation of Gardet and Anawati seems to rest mainly on the testimony of the eminent al-Ghazālī (d.1111), who grew increasingly lukewarm toward *kalām* in his later years, and of the famous historian Ibn Khaldūn (d.1406), who thought that *kalām*

Al-Sanūsī. Khaled El-Rouayheb, Oxford University Press.
 DOI: 10.1093/oso/9780197835630.003.0003

was not much needed in his own day since the old heresies had been defeated. The interpretation also fit well with two more general assumptions that have been widely shared among Western scholars of medieval Islamic thought. The first, advocated by eminent figures such as Wilfrid Cantwell Smith, Josef van Ess, and George Makdisi, is that "orthopraxy" was historically more important in Islam than "orthodoxy," and that law rather than theology is "Islam's ideal religious science."[2] The second is the tendentious view, expounded by philosophers such as Averroes (d.1198) and accepted uncritically by many modern scholars, that the method of the Aristotelian philosophers is demonstrative syllogism (*burhān*) that yields certainty, whereas the Islamic theologians use mere "dialectic" (*jadal*) that at best yields opinion.[3]

Nevertheless, the view that Islamic theology is essentially dialectical and apologetic extrapolates too readily from the evidence of a select number of (unsympathetic or lukewarm) medieval authors and does not do justice to the self-conception of the theologians themselves. As I will show in this chapter, *kalām* for Sanūsī is a demonstrative, not a dialectical science, and a mastery of its essentials is a religious duty incumbent on every adult and sane Muslim, regardless of the presence or absence of infidels and heretics. A nominal Muslim who has no inkling of the rational basis for belief in God and the prophecy of Muḥammad is, Sanūsī declared, at best a sinner who is neglecting a religious duty and at worst not strictly a believer at all.

1 Imitation in the Ashʿari tradition

A better sense of the theologians' own assessment of the aim of their discipline can be obtained from the relevant discussion in *The Guidance* by the great Ashʿarī theologian al-Juwaynī (d.1085), a teacher of the now better known al-Ghazālī (d.1111). As mentioned in the previous chapter, Juwaynī's work was widely studied in North Africa from the twelfth to the fifteenth century and elicited numerous commentaries. The opening section of *The Guidance*, after the preamble, tells the reader that the first duty of a Muslim of legal age and sound mind is to intend to reason correctly so as to achieve knowledge of the creation of the world.[4] This statement on the first duty of a Muslim is then followed by brief sections on "reasoning" or "ratiocination" (*naẓar*) and its ability to yield what Juwaynī calls *ʿilm* or *maʿrifa*, i.e., justified knowledge that contrasts with ignorance, doubt, and surmise.[5] This, in turn, is followed by sections that present Juwaynī's proof for the existence of God, a cosmological proof that tries to show that the world cannot be pre-eternal and must have been brought into existence by a creator.[6] In short, Juwaynī's work clearly expounds the view that the first duty of a Muslim is to exercise his or her reason so as to prove—or learn an already available proof for—the existence of God.

One of the commentaries on *The Guidance* that most influenced Sanūsī was written by the Egyptian scholar al-Muqtaraḥ (d.1216). The commentary presented two views within the Ashʿarī school on the duty of engaging in reasoning.[7] According to one view, ordinary, non-scholarly believers are not obliged to reason their way to belief in God and the truth of Muḥammad's prophecy. Reasoning is, on this account, a collective duty of the Muslim community. As long as some Muslims—the scholars—took on the duty, the common run of Muslims need not do so and can rest content with following the lead of the specialists. This "following the lead of specialists" was termed *taqlīd* ("imitation" or "conformism"), so this view was often phrased as *taqlīd* being permissible with respect to the fundamentals of religion (*uṣūl al-dīn*). The ordinary, unlearned believer did nothing wrong by leaving off reasoning and simply accepting true dogma from theologians. The supporters of this view, al-Muqtaraḥ wrote, often invoked the practice of the Prophet and his companions who accepted the mere profession of faith from people who were often unlearned and uncouth, without any indication that they required the profession to be based on intricate theological argument.

The opposing view, to which al-Muqtaraḥ inclined, was to insist that reasoning is an individual and not just a collective duty. Every legally responsible Muslim must exercise his or her reason to ascertain the existence of God and the truth of Muḥammad's prophecy, and mere imitation is unacceptable when it comes to these fundamentals of the faith. In support of the view, al-Muqtaraḥ quoted eminent companions of the Prophet Muḥammad who had urged their fellows not to base their belief on mere conformism. Ibn Masʿūd (d.652 or 653), for example, was reported to have said, "Don't be someone who is weak of character (*immaʿ*), such that if people do not believe then you don't believe, and if people believe then you believe." ʿAlī ibn Abī Ṭālib (d.661), the Prophet's cousin and son-in-law, was reported to have contrasted those who have or seek knowledge with the "savage rabble" (*hamaj raʿāʿ*) who mindlessly follow the loudest voice and the strongest gust of wind. As for the Prophet and his companions accepting the verbal profession of faith, this is to no avail, al-Muqtaraḥ wrote. Both sides of the argument agree, he stated, that someone who utters the profession of faith should be treated legally as a Muslim in this world. But both sides also agree that mere utterance is insufficient for salvation; the "hypocrite" (*munāfiq*) who goes through the motions with no inner conviction is, by common agreement, not a believer in the eyes of God and will not be saved in the hereafter. Furthermore, the view that *taqlīd*—imitation or conformism—is sufficient in the principles of religion leads to a dilemma. It is clearly absurd, according to al-Muqtaraḥ, to suggest that the unlearned can follow whomever they wish. They are required to follow the lead of the right specialists, as opposed to infidels or heretics. But how are the unlearned to know who is the right specialist without exercising their own reason?

One point that is left unanswered in al-Muqtaraḥ's discussion is the following: Granted that reasoning is incumbent on all Muslims of sound mind and legal age, what is the status of those who neglect that duty? Some held that the imitator is a sinner for neglecting a duty, others that the imitator lacks true knowledge of the fundamental tenets of the religion and hence is not fully a believer. The two competing answers to this question could be seen as distinct positions. Accordingly, Sanūsī presented three views within the Ashʿari school on imitation in matters of creed, rather than the two delineated by al-Muqtaraḥ:

The first view is that conformism or imitation is a perfectly acceptable way to acquire religious belief. Going beyond the stage of imitation and acquiring knowledge through reasoning is a collective but not an individual duty. Some members of the class of religious scholars should pursue natural or rational theology and thus be in a position to allay doubts, answer questions, and clarify the proper understanding of the articles of faith. But it is not necessary—and may even be dangerous—to ask this of all believers. Perhaps the most prominent exponent of this position within the Ashʿari school was the famous Ghazālī.[8] Among Sanūsī's North African contemporaries, this was the position of the Tunisian scholar and judge Muḥammad al-Bakkī al-Kūmī (d.1510).[9]

The second position is that reasoning is the individual duty of every adult and sane person, and the believer who willfully remains at the stage of *taqlīd* is a sinner who is shirking a religious duty. Among Sanūsī's North African contemporaries, this position was upheld by the Tunisian scholar Aḥmad al-Qalshānī (d.1459) and by Sanūsī's compatriot and rival Ibn Zakrī (d.1494).[10]

The third position is that reasoning is a condition (*sharṭ*) for religious belief (*īmān*). A person who is nominally a Muslim but willfully remains at the stage of imitation is not only a sinner but has no *ʿilm* or *maʿrifa* (i.e., justified, secure knowledge) of the fundamental tenets of the creed and is therefore not truly a believer in the eyes of God. Such a person remains a Muslim legally but—like a hypocrite who utters the profession of faith—will not obtain salvation on the Day of Judgment. There is evidence that this was the view of some early Ashʿaris. Abū Isḥāq al-Isfarāyinī (d.1027), for example, wrote in one of his works:

> When a person believes this [i.e., the fundamental articles of faith], the literalists (*ahl al-ẓāhir*) say that he truly has faith (*īmān*): that he is one of those on whose behalf the Prophet will intercede and that he will ultimately achieve paradise. The expert theologians, however, say that this is not the case until his belief (*iʿtiqād*) in what we have set forth becomes, as we have explained, a real knowing (*maʿrifa*) and he thus belong to the number of those who know (*al-ʿārifūn*) and be no longer counted among those who simply repeat the statements of others (*al-muqallidūn*).[11]

ʿAbd al-Qāhir al-Baghdādī (d.1037), though he personally preferred the view that the imitator is a sinner, attributed the following view to Abū l-Ḥasan al-Ashʿarī (d.935), the eponym of the theological school to which Baghdādī himself belonged:

> Some claim that the one who believes the truth is, by virtue of this belief, not an infidel (*kāfir*), for infidelity and believing the truth with respect to monotheism and prophecy are opposed. But such a person does not deserve the name "believer" (*muʾmin*) unless he knows the truth concerning the creation of the world and the unity of its creator and the correctness of prophecy by means of some of the proofs, whether or not he can express these verbally or not. This is the position of al-Ashʿarī. The one who believes the truth on the basis of imitation (*taqlīd*) is not, in his view, a polytheist or infidel, though he does not call him unqualifiedly "a believer."[12]

Such views make it understandable why Ashʿaris were sometimes accused by opponents of denying the "faith of the imitator" (*īmān al-muqallid*). The charge had surfaced during the brief persecution of Ash'aris in Seljuk-ruled Khurasan in the mid-eleventh century, leading the famous theologian and mystic al-Qushayrī (d.1072) fervently to deny the charge.[13] In the aftermath of the persecution, it appears that especially eastern Ash'aris tempered their position on this point or expressed it more cautiously.[14] In the Islamic West, there may have been less pressure for Ash'aris to adopt a more lenient position. But even in that region, the claim that the imitator is not fully a believer was clearly controversial, and the evidence suggests that the majority of theologians in Sanūsī's time preferred to say either that imitation is sufficient for ordinary, non-scholarly Muslims or that it is simply a sin that does not take a person outside the bounds of faith.

Of the Ash'ari works that influenced Sanūsī, the one that comes closest to the third, radical position is *The Intermediate in Creed* by Abū Bakr Ibn al-'Arabī (d.1148), mentioned in the previous chapter as one of the early prominent Ash'aris in the Islamic West. Ibn al-'Arabī wrote:

> Even though we say that justified knowledge is a duty, and that reasoning leading to this is a duty, some of our fellow Ash'aris say that the one who has true beliefs about God and whose beliefs about His attributes are accurate is a believer and a monotheist. But this is not the case, for the most, except for the one who reasons, and even if it is true of the one who does not reason, there is no safeguard from the belief being shaken. So, according to us, one must know every article of faith by a proof, and the belief is to no avail unless it proceeds from this proof.[15]

Ibn al-'Arabī then spelled out what this meant for the nominal believer who did not engage in ratiocination. First, he presented the received view:

> What if he dies [before reasoning] and his beliefs about God are appropriate, or if he is unable to reason? Some of them [i.e., of

> Ibn al-ʿArabī's fellow Ashʿaris] claim that he is a believer. If he is able to reason but does not reason, then the Ustādh Abū Isḥāq [al-Isfarāyinī (d.1027)] said that he is a believer but a sinner for leaving off reasoning, and he based this on the principles of the Shaykh Abū l-Ḥasan [al-Ashʿarī].[16]

Ibn al-ʿArabī then added his own, less sanguine position on this issue:

> As for him being a believer when the absence of reasoning is due to inability or death, this is clear, God willing. As for his being a believer while being able to reason but not doing so, this is a position whose truth is doubtful to me, and I do not at present know whether it is true.[17]

As will be seen in the following section, Ibn al-ʿArabī's position is the one that Sanūsī upheld in his major theological works. It amounts to rejecting the first of the three main positions (imitation is sufficient for ordinary, unlearned believers) and leaving it open whether it is the second position (imitation is a sin) or the third position (imitation is incompatible with being a believer) that is correct.

The discussion of the permissibility or otherwise of imitation in matters of creed was complicated by a further disagreement. Most contributors to the controversy clearly assumed that the common people were imitators. On that account, the position that an imitator is a sinner or not fully a believer would have serious—if only otherworldly—consequences for the majority of nominal Muslims. But some scholars demurred and held that ordinary, unlearned believers are not imitators at all. The common run of believers, they argued, often indulge in inferences from the intricate wonders of creation to the existence, power, and wisdom of the Creator, or from the inimitability of the Quran to the truth of Muḥammad's prophecy. It is true that unlearned Muslims are unfamiliar with the technical terms and precise modes of argumentation of the discipline of kalām, but this does not make them imitators who unthinkingly accept the basic articles of faith. An exponent of such a view was Sanūsī's North African contemporary Aḥmad Zarrūq (d.1493), one of the most eminent Sufis in the Islamic tradition. In his commentary on the creed of Ghazālī, Zarrūq wrote:

> There has been disagreement about imitation in the principles of religion . . . The chosen position is that if he [i.e., the imitator] takes on the view of someone else while leaving room for doubt and false imaginings, then it is not acceptable. Otherwise, it is acceptable, though he is a sinner for leaving off reasoned inference.[18]

This reads like an expression of the second of the three positions outlined above. But Zarrūq went on to neutralize the apparent exactingness of the position by writing:

> One of the verifying scholars has said: The disagreement concerns the one who is raised in the high mountains or east of China or on an island and does not contemplate the world, and then a human tells him what is incumbent, and he assents. As for the one who grows up in the lands of Islam and praises Allah when he sees His work and contemplates His marvels, he is indulging in a kind of inference which takes him beyond imitation.[19]

This addition makes Zarrūq's position much less radical and demanding than it seems to be at first sight. Yes, it is a sin to accept the basic articles of faith unthinkingly without reasoning, but ordinary, unlearned believers do not do this. There is therefore no danger that the censure of imitation would lead to declaring the majority of nominal Muslims sinners or worse.

Another of Sanūsī's contemporaries, the aforementioned Tunisian judge al-Bakkī al-Kūmī expressed the same view, writing:

> The subject of controversy . . . is not those who grew up in the lands of Islam, its towns and villages and deserts, and among whom the Prophet and his miracles are known by numerous, indubitable reports, nor those who give thought to the creation of the heavens and the earth and the difference of night and day. All of these are among the people of reasoning and inference. Rather it is the one who grew up on a mountain-top, for example, and has not given thought to the realms of the heavens and the earth, and a human tells him what he ought to believe, and he believes what he is told without deliberation and reflection.[20]

As will be seen in the following sections, Sanūsī was considerably less sanguine about the state of the ordinary, unlearned Muslims of his age.

2 Sanūsī's condemnation of imitation

All Sanūsī's major theological works include an impassioned condemnation of imitation (*taqlīd*). In his *Long Creed*, he wrote:

> The first duty incumbent before anything else on the person who reaches the age of maturity is to exercise his mind on what will lead him with certain demonstrations and clear proofs to knowledge of his Lord [. . .] and not to be satisfied with the lowly occupation of imitation (*taqlīd*), for this does not avail him on the Last Day according to many verifying scholars. (K 83)

In the introduction to his commentary on the *Middle Creed*, Sanūsī wrote:

> We praise and thank Him for countless bounties, the most precious of which is what He, may He be exalted, has bestowed of the bounty of faith (*īmān*) and coming forth from the darkness and prison of imitation (*taqlīd*) concerning the creed to the spacious light of correct reasoning that reveals the quintessence of certainty (*yaqīn*). (W 121)

In his commentary on the *Short Creed*, he wrote:

> Lowly imitation (*al-taqlīd al-radī'*) is at the root of the unbelief of the idolaters, who say "We found our forefathers following a religion, and we are guided upon their traces" [Quran 43:22]. For this reason, the verifying scholars (*muḥaqqiqūn*) have said: Imitation in the tenets of the creed is not sufficient. One of the religious dignitaries said, "There is no difference between an imitator being led and an animal being led." (S 290)

In the previous section, three positions within the Ash'arī school on imitation in the principles of religion were outlined: (i) it is permissible for ordinary, unlearned Muslims to accept the creed by imitation of the learned; (ii) it is incumbent on all mature and sane Muslims to strive to ascertain the rational grounds for the articles of faith, and it is a sin not to do so and remain at the stage of imitation; and (iii) mere imitation does not yield true knowledge of the fundamental articles of faith, and the imitator is, accordingly, not fully a believer. In his three main theological works, Sanūsī unequivocally rejected the first of these options. The question of whether it is the second or third option that is correct he tended to leave open—his various statements tend to be studiedly compatible with either position:

> It [imitation] is insufficient for salvation in the view of many verifying scholars. (K 87)

> In sum, that which has been related by many mainstream Sunnis and verifiers among them is that imitation is not sufficient in matters of religious creed. (K 144)

> This is a short compendium the understanding of which will raise—if God wills—the legally responsible person from the stage of imitation, concerning whose sufficiency for faith there is disagreement, to correct reasoning, concerning whose sufficiency there is a consensus. (W 87)

In his commentary on *The Short Creed*, he expressed a guarded preference for the position that the imitator is not strictly speaking a believer at all:

> The true position indicated by the Quran and Tradition (*sunna*) is to hold that correct reasoning (*al-naẓar al-ṣaḥīḥ*) is incumbent [on every sane adult] while hesitating concerning whether it is a condition for faith or not, and the more plausible position (*al-rājiḥ*) is that it is indeed a condition for faith. (S 129)

Regardless of whether imitation is a sin or outright unbelief, Sanūsī considered it the duty of the individual to engage in theological reasoning and thus go beyond merely imitating elders and peers. Specifically, every believer should know each tenet of the creed along with at least one demonstration of it. Sanūsī used the term "demonstration" (*burhān*) in its technical sense in logic: a valid inference from proven or indubitable premises. As Sanūsī was well aware, Arabic logicians typically recognized that there are formally valid inferences that are not demonstrative: for example, a dialectical (*jadalī*) inference would consist of premises that are accepted by all parties in an argument, and a rhetorical (*khiṭābī*) inference would consist of premises that elicit emotional assent from listeners. Theology for Sanūsī must rest on demonstrative inferences: its premises must not just be emotionally congenial or accepted for the purposes of the argument at hand but be indubitable or proven. He wrote, "In sum, what is to be relied upon of these kinds in correctly establishing religious creeds is the first, which is demonstration" (K 139).

When comparing Sanūsī's discussion with that of his North African contemporaries—al-Bakkī al-Kūmī, Qalshānī, Zarrūq, and Ibn Zakrī—what stands out is not only the vehemence of Sanūsī's disparagement of imitation but also the space he allocated to the issue. A recent edition of his *Commentary on the Long Creed* devotes almost fifty pages (K 141–89) to the question of imitation, compared to a few sentences or a handful of pages in the work of his aforementioned contemporaries. In what follows, I will outline Sanūsī's arguments against imitation as presented in the *Commentary on the Long Creed*, his most extensive treatment of the issue.

A starting point for Sanūsī is what he takes to be uncontroversial, namely that creedal conviction must be firm and unshakeable. Judgments come with five grades of epistemic commitment:

(i) Knowledge (*ʿilm*), which is firm conviction based on proof
(ii) Belief (*iʿtiqād*), which is firm conviction not based on proof
(iii) Supposition (*ẓann*), which is deeming a judgment more likely than not
(iv) Doubt (*shakk*), which is wavering between a judgment and its negation
(v) Misgiving (*wahm*), which is deeming a judgment more likely false than true.

Creedal commitment cannot, by common agreement, be based on (iii), (iv), or (v). It is also uncontroversial that (i), unwavering conviction based on proof, is sufficient. This leaves option (ii), unwavering commitment not based on proof. Such belief can be true or false—the imitators among infidels and heretics have this kind of unwavering commitment that is false. The question is whether *true* belief that lacks proof is sufficient as a basis for creed. Sanūsī's position is laid out at the outset, thus:

> The position of the majority and the verifying scholars of Sunnis such as al-Ash'arī and al-Bāqillānī and al-Juwaynī and others is that it [mere belief not based on proof] is not sufficient with regards to religious creed. This is the truth of which there is no doubt. (K 142)

Sanūsī adduced three main arguments for this position. First, the Quran on numerous occasions commands believers to have knowledge (*'ilm* or *ma'rifa*) or insight (*baṣīra*), not mere belief. Other passages order believers to engage in deliberation (*tafakkur*) and ratiocination (*naẓar*) leading to acknowledgment of God's Power, Knowledge, and Oneness.

Second, it is also beyond dispute that believers are obliged to follow the example of the Prophet, and the Prophet was most certainly not an imitator who believed without proof.

Third, Sanūsī adduced the same argument that we encountered in al-Muqtaraḥ's discussion in the previous section: The believer is not free to imitate anyone but must imitate those who have the correct creed. But how can one know which person to imitate unless one reasons? Sanūsī anticipated that one might counter the argument by pointing to the legitimacy of "imitation" (*taqlīd*) in Islamic law. But he rejected the analogy. In legal matters, a believer may choose to follow the lead of specialist scholars of a certain legal school on the basis of less-than-certain conviction. The differences among the legal schools pertain to issues on which there is no room for demonstrative certainty, only plausibility. And God will, by common agreement, not hold ordinary believers or legal specialists to account for well-intentioned mistakes in disputed legal matters that do not admit of certainty (K 146).

Sanūsī next tried to disarm some of the arguments in favor of the sufficiency of imitation. One such argument has already been mentioned in connection with the discussion of al-Muqtaraḥ above: The Prophet accepted into Islam the unlearned and rustic who merely uttered the two professions ("There is no god but

Allah" and "Muḥammad is Allah's Messenger"), without inquiring into their reasons. But Sanūsī, like al-Muqtaraḥ, replied that this merely shows that the profession is sufficient to be treated as a Muslim in this world. It does not show that this is sufficient for salvation. The Prophet even treated as Muslim those he knew were hypocrites (*munāfiqīn*) who outwardly professed Islam while inwardly rejecting it, though no one would claim that the hypocrites are saved in the Hereafter (K 146–7).

Another argument for imitation is that the venerable companions of the Prophet did not know the technical terminology of kalām and yet surely no one would suggest that their belief was lacking. As even some theologians admitted, paradise would be very empty if it were confined to those who mastered the abstruse terminology and arguments of kalām. To this, Sanūsī's replied that to suggest the companions were mere imitators is to insult that most excellent of generations. It is also to suggest, absurdly, that they did not heed the Quranic injunctions to know and contemplate, or that they did not understand the arguments given in the Quran in favor of monotheism, the truth of Muḥammad's prophecy, and bodily resurrection. Sanūsī adduced several reports supporting the view that the great companions of the Prophet far surpassed all later scholars in religious knowledge. As for the technical terms of kalām, Sanūsī pointed out that these are not an end in themselves, just like the technical terms of Arabic grammar are not an end in themselves. The technical terms of Arabic grammar were instituted once the pristine knowledge of the language in earliest times had been corrupted by later usage and by later converts who learned Arabic as a non-native language. Similarly, the technical terms of natural theology were instituted once the pristine creed had been sullied by doubt and heretic innovation (K 162–72).

Another argument for the sufficiency of imitation is that 'Umar b. 'Abd al-'Azīz (r. 717–720), generally recognized as the most pious of Umayyad Caliphs, reportedly advised someone to cling to the faith of old people. Sanūsī responded by interpreting this to mean the following: As heresies began to appear in the time of this Umayyad Caliph, he advised people to follow the creed of old people who still maintained the pure beliefs of the earliest generation. It cannot be, Sanūsī insisted, that the Caliph was urging believers to forego learning and the refutation of heretics. What religion would remain to the old had it not been for the heroic efforts of scholars to defend the pristine creed and refute the machinations of heretics? Sanūsī added that it may well have been the case that in those more virtuous times, old people knew the basics of the creed. But in his own age, ignorance of creedal matters was widespread. There is no concerted effort, he wrote, to teach the principles of religious creed to women, children, and the rural folk. As for slaves, they are often not taught at all, "as if they are brute animals in the eyes of their masters and are not under any religious obligation" (K 161). In general, Sanūsī bewailed—with characteristic pessimism and verve—the state of knowledge in his own time:

> You will find the minds of most people of this age to be rigid and unwieldy, inclined to matters of no importance. If advised, they reject, and if taught, they do not learn, and if instructed, they do not understand, and if made to understand, they soon forget, and if some understanding remains, they become vain and use it to advance in this world and get close to tyrants. (K 161)

Yet another argument for the admissibility of imitation is that some imitators are more unshakeable in their faith than those who indulge in kalām-theology. Sanūsī replied that this is to beg the question. The very point at issue is whether an imitator has faith (*īmān*) in the full sense of the term. It will clearly not do to address such a question by presupposing that an imitator is a believer and then assert that his or her belief is more entrenched than that of a theologian. The only non-circular argument here may be that some imitators lead lives of outward piety and asceticism, while some learned scholars are impious and avaricious. But this is neither here nor there. Imitation is not invariably or even normally linked to piety, nor is learning linked to worldliness and sin. Non-Muslim ascetics sometimes lead lives of outward piety and asceticism, though by common agreement this is to no avail in the Hereafter (K 148–51).

The upshot is that some degree of reasoning is incumbent on every sane and mature person. Sanūsī wrote:

> The imitator should not find comfort in his strong resolution and pious demeanor, for a counterexample (*naqḍ*) is the resolve of Jews and Christians and idolators and their like in imitating their religious leaders and fathers who are misled and mislead. (K 177)

Strong resolve is not, Sanūsī pointed out, an indicator of truth. It is rather an indicator of having grown up in a certain community with certain deeply held beliefs. Rather than appealing to one's strength of resolve, one should rather introspect and ask oneself why one has certain religious convictions. If one cannot answer that question, then one is a mere imitator. To progress beyond that stage and achieve insight (*baṣīra*) requires engaging in demonstrative reasoning (K 177).

Sanūsī then dealt with two further objections to his position. The first is that the Quran and hadith are sufficient to establish the creed. Sanūsī's answer was, first, that the fact that the Quran and hadith are prooftexts can only be known through natural reason, and second, that natural theology is necessary for a correct understanding of the Quran and hadith, and more specifically for knowing when scriptural passages should be understood literally and when figuratively. Just taking everything in scripture literally leads to crude anthropomorphism and is therefore one of the sources of heresy or unbelief (K 178).

Another possible objection to Sanūsī's call for ratiocination is to claim that true knowledge (*ma'rifa*) comes about through asceticism and supererogatory practices rather than reasoning. Sanūsī's response was that such pious practices presuppose knowledge and cannot lead to it. How, he asked, can one serve without knowledge of the One served, or practice supererogatory acts of worship without knowing the One worshipped, or obey without knowing the One obeyed? Of course, Sanūsī—who was himself initiated into Sufi practices—agreed that once creedal knowledge is obtained, supererogatory and purificatory practices can be of immense benefit and can, in turn, promote one's station from correct belief (*īmān*) to that of charity (*iḥsān*). But he insisted that such practices presuppose proper creedal conviction and therefore cannot ground it. Brahmins and Christians indulge in extreme ascetic practices and yet remain infidels, and this is all the proof one needs for the claim that proper creedal conviction is the ground for ascetic and supererogatory practices, not the other way round (K 178–9).

Sanūsī reiterated his position on imitation at length in his *Commentary on the Middle Creed* (W 148–93, 346–54). But he added a significant qualification. Each individual is best placed to tell whether he or she is an imitator or not. It is not a condition for being a non-imitator that one is able to expound the underlying arguments to others or address questions and doubts. It would therefore be inappropriate to challenge ordinary believers and ask them about their beliefs and proofs. Rather, one should adhere to the general principle of "thinking well" (*ḥusn al-ẓann*) of one's fellow Muslims, whether learned or unlearned. Sanūsī wrote:

> We should not think ill of the belief of any Muslim, commoner or not, for knowledge is in the heart, and it is sufficient to progress beyond imitation to have a general proof. It is not a condition that he be able to organize it [i.e., the proof] in the way scholars do, nor to repel doubts, nor to express it verbally . . . Even many scholars have difficulty expressing what is in them of various sciences, so how can one expect more of the commoner? Yes, if an individual expresses something that indicates a corrupt creedal

belief, then it is incumbent to instruct him with kindness and dispel the ailment as far as possible. (W 351–2)

3 Did Sanūsī moderate his position in later works?

Some of Sanūsī's shorter creedal works, which were written later in his life, suggest a less uncompromising stance on imitation. In his *Commentary on the Preliminaries*, for example, he wrote:

> There is disagreement concerning the common run of believers imitating Sunni scholars in the principles of religion: Is this sufficient or not? Many verifying scholars have said that this is sufficient if it is accompanied by a determination to be right, especially in the case of those for whom understanding proofs is difficult, and God knows best. (M 200)

In his *Commentary on the Shortened Short Creed*, Sanūsī wrote:

> If certain conviction that corresponds to actual fact occurs to him [i.e., the adult, sane person] but is neither evident nor the conclusion of demonstration but is from imitation, then there are a number of opinions and views, of which the most correct is that he must seek a demonstration leading to knowledge when he has the aptitude for understanding it. (SS 130)

In his commentary on Ḥawḍī's creedal poem, Sanūsī wrote:

> Among Sunni scholars there are some who distinguish between the one who has aptitude and intelligence and can understand the proofs that lead to knowledge, and the one who does not have this aptitude, who need not reason and for whom imitation is sufficient.[21]

Such passages suggest that in some later works, at least, Sanūsī adopted a somewhat more accommodating tone, carefully leaving open the possibility that not all legally mature believers may have the aptitude to study the proofs that lead them beyond the stage of imitation. The evidence, to be sure, is not conclusive. The relevant passages are short, and the exact wording allows for a number of interpretations. But the tone does seem more forgiving than the one adopted in his three main creedal works—the commentaries on the *Long*, *Middle*, and *Short* Creeds. We know that Sanūsī's creedal classes were attended by commoners, not just full-time students.[22] It may be that Sanūsī came to realize that unlearned commoners had difficulty understanding and assimilating the content of even the *Short Creed*. It was mentioned in the previous chapter that the *Shortened Short Creed* was written for one of his students' father who found the *Short Creed* too long. This would hardly be the only example of a man immersed in the scholarly life coming to realize that what he deemed straightforward and uncomplicated was in fact baffling to the unlearned.

Sanūsī's later view on imitation may, however, have been more complex than a simple shift away from an earlier, more strident position. As mentioned earlier in this chapter, the discussion of the admissibility of imitation in the principles of religion intersected with another question. While most discussants assumed that the ordinary, unlearned Muslims were imitators, some expressly dismissed the idea. Sanūsī's contemporaries Zarrūq and al-Bakkī al-Kūmī were quoted above as opining that an "imitator" was someone who grew up on the margins of civilization, on an isolated mountain top or island. Ordinary Muslims were not imitators at all—they regularly made inferences from the grandeur and order of the world to the existence of God, or from the miracle of the Quran to the truth of Muḥammad's prophecy. There is no reason to think that Sanūsī ever came round to such a rosy view of the religious beliefs of the common people of his time. He wrote:

> Even weaker . . . is the statement of one of our contemporaries that there is no imitator amongst the believers, commoners as well as elite, and that justified knowledge (*ma'rifa*) obtains for them all, the sole difference being in the degree to which they can or cannot express what is in their hearts . . . This person does not impose any conditions at all but makes justified knowledge obtain for anyone called a "believer" without the necessity of reasoning. There is no concealing the fact that this statement is false and that there is consensus that the opposite is true, for it is known without a shadow of doubt that the tenets of the creed are not all self-evident, rather some require subtle reasoning. How could this not be the case when this noble community alone has disagreed in matters of creed to such an extent that they have divided into 73 sects of which only one is right?[23]

Whereas Zarrūq, al-Bakkī al-Kūmī, and Ibn Zakrī saw the "imitator" as a liminal figure, located on the margins of human society, Sanūsī passionately denounced what he saw as widespread creedal ignorance among the common people. Heresies such as anthropomorphic conceptions of God, belief in natural causation, that God undergoes change, and that God acts for a final cause were, he believed, rampant among the unlearned. Many nominal believers were therefore not even "imitators" of correct creedal views and, as such, were at risk of damnation. He wrote:

> As for the common people, most of them do not care to attend the classes of the scholars or attend the people who uphold rightness and one may verify amongst them belief in anthropomorphism, that God is in a certain direction, that natural entities have causal powers, that God's actions have a final cause, that His Word consists of letters and sounds, and that He, like humans, sometimes speaks and sometimes is silent . . . Some of these beliefs constitute unbelief by consensus of the learned scholars, while concerning the other beliefs there is disagreement

> [whether they constitute unbelief or are just erroneous] . . . By God! Had it not been for His kindness, may He be exalted, and His enabling us to engage with learning and its people, we would have been wallowing in the gorges of the partisans of falsehood. How strange it is when a rational person is ignorant of necessary truths and does not recognize his own state before engaging with learning and does not recognize the state of the common people! (K 181–2)

Another passage strikes a similar pessimistic tone:

> As for our own times, the Right Path (*al-sunna*) is by comparison to reprehensible innovations as rare as a white hair on the skin of a black bull. One who does not expend himself today in acquiring knowledge and taking it from well-versed scholars—and how rare are these today, especially in this science [i.e., *kalām*]!—will die in a state of heretical innovation or unbelief without even realizing it. Most people today have not even attained the rank of believers by imitation but rather remain in the rank of corrupt beliefs and heedless ignorance. This is due to nothing else but the approach of the Hour and the scarcity of knowledgeable, upright scholars and decent, clever students, as well as the abundance of the people of the nether world who are impressed with what they think they know and who are misled and mislead. (K 171–2)

The only cure, Sanūsī insisted, is to combat creedal ignorance through teaching, and this teaching, in turn, is most effective if the rational grounds of the creed are taught at the same time. In other words, it is not that the common folk had correct beliefs but lacked the proofs. Rather, ignorance of theological reasoning (*naẓar*) tended to go hand in hand with gross creedal error (W 178). Accordingly, all Sanūsī's creedal works, including those that seem more lenient toward "imitation," stand out by systematically giving both the articles of the faith and at least one proof for each article.

It cannot be ruled out that Sanūsī became more accommodating of "imitation" in his later years. But the evidence is circumstantial rather than definitive, and it is possible to give an alternative explanation of the more lenient tone in some of his writings. The works that express a more hardline stance toward imitation also tend to be longer and more demanding, presumably having been addressed to serious students who could be trusted to have the correct creedal beliefs already, and Sanūsī accordingly focused on urging them to learn proofs and progress beyond the stage of imitation. The works that express a more accommodating stance tend to be shorter, accessible works, presumably aimed at beginning students or the unlearned. This group may still have been under the sway of popular beliefs that Sanūsī considered heretical: anthropomorphic conceptions of God, the belief in natural causation, the belief that God's eternal Speech is in Arabic, and the belief that God's attributes change. When addressing such people, he may well have emphasized the paramount importance of getting the creedal beliefs right, a step that, even according to his earlier, more hardline works, is indubitably more urgent than going beyond "imitation."

There is, in other words, some reason to believe that Sanūsī's attitude to "imitation" did not necessarily soften, but that—when addressing beginning students and the unlearned—his campaign against imitation took a back seat to the more urgent task of rectifying what he considered widespread and serious ignorance of the correct creed.[24]

4 "Fossilized Conservatism"?

An earlier generation of scholars writing in English tended to dismiss Sanūsī as a "vulgarizer" or an exponent of "fossilized conservatism."[25] The assessment was largely based on a cursory look at his shorter creedal works, explicitly aimed for ordinary believers or young students. These do indeed appear to popularize

Islamic theology and present the arguments behind the articles of faith in a systematic but truncated and dogmatic form, without in-depth discussion of the positions and arguments of opposing theological schools. However, to see nothing but vulgarization and dogmatism in these works is to miss the point. As will be clear from later chapters, Sanūsī wrote longer, more detailed theological works that cannot plausibly be written off as popularizations, and these engage in detail with internal disagreements within Ashʿarism and with the positions and arguments of other schools. He wrote shorter, more accessible creedal works, not because he had nothing more advanced to say, but because he thought it of ultimate importance that ordinary Muslims, including the unlearned, both men and women, should know the core articles of their faith and their rational proofs so that they could emerge from the "darkness and prison" of unthinking conformism to the "spacious light" of reasoned certainty. Rather than "fossilized conservatism," this was a radical project that was met with hostility by many of Sanūsī's contemporary scholars, including some of the most prominent ulema of Tlemcen in his time. In the words of his student Mallālī:

> When the Shaykh [i.e., Sanūsī] composed some of his creeds and disseminated them with the intention of benefitting Muslims, many of the scholars of his time, ignorant of his true worth, criticized him for this, impugned his honor, and made accusations that were not befitting of his station. They claimed, by their corrupt imaginings, that what the Shaykh had done by making the creed known is a major innovation (*bidʿa*) and that piety calls for refraining from this. When the Shaykh heard this, his mood changed dramatically, and he remained sad and dejected for around three days. (MQ 287)

In the previous chapter, it was mentioned that Sanūsī had tense or hostile relations, partly related to his radical stance on "imitation," with some of the most prominent religious scholars of Tlemcen in his time: The Chief Judge Muḥammad al-ʿUqbānī (d.1467), the Imam of the Grand Mosque Ibrāhīm al-ʿUqbānī (d.1475), and the Mufti Ibn Zakrī (d.1494). The last-mentioned scholar explicitly made the accusation that teaching commoners the rational proofs underlying the creed is a reprehensible "innovation" (*bidʿa*). He wrote (in verse):

> There are no reports that the pious ancestors
> Undertook reasoning (*naẓar*) with commoners.
> Doing so is an impious innovation (*bidʿa*),
> Which calls out to all for rectification.
> [. . .]
> The ones with faith (*īmān*) should not be asked for demonstration.
> Exposing gaps in their knowledge is not part of pious tradition.
> Provoking the ill-prepared with demands for validation,
> Will do nothing but lead them to perdition.

It is clear that Ibn Zakrī was here taking aim at Sanūsī, as a sixteenth-century commentator on these words acknowledged.[26] The commentator, the Moroccan scholar Aḥmad al-Manjūr (d.1587), whose teachers had studied with students of Sanūsī, glossed Sanūsī's hardline position on imitation thus:

> This from the Shaykh, may God have mercy on him and may we benefit from his knowledge, is very severe concerning the imitator. It is said that, because of this, his contemporaries in Tlemcen, such as Ibn Zakrī, challenged him and condemned him for declaring the imitator an infidel (*takfīr al-muqallid*).[27]

Despite the initial resistance from some quarters, Sanūsī's reputation had grown considerably by the time of his death and would soon thereafter overshadow that of his local opponents. As will be outlined in the concluding chapter, his creedal works elicited widespread enthusiasm, and within a century of his death came to dominate the teaching of theology in the Maghreb, from whence they spread to West Africa, Egypt, Sudan, the Levant, the Hejaz, and even as far away as the Malay Archipelago. The idea that imitators may not be true believers remained very controversial. But even many scholars who thought that imitation in the principles of the creed is merely a sin, or perhaps not even a sin at all for the unlearned, obviously still thought that a little learning is not a dangerous thing and that Sanūsī's creeds effectively conveyed to the common folk what they should believe—and why.

4
What Every Believer Should Know

The previous chapter dealt with Sanūsī's radical stance on "imitation" (*taqlīd*) and his insistence that all adult and sane believers are obliged to know both the core articles of faith and at least some of their rational proofs, as opposed to simply accepting what they are told by elders and peers. At the same time, Sanūsī did not demand that all believers become expert theologians who could refute the arguments of heretics and infidels. The question then becomes just how much ordinary believers should know in order to go beyond the status of "imitator." Sanūsī's shorter creedal works will give the reader a sense of the answer. The following exposition will survey the contents of his widely studied *Commentary on the Short Creed*, supplemented on occasion with his *Commentary on the Shortened Short Creed*. My discussion will touch on topics and arguments that will be dealt with in greater detail in later chapters. Readers who find certain arguments undeveloped or unconvincing are asked to keep in mind that the purpose of this chapter is not to give a detailed exposition and evaluation of the arguments. It is rather to give a sense of what Sanūsī wanted all believers to know.

A predictable tension is apparent throughout Sanūsī's shorter theological works. He wanted ordinary believers to be familiar with rational arguments for the central articles of faith but was consciously addressing non-specialists, not advanced students or fellow expert theologians. Finding the right balance between being compelling and yet accessible is, of course, not straightforward. A standing risk is that one fails on both counts, by presenting arguments that are at once too abrupt to be convincing to the specialist and too compressed to be properly understood by the

Al-Sanūsī. Khaled El-Rouayheb, Oxford University Press.
 DOI: 10.1093/oso/9780197835630.003.0004

unlearned. However, the sheer historical influence of Sanūsī's works, the fact that they were so widely studied for centuries in such a large area of the Islamic world, suggests that his attempt should not be dismissed out of hand.

1 What is necessarily and impossibly true of God

Sanūsī asserted in both his *Short Creed* and *Shortened Short Creed* that every legally responsible believer is obliged to know what is necessarily true of God, what is impossibly true of God, and what is contingently true of God. He or she is also obliged to know what is necessarily, impossibly, and contingently true of God's prophets. The necessary (*al-wājib*) is that which the mind cannot conceive to be false, either immediately or evidently (*ḍarūrī*), such as the principle of non-contradiction, or through reasoning (*naẓarī*), such as the existence of God. Impossibility (*al-mustaḥīl*) is that which the mind cannot conceive to be true, again either evidently or upon reflection. The contingent (*jā'iz*) is that which the mind can conceive to be the case or not to be the case—whether it is one or the other depends on sense-perception, experience, introspection, or revelation. Sanūsī gave the following elegant example of the three types of "rational judgment" (*ḥukm 'aqlī*): Reason tells us that it is *necessary* that a body is either in motion or at rest, that it is *impossible* that it is neither in motion nor at rest, and that it is *contingent* that it is one rather than the other (S 121–5; SS 93–4, 132–40).

What is necessary for God are the following twenty attributes (S 90–2):

(1) Existence (*wujūd*).
(2) Pre-eternality (*qidam*).
(3) Everlastingness (*baqā'*).

(4) To be different from anything that comes-to-be (*mukhālafat al-ḥawādith*).
(5) Self-subsistence (*qā'im bi-nafsihi*), i.e., not being an attribute that inheres in a substance.
(6) Oneness (*waḥdāniyya*).
(7) Power (*qudra*).
(8) Will (*irāda*).
(9) Knowledge (*ʿilm*).
(10) Sight (*baṣar*).
(11) Hearing (*samʿ*).
(12) Speech (*kalām*).
(13) Life (*ḥayāt*).
(14) Being powerful (*kawnuhu qādir*).
(15) Being a willer (*kawnuhu murīd*).
(16) Being knowledgeable (*kawnuhu ʿalīm*).
(17) Being alive (*kawnuhu ḥayy*).
(18) Being a hearer (*kawnuhu samīʿ*).
(19) Being a seer (*kawnuhu baṣīr*).
(20) Being a speaker (*kawnuhu mutakallim*).

What is not possibly true of God are the negations of the necessary attributes: non-existence; coming-to-be; passing away; being similar to created things; being an attribute inhering in a substance; being one of many entities of the same type; not having power, will, knowledge, sight, hearing, speech, or life.

2 Different types of divine attribute

The Ashʿarī tradition to which Sanūsī belonged tended to recognize different types of divine attribute. These are as follows:

(i) "Per se attributes" (*ṣifāt nafsiyya*). The precise understanding of such attributes is elusive, for various kalam theologians gave differing and sometimes incompatible definitions. (The topic will be dealt with in more detail in Chapter 7.) In the later commentary tradition on the *Short Creed*, "existence" was typically presented as the sole per se attribute of God. But as will be shown later, Sanūsī wavered on this point, expressing differing views in different works. In his *Commentary on the Short Creed*, he wrote that it is only with some latitude that existence is considered an attribute at all. "Exists" can be predicated truthfully of an entity but arguably does not denote something additional to—and inhering in—that entity itself (S 142–3). The mainstream Ash'arī tradition, from an early period, rejected the view that there are non-existent entities.[1] It accordingly tended to reject the view that existence is an attribute inhering in some entities but not others. Rather, saying that X is an entity and saying that X exists were held to be two different ways of expressing the same fact.

(ii) "Attributes of negation" (*ṣifāt salbiyya*), such as "being unlike created entities." These were also standardly presented as truthfully predicated of an entity but not real attributes inhering in that entity. Attributes (2)–(6) above were considered negative attributes by Sanūsī. Their import is that God is *not* generated, *not* corruptible, *not* like generated things, *not* an attribute inhering in a locus, and does *not* have an equal or a like.

(iii) "Entitative attributes" (*ṣifāt al-ma'ānī*). These were believed to be real, positive attributes inhering in an entity, not reducible to the entity itself nor to negations or relations. Attributes (7)–(13) were held to be the "entitative attributes" of God: Power, Will, Knowledge, Life, Speech, Sight, and Hearing.

(iv) "Entitative states" (*ṣifāt ma'nawiyya*). Some early theologians, both of the Mu'tazilī and Ash'arī schools, had postulated attributes called "states" (*aḥwāl*) that are themselves neither existent nor non-existent. Attributes

(14)–(20) were classified as entitative states: being powerful, being a willer, being knowledgeable, being alive, being a hearer, being a seer, and being a speaker. These "states" are qualifications that are entailed by the entitative attributes inhering in God but are not themselves existing or non-existing. For example, the real attribute of Knowledge inhering in God logically entails God's state of being knowledgeable and, vice versa, God's state of being knowledgeable logically entails God's possessing the attribute of knowledge. The theologians who rejected states did not accept this category of attribute. The theory of "states" will be discussed further in Chapter 7.

Is the distinction between these four kinds of divine attribute part of what Sanūsī expected the ordinary believer to know? The question does not admit of a hard and fast answer. On the one hand, when Sanūsī later wrote the *Shortened Short Creed*, abridging the *Short Creed*, he left out the "entitative states" altogether, confining himself to the first thirteen divine attributes. On the other hand, as will be seen below, some of the proofs adduced by Sanūsī for God having these thirteen attributes presuppose knowing the difference between the first three types of divine attribute, i.e., the difference between per se, negative, and entitative attributes.

3 Proof of God's existence

As one would expect from Sanūsī's views on imitation, the claim that a certain attribute is necessarily true of God is accompanied by a proof. For the assertion that existence is necessarily true of God, Sanūsī wrote in his *Short Creed*:

> As for the demonstration of His existence, this is the origination of the world. For if it did not have an originator but came to be

> by itself, then it follows that one of two equally possible items comes about without a reason, which is absurd. And the proof for the origination of the world is that it is co-implied by originated accidents, such as motion and being stationary. And that which is co-implied by what is originated is itself originated. The proof for the origination of accidents is the observation of their changing from nonexistence to existence and from existence to nonexistence. (S 92–3)

In his commentary, Sanūsī unpacked this (S 206–8). Following a long-standing tradition of Islamic kalam-theology, he argued that bodies cannot exist without non-essential attributes, so-called "accidents" (*aʿrāḍ*), and these accidents are changing or changeable. A given body, for example, is sometimes in motion and sometimes not, increases or decreases in size, and changes from one color to another. Even if some of these accidents are not observed to change, they are clearly "contingent" in the above-mentioned sense that the human mind cannot tell a priori which of these accidents obtain but must instead rely on sense-perception. Given that they are contingent, they require a cause that determines that one accident is realized as opposed to other, equally possible accidents—for example, why a body is here rather than there, or why it has a particular size rather than being a bit larger or smaller. It is also clear that a body cannot exist without having a specific spatial location, a certain size, and a certain color. Sanūsī then applied a general principle widely accepted in kalam theology, namely that if a body cannot exist without caused and originated accidents, then it must itself be caused and originated. So, all bodies in the world are originated as opposed to pre-eternal. If the world is originated, then it must have an originator. It is inconceivable that the world should have come about without sufficient reason, without an entity that causes the world to exist rather than not exist.

We will encounter a more detailed version of this "argument from accidents" in Chapter 6 devoted to Sanūsī's proofs for the existence of God as presented in his longer, more advanced theological works. As will be clear then, Sanūsī was aware that the argument faced some objections. It is not evident, for example, that the "world," defined as everything other than God, exclusively consists of bodies and their accidents. Such a physicalist premise would have been unacceptable to Aristotelian–Neoplatonist philosophers. Nor is it evident why originated attributes cannot be successively true, ad infinitum, of eternally existing bodies. In Aristotelian–Neoplatonist cosmology, the stars and planets are pre-eternal, and yet some of their accidents—their spatial positions—are constantly changing as they revolve around the Earth.

As is plain from his more advanced works, Sanūsī thought he could answer such objections. The question, however, is whether he thought the ordinary believer should be able to do so. It seems that he did not. When discussing the question of imitation, he wrote that ordinary believers were not tasked with refuting the doubts and counterarguments of heretics; that was the preserve of specialist theologians (S 134). But it then seems to follow that Sanūsī expected the ordinary believer to have unwavering certainty in the core tenets of the faith on the basis of arguments that could be—and historically had been—subjected to criticism from other philosophical and theological groups, criticisms that the ordinary believer would not be able to answer. It is not clear why this should not be considered imitation. Differently put, Sanūsī's campaign against imitation threatens to result in the implausible demand that every believer should become a specialist theologian who devotes a large part of his or her life to assessing the arguments of competing theological and philosophical groups. This was precisely the argument of those Islamic thinkers who thought that nothing good could come of exposing ordinary believers to the proofs of kalām theologians.

Though such an objection is understandable, it is hardly decisive. Sanūsī might reasonably have replied that it is absurd to say that believers should only be exposed to arguments behind the core tenets of the creed if they intend to become specialist theologians who can engage with opposing philosophical and theological schools. By the same logic, one should not expose believers to any of the Scriptural grounds for various legal rulings unless they intend to become independent jurists who can engage with the complex arguments of competing Islamic legal schools. Having said this, it seems difficult to avoid the conclusion that imitation is a matter of degree, as was often recognized in the field of Islamic legal theory, rather than—as Sanūsī often suggested—a clear-cut distinction between those who know the proofs and those who do not.

4 Proofs of God's attributes of negation

Sanūsī next turned to the proofs for the attributes of negation that are necessarily true of God: pre-eternality, post-eternality, being different from all generated things, not inhering in a substance, and being unique. The arguments here are regularly presented in the form of modus tollens, i.e., arguments of the following form:

If X is not true of God, then Y
Y is false
∴ X is true of God

If, for example, pre-eternality is not true of God, then God would be generated. But this is absurd, for it would mean that the only explanation for the existence of the world would be an infinite chain of causes, a circular chain of causes, or that the world came about by chance, without a sufficient cause, all of which are absurd. Ergo, pre-eternality must be true of God.

Given that God is pre-eternal, it is impossible that God should have attributes that entail origination. If, for example, God is mobile or stationary, and given that these accidents entail being caused and originated, then God would be caused and originated, which has just been shown to be absurd. If God has a certain physical size or a certain color, then—given that physical size and color are contingent and therefore originated—God would be originated, which is absurd. More generally, the starting point for the proof for the existence of God is that entities whose attributes are contingent and generated must themselves be contingent and generated. And it has already been established that God is pre-eternal and exists necessarily. Ergo, generated attributes cannot inhere in God (S 183–6; SS 151–3).

On this basis, Sanūsī rejected a literal interpretation of passages from the Quran and hadith that might suggest that God is in a certain direction ("upward"), has a face and hands, seats Himself on a throne, sometimes moves down to the lower heavens, sometimes speaks and is sometimes silent, is sometimes angered and sometimes pleased. Such literalist interpretations of Scripture, he insisted, is one of the principles of unbelief (*kufr*) (S 292). His remark underlines the inaccuracy of the assumption, shared by many modern Western scholars, that the Ashʿarīs were literalists who, like Ḥanbalī fideists, simply accepted all such apparent anthropomorphisms in Quran and hadith "without asking how."

As for why it is impossible that God is an attribute inhering in something else, Sanūsī wrote:

> If He were in need of a locus, then He would be an attribute. And an attribute does not itself possess entitative attributes or states. And our Lord, most Exalted and High, necessarily possesses these. So, He is not an attribute. (S 93–4)

Sanūsī, in his commentary, explained that "entitative attributes"—in other words, real attributes inhering in a subject—can only be true of substances, on pain of generating an infinite regress. The per se and negative attributes, by contrast, can be true of both substances and attributes. If I say, for example, that the existence of God itself exists, this does not entail an infinite regress of existing attributes because existence is only nominally (or linguistically) an attribute and does not denote a real quality inhering in God. And if I say, for example, that God's Knowledge is non-originated, then this, too, does not generate an infinite regress because "non-origination" is a negation and not a real quality inhering in the divine attribute of Knowledge. But God's Knowledge cannot itself be said to be knowing or willing, for that would generate an infinite regress of existing attributes: one could then ask if these positive attributes of knowing and willing that inhere in God's Knowledge are themselves knowing or willing, and so on ad infinitum (S 215–7; SS 159–60).

As for the proof for God's oneness, it again takes the form of modus tollens: If we suppose that there are two divine beings, then an absurdity arises. If the two divine beings will the same things, then this entails causal overdetermination (*taḥṣīl al-ḥāṣil*), i.e., that one effect has two different sufficient causes, which is absurd. If the two divine beings will different things, then at least one being's will must be inefficacious. But this is absurd: a divine being is such that the reach of its power and will extends to all that is not impossible, and furthermore there would be no explanation for the fact that one god's will and power trumps the will and power of the other (S 218–23).

The foregoing argument against the possibility of more than one God is known in the Islamic theological literature as "the demonstration from mutual hindering" (*burhān al-tamānu'*). In all his major theological works, Sanūsī extended the point to show that only God has causal power. If we suppose that a human being has causal power, then the same absurdity results. God's Power and Will are directed at all that is contingent, i.e., neither necessary nor impossible. Another being's efficacious will and power either coincide with God's Will and Power, in which case we have causal overdetermination, or do not coincide with God's Will and Power, in which case they are nullified. In either case, no other being can have a causally efficacious will and power. This is often referred to as the doctrine of "occasionalism" and will be discussed further in Chapter 7.

Sanūsī was careful to explain that he did not deny that humans have power and will at all. Humans have power and will, and these are directed at certain things, i.e., they are power and will *to do something.* It is just that such human power and will have no causal effect. An analogy is human knowledge: it is directed at certain things, i.e., it is a knowledge *of something.* But knowledge does not have any effect on the things known. Similarly, humans can will certain things, but their will does not have any effect on the things willed. This is the notorious Ashʿarī doctrine of "acquisition" (*kasb*): Humans assume or "acquire" responsibility for the actions that their will and power are directed toward, even though their will and power do not have causal efficacy, for all bodily movements are direct creations of God. The doctrine of acquisition will also be discussed in greater detail in Chapter 8.

5 Proofs of God's entitative attributes

Entitative attributes are those that cannot be reduced to the entity itself (like existence) or to negations (like pre-eternity and uniqueness). The Ashʿarī tradition recognized seven such core attributes of God: Power, Will, Knowledge, Life, Speaking, Hearing, and Seeing. The first four were held by Sanūsī to be known through pure reason, without resort to revelation. The fact that the world is created shows that God has power. The fact that the world is in just one of many possible ways shows that God has will. Will and power presuppose knowledge. And all three attributes—Power, Will, and Knowledge—presuppose Life. The four core attributes must be pre-eternal. If they were generated, then one would have to suppose that they came about through a different, pre-existing power, will, knowledge, and life, which leads to an infinite regress (S 224–5).

Three of these four attributes are such that they logically entail an intentional object. Power is a power to do *something*; will is a will to do *something*; and knowledge is knowledge of *something*. Life, by contrast, has no such intentional object—the attribute of life does not point beyond itself. The object of divine power, will, or knowledge is, in the parlance of kalam theology, the "attachment" (*muta'allaq*) of the attribute.[2] Sanūsī explained that God's Power and Will attach to all that is contingent, whereas God's Knowledge attaches to what is contingent, necessary, and impossible. In other words, all that is neither necessary nor impossible falls under God's Power and Will, whereas what is contingent, necessary, and impossible falls under God's Knowledge. With respect to God's Power, this is perhaps not surprising from a mainstream theistic perspective. It is at first sight more surprising that God's Will also attaches to all that is possible. God's Will determines which of the many things that fall under God's Power actually comes to pass. Accordingly, one might have expected that what falls under God's Will is a subset of what falls under God's Power, in other words, that God's Power attaches to what is possible whereas God's Will attaches to what is actual. Indeed, such an understanding seems implicit in Sanūsī's proof for God's possession of Will: God's Power has an equal relationship to all that is possible; given that the world is in just one of several possible ways, this shows that God in addition possesses a Will (K 262–3). But this invites the question how the attachments of divine power and divine will can nevertheless be the same. Sanūsī did not address this issue in his shorter theological works, and a fuller discussion of the issue will be deferred to chapter 8.

Three further, entitative divine attributes are known through revelation: Speech, Sight, and Hearing. One might ask if appeals to revelation are legitimate at this foundational stage of the theological argument, and if they are, why they cannot be appealed to across the board to establish all the divine attributes. The answer reveals a considered systemic logic, refuting the common view that kalam theology was merely an ad hoc, apologetic enterprise. Sanūsī carefully explained that the four former attributes must be established independently of revelation. This is because they are needed to establish the veracity of prophecy. A miracle is a supernatural rupture of the customary order of creation that appears in support of a person's claim to being an emissary of God. Appealing to the miracle in support of a prophet's claim presupposes, according to Sanūsī, that it has already been shown to be an act of God, and this in turn presupposes that it has been shown that God exists, has the Power and Will to do the act, and has the Knowledge and Life that are preconditions of willed action. In other words, one must show that God exists and has Power, Will, Knowledge, and Life *before* one can appeal to a miracle in support of a claim to prophecy, and therefore *before* appeal to revelation.

Given that all that occurs in the world is the direct creation of God, and is in accord with God's Will, it follows that the miracle is also a direct creation of God and in accordance with God's Will. If this miracle occurs in clear support of a claim to being an emissary of God, then there is no doubt that the claim is true. Sanūsī, using an analogy already used by Ghazālī, argued that if a person were to claim in front of a crowd of people, in the presence of a king, to be the king's spokesperson, and called on the king to support his claim by doing something very unusual, whereupon the king were to stand and sit three times in quick succession, for example, then all those present—and all those who hear of the incident from so many independent witnesses that the truth of the report is certain—would know without a doubt that the king has endorsed the person's claim.[3] Once the miracle and the veracity of prophecy are established by natural reason, further attributes of God can be established through revelation (S 226; SS 173–5).

6 What is contingently true of God

What is contingently true of God, i.e., what is neither necessarily nor impossibly true of God, is everything God freely chooses to do: create the world, create human beings, impose obligations on them, reward and punish them, send forth prophets, and so forth (S 204–5; SS 182–5). These are called, in the parlance of kalam theology, the "attributes of divine acts" (*ṣifāt al-af'āl*). As shown earlier, there are no contingent and generated attributes of the divine self, for anything with contingent and generated attributes is itself, according to Sanūsī, contingent and generated. Strictly speaking, it is the "creation of the world," for example, and the "sending forth of prophets" that are contingent, not the Divine Power and Will to do so.

Given that God is the sole cause, and that all God's real attributes are pre-eternal and necessary, it may be natural to think that all effects must be necessary. Sanūsī need not have disagreed with this. But, as shown above, he defined "the contingent" as that which human reason cannot ascertain to be the case without relying on sense-perception, repeated experience, introspection, reports from others, or revelation. In this sense, things that are metaphysically necessary can still be said to be epistemologically contingent. For example, God's sending forth prophets is in a sense necessary given God's pre-eternal Power and Will to do so. But the sending forth of prophets is nevertheless contingent in the sense that humans cannot tell by pure reason, without appeal to revelation, whether it is the case.

Sanūsī's view that it is contingent that God sends forth prophets is typical of the Ash'ari school of theology. The opposing view, advocated by the earlier Mu'tazili school and in later centuries by Shi'is and Māturīdi Sunnis, is that it is necessary, i.e., knowable through pure reason without resort to revelation, that God sends forth prophets.[4] Sanūsī associated such a view with the more general position that natural reason can determine what is objectively good and bad (*taḥsīn wa taqbīḥ 'aqlī*) and that such determinations apply to what God should or should not do. On that view, unaided human reason can determine that it would be contrary to justice or wisdom for God not to send prophets to guide humans. Ash'ari theologians typically rejected such a view. God, for them, is unconstrained by human interests or human notions of what is good or bad, and the only limits on what He can do is outright logical impossibility. In his *Commentary on the Shortened Short Creed*, Sanūsī wrote:

> Similarly, among the contingent truths is that God the Exalted sends forth His prophets, peace be upon them. That which God has determined of the worldly and otherworldly benefits of [sending] them is His free gift [to humans] . . . No one has any claims upon God, neither to be rightly guided nor to have worldly or otherworldly interests maintained. The Muʿtazilis have imposed upon God—through reason—the sending forth of prophets, on the basis of their corrupt principle that God the Exalted is bound to do what is beneficent and best [for humans]. (SS 184)

The issue at stake here—whether unaided human reason can discover standards of goodness and fairness that God is obliged to respect—is one that will be treated more fully in Chapter 9. But Sanūsī gave the beginning or non-specialist reader of his shorter creeds a prima facie powerful argument: If God were obliged to do what is best for humanity, then there would be no "corruption" (*fasād*): no evil, no pain, no illness, no death, no prohibitions, no hellfire, and no final judgment. But such evils and tribulations are known to exist. Ergo, God is not obliged to do what is best for humanity. Sanūsī wrote:

> If it were incumbent upon God to do what is good or best for His creatures, as the Muʿtazilīs claim, there would be no worldly or otherworldly tribulation, nor would any command or prohibition be imposed, and this is seen to be false. As for the good outcomes that are supposed to come out of such tribulations and impositions, God is capable of granting such good outcomes

without hardship, tribulation, or imposition. Furthermore, such good outcomes are not general to all those who are faced with tribulation or impositions, for there is no doubt that tribulation and imposition in the case of those who are destined to be infidels is a sore punishment and exposure to eternal damnation [with no ultimate good]. (S 204–5)

7 What is necessarily and impossibly true of God's prophets

Sanūsī's creed continued by presenting what is necessarily true of God's prophets, namely (S 95; SS 97–8):

(i) Truthfulness, in the sense of not uttering falsehoods when making pronouncements on points of creed or law.
(ii) Sincerity, in the sense of not committing sins, knowingly or unknowingly.
(iii) Not holding back anything that God has ordered them to reveal.

What is impossible of God's prophets is the opposite of these three. Sanūsī's arguments for these points again take the form of modus tollens:

If X is not true of the prophets, then Y
Y is false
∴ X is true of the prophets

For example, if the prophets commit sins, then their followers would be dutybound to commit sins, for they are commanded to follow the example of the prophets. But the followers are not dutybound to commit sins, so prophets do not commit sins. (To be clear, they do not commit sins *after* being anointed as prophets;

there is no necessary commitment to them being sinless beforehand.) Further, if the prophets are not truthful, then it would follow that God is not truthful, for God's creating miracles at the hands of the prophets in support of their claims to prophecy is tantamount to authenticating their claims. But it is impossible that God is not truthful. So, the prophets must be truthful.

One might wonder if Ashʿarī theologians can help themselves to the premise that God must be truthful. If, as Sanūsī affirmed, "No one has any claims upon God, neither to be rightly guided nor to have worldly or otherworldly interests maintained," then it is not immediately apparent how we can rule out that God misguides humanity by revealing falsehoods to His prophets. After all, Ashʿarīs—accepting the plain sense of numerous Quranic verses and hadith reports—tended to maintain that God misguides *some* people, namely the infidels, making them impervious to His prophets' message, thus inviting the question how we can then rule out that God misguides *all* people. This very argument was historically raised by Islamic opponents of Ashʿarism: If lying cannot be determined to be evil by natural reason, then it is not impossible that God lies, and if it is possible that God lies, then trust in revelation is undermined.[5]

In his shorter creedal works, Sanūsī briefly gave the following argument for why it is impossible that God is not truthful: God's eternal, uncreated attribute of Speech must be in accordance with God's eternal, uncreated attribute of Knowledge, and speech that is in accordance with knowledge must be true (S 236; SS 189). Thus stated, the response is surely too brief and undeveloped to be compelling. Sanūsī discussed the issue at greater length in his longer theological writings, as will be seen in Chapter 9.

On the basis of the necessary truthfulness, sincerity, and forthrightness of prophets, Sanūsī asserted that believers should deny popular reports derived from the Hebrew Bible or certain Islamic traditions according to which prophets could indulge in sinful or inappropriate behavior or forget or confuse certain parts of revelation (S 244; SS 186–94). Such a dismissal might strike modern readers as narrowly dogmatic. It is important to keep in mind, however, that the attitude was reflective of an epistemological position widespread among Islamic scholastic theologians and legal scholars. The great majority of reports about the sayings and doings of the Prophet—even those that were widely accepted as formally "correct" (*ṣaḥīḥ*)—were held at best to yield plausibility that might be good enough for legal purposes. Such traditions met certain formal criteria, specifically that the chains of transmission do not contain gaps and only consist of individuals reputed to be honest and sound of mind. But this only showed that it is *probable* the Prophet had actually said or done such-and-such, not that it is *certain* he had done so. The prevalent view was that only so-called *mutawātir* reports could yield certainty, having been relayed by so many and independent witnesses, at each link in the transmission, that it would be incredible if the report were false—an example would be reports that a historical figure such as Napoleon existed. If there were any such *mutawātir* hadith at all—which many Muslim scholars doubted—they were generally held to be very few.[6] The majority of "correct" (*ṣaḥīḥ*) hadith—let alone reports judged to be less plausible (*ḥasan* or *ḍaʿīf*)—did not qualify as such. Such reports were therefore not believed to yield certainty and could accordingly be overruled by demonstrative reasoning. For example, rational theologians considered demonstrative reasoning to establish conclusively that God cannot be an object in space, and they accordingly interpreted non-literally hadith reports that speak of God descending to the lower heavens on certain nights of the year. Similarly, rational theologians—like Sanūsī—held that the truthfulness and infallibility of a prophet can be established by demonstrative reasoning, and they therefore thought themselves entitled to overrule isolated and non-certain reports that contradicted this, such as the notorious story of the Satanic verses according to which Satan had once managed to interpolate certain praises of the pre-Islamic gods of Arabia into the divine revelation without the Prophet Muḥammad noticing this.[7]

8 What is contingently true of the prophets

The contingent attributes of prophets are human accidents such as sleeping, eating, illness, pain, and death. The proof is that prophets actually were subject to these accidents, and if they were *in fact* subject to such accidents, then it must have been *possible* for them to be subject to them. Sanūsī wrote:

> As for what is contingently true of the prophets, peace be upon them, these are human accidents that are not contrary to their exalted rank, such as illness and the like, the proof of this being that such [accidents] have been witnessed in their case. (SS 98)

It seems to have been common among later Ashʿari theologians who taught and commented on Sanūsī's works to interpret "human accidents that are not contrary to their exalted rank" to mean, for example, that a prophet must be male, freeborn, of good lineage, free from physical blemishes that elicit aversion (such as leprosy), and even an urbane townsman as opposed to a rustic country dweller.[8] Sanūsī himself did not interpret "contrary to their exalted rank" in these terms but as referring to sinful or inappropriate behavior. He wrote:

> Our saying, "that are not contrary to their exalted rank" is to guard against the belief... that the prophets, peace be upon them, can be tarnished by sinful or untoward behavior (*al-maʿṣiya wa l-makrūh*) and the like. (SS 203)

It is surprising that some later Ashʿaris, officially committed to occasionalism and divine voluntarism, should seek to impose rationally determined limits on whom God can choose as a prophet, limits that look suspiciously like the rational conditions for prophecy adduced by Muʿtazilis and Shi'is. If indeed, as Sanūsī was quoted above as stating, "No one has any claims upon God, neither to be rightly guided nor to have worldly or otherworldly interests maintained," then it is difficult to see how we can determine, through natural reason and prior to revelation, that if God sends forth a prophet, then this prophet must be male, freeborn, free from bodily disability, etc. The standard argument for imposing such limits on God's freedom to choose a prophet is that a female, a slave, or a disabled person would not elicit the requisite respect or deference to fulfill the duties of prophethood. But surely an Ashʿari occasionalist should say that there is nothing to prevent God from creating respect in a community even if their prophet is a woman, a slave, or disabled. And even apart from that point, an Ashʿari voluntarist should say that God is not obliged to do what is most aligned with human emotions and prejudices.

It is clear that Sanūsī, at least, had no sympathy for the idea that we can rule out certain characteristics of prophets on the grounds that this would elicit negative sentiments among the faithful. When, in his *Commentary on the Long Creed*, he discussed the question whether prophets can commit major sins before their prophetic career, he mentioned that Shi'is and Muʿtazilīs rule this out on the grounds that "the committing of sins would lower their status among people and repel hearts from following them, which contradicts the wisdom of sending forth prophets, and so is rationally bad." Sanūsī dismissed such arguments, writing:

> The mainstay of both groups [i.e., Shīʿīs and Muʿtazilīs] is declaring things bad by natural reason . . . And we have already spoken of the error of declaring things good or bad by natural reason. (K 573).

The only ground for declaring that prophets are free from major sins before prophecy, according to Sanūsī, would be revelation (*samʿ*).

Furthermore, Sanūsī must have been aware of the following passage from a work that he regularly cited with approval, the aforementioned Egyptian Ashʿari scholar al-Muqtaraḥ's commentary on Juwaynī's *Guidance*:

> The Muʿtazilis have rejected the possibility that a woman could be a prophet. They said, "The rank of prophecy is tied to the perfection of reason, and she is deficient in reason. It is therefore rationally abhorrent to grant her, with this deficiency, the exalted position of being in charge of humankind." This is silly (*sakhīf*). There may be a woman who is greater than men, and Muslims are in agreement that [the Virgin] Mary was better than the men of her age except for prophets. If God were to send forth a woman as a prophet, deficiency would not be true of her. And the assumed perfection of men could be created [by God] in women, and with this perfection she would increase in her insight and swiftness of apprehension of the relative strengths of opinions and of the arts of governance. This is not impossible for women, and thus what they [the Muʿtazilis] have fancied has been refuted.[9]

9 The two professions

Having expounded what is necessarily, impossibly, and contingently true of God and God's prophets, *The Short Creed* went on to discuss the "two professions" of Islam: "There is no god but Allah, and Muhammad is Allah's Messenger." Sanūsī tried to show that this encapsulates all the articles of faith that had been expounded and demonstrated earlier. The meaning of being divine, he wrote, is to be independent of everything else and to have everything else be dependent on oneself. The creedal points outlined in the previous sections are all, Sanūsī argued, in accordance with this definition (S 279–88).

The criterion that a divine entity should be independent of everything else corresponds to God's being a necessary existent, pre-eternal and post-eternal, self-subsisting, and unlike any contingent entity. It also corresponds to the Ashʿarī principles that there is no final cause for God's actions and decrees and that it is not incumbent on God to do what is good or best for creatures, for this would entail that somehow God's perfection depends on the realization of these outcomes.

The criterion that everything else should depend on a divine being corresponds to the principles that God's Knowledge, Power, and Will encompass all created substances and accidents; that God has no partner or equal, for this would entail that creatures are not, after all, dependent on God alone; that the world in its entirety is created and nothing else besides God is pre-eternal; and that nothing but God has the power to bring anything into existence.

As for the second profession, "Muhammad is Allah's Messenger," it recapitulates the above-proven principles that prophets must be truthful and sincere, and that what they reveal of truths that cannot be known through pure reason must be accepted, for example that God is a Speaker, a Seer, and a Hearer, that there will be bodily resurrection, and that there will be a Judgment Day. The second profession also confirms that human accidents—such as being born, growing up, eating, sleeping, falling ill, growing old, and passing away—are true of God's prophets. The fact that they are human reinforces their stature as exemplary servants of God who overcome human ailments and temptations. It also adds support to the creed if prophets are humans who cannot ward off pain, illness, and death, let alone bring about astounding miracles on their own accord. This also discourages believers from going to extremes in venerating them, as Muslims believe Christians have exaggerated the esteem proper to Jesus. The Quran itself (Q 5:75) rejects the divinity of

Jesus and his mother by adducing the fact that "They both used to eat food" (S 293–7).

10 Is the average believer expected to be a philosopher?

The Maghreb had known shorter creedal works addressed to non-specialists for centuries before Sanūsī. The influential *Epistle* of Ibn Abī Zayd al-Qayrawānī (d.996) includes a brief creedal introduction followed by an outline of the essentials of Islamic law.[10] The monumental *Revival of the Religious Sciences* by al-Ghazālī (d.1111) includes an introductory chapter giving the basics of the creed, a chapter that seems to have circulated independently and elicited self-standing commentaries by later Maghrebi scholars such as Sanūsī's contemporary Aḥmad Zarrūq (d.1493).[11] The short *Guide* of the founder of the Almohad movement Ibn Tūmart (d.1130) also outlined the articles of faith, and there is evidence that the work was taught by Almohad preachers to ordinary believers.[12] Also influential was the *Notification of the Rules and Principles of Islam* by the eminent Maghrebi scholar and judge al-Qāḍī ʿIyāḍ al-Yaḥṣubī (d.1149) that covers the five pillars of Islam, including an explanation of the "two professions": there is no god except Allah, and Muhammad is Allah's messenger.[13] Qāḍī ʿIyāḍ's work bears some resemblance to Sanūsī's shorter creeds, specifically its organization of the creedal presentation in terms of what is necessarily true of God, what is not possibly true of God, and what must be affirmed on the basis of revelation. But all the mentioned creedal works simply list the articles of faith, without systematically adducing their proofs. In this sense, Sanūsī's shorter creeds stand out as distinctive, and it is understandable that some of his contemporaries reacted so strongly and negatively to what they saw as the "innovation" of adducing rational proofs in creedal works intended for beginners and ordinary believers.[14]

Some modern observers have also been baffled by Sanūsī's shorter creeds. W. Montgomery Watt, in his *Islamic Philosophy and Theology* (1st edition 1962, 2nd edition 1985), noted that Sanūsī's *Short Creed* was popular for centuries in Islamic Africa and expressed astonishment at the demands it made on the reader. Especially the distinction between various types of divine attribute led Watt to exclaim, "it is clear that the average believer is expected to be a philosopher!."[15] Watt's reaction is perhaps understandable. We have seen that Sanūsī's shorter creedal works presuppose that the reader follow rational arguments for: the existence of God; why there cannot be more than one God; why created things are causally inert; why God must have the attributes of power, will, knowledge, and life; why real, positive attributes can only inhere in substances, not in attributes; why prophets must be truthful and sinless; and also understand the distinction between merely nominal attributes like "existence," negative attributes like "being pre-eternal," positive, entitative attributes like power, will, and knowledge, and the contingent attributes of divine acts. One might wonder just how many of Sanūsī's unlearned contemporaries, even assuming that they had the inclination and time to make the effort, would have been able to follow these arguments and distinctions.

On the other hand, such armchair skepticism has to contend with the sheer popularity of Sanūsī's shorter creeds. Despite the initial animadversions of some of the leading scholars of Tlemcen, these creeds made a deep impression on many of Sanūsī's contemporaries. Historical sources attest that they quickly became popular in the Maghreb, even beyond prestigious, urban madrasas. There is evidence that they were studied in mosques, Sufi lodges, and fortified settlements (*ribats*) that served as bases for warfare against the Portuguese and Spaniards who had managed to conquer a number of North African coastal towns in the fifteenth and sixteenth centuries.[16] A Moroccan scholar active in the late sixteenth and early seventeenth centuries noted that craftsmen (*aṣḥāb al-ḥiraf*) in his region were keen on Sanūsī's creeds and did not know any other.[17] In later generations, Berber, Fulfulde, Turkish, Javanese, and Malay translations or adaptations of the *Short Creed* were made, and some of these were still in use in the nineteenth century when the printing press came to be firmly established in the Islamic world. The fact that Sanūsī's *Short Creed* was rendered into various vernaculars also suggests that its influence was not confined to intermediate or advanced madrasa students who, even in non-Arab parts of the Islamic world, would typically have studied works in Arabic.

The endurance and geographic spread of Sanūsī's popularity, prior to state-imposed mass education, defy a straightforwardly "political," top-down explanation. After all, what explanation of that sort could account for the popularity ranging over three or four centuries and different polities, continents, linguistic areas, mystical orders, and legal schools? A satisfactory study of the reception of Sanūsī's short creeds is likely to be complex and involve a series of localized "thick descriptions." But it seems plausible to assume that the creeds would not have achieved such popularity with teachers, scholars, holy warriors, and Sufis had their contents been impenetrable to the novice students, disciples, and more committed ordinary believers who chose to listen to them.

A very different perspective from Watt's was presented by the German orientalist Max Horten (1874–1945). During the First World War, Horten translated the *Short Creed* into German, with an introduction in which he stated—with some exaggeration—that the creed was known throughout the Islamic East. He noted that its abstract contents could nevertheless be difficult to understand for the averagely educated European of his day. This was, he wrote, because modern Europeans had become unfamiliar with the Greek philosophical and logical concepts that underlay this popular catechism. Even semi-educated Muslims were, by comparison, more conversant with this aspect of the "Hellenistic heritage." He criticized the tendency of Western scholars to avoid engagement with such catechisms, which he believed formed the heart of the

Islamic worldview, and instead focus on secondary legal issues and ritual practices.[18]

Horten's alternative perspective is itself not beyond dispute. But it is worthy of serious consideration, and not only for the striking suggestion that the average Muslim of the early twentieth century was more conversant with Greek-inspired philosophical and logical ideas than the average Western European. It is also salutary to juxtapose its perspective to later dominant currents in the study of Islamic thought that assumed that "orthopraxy" is more important in Islam than "orthodoxy," that creed and theology occupy a much more marginal position in Islamic than in Christian religious consciousness, and that law rather than theology is at the heart of the Islamic religious experience. Such views never deserved their hegemonic status and have rightly been challenged in recent years.[19] They are based on ignoring or explaining away the abundant evidence for the importance of creedal beliefs in Islamic history and in the contemporary Muslim world. The early theological disputes between Muʿtazilīs and their opponents did not inevitably, or even normally, reflect legal or ritual differences; many of the Muʿtazilīs belonged to the same schools of law as their opponents, especially the Shāfiʿī and Ḥanafī schools.[20] With the exception of the minority Khārijite sect, mainstream Muslims agreed that transgressions of the law—serious as they might be—do not exclude a person from the community of believers. At the same time, pronouncing nominal Muslims to be infidels (*takfīr*) was regularly done on the basis of belief. The early Ḥanbalīs pronounced those who believe that the Quran is created to be infidels.[21] Muʿtazilīs, in turn, often accused of infidelity those nominally Muslim groups that have anthropomorphic views of God, believe that there are numerous and pre-eternal divine attributes, or hold that humans are compelled in their actions by God.[22] Ghazālī famously deemed certain ideas of the Aristotelian–Neoplatonist philosophers to be beyond the pale of Islam: the belief that the world is pre-eternal, that God does not know changing particulars in the sublunar world, and that there is no bodily resurrection. The panentheism of the mystic Ibn ʿArabī (d.1240) and his followers was also often condemned as infidelity.[23] Closer to Sanūsī's time and region, influential fatwas from fourteenth-century jurists in Béjaïa (in modern-day eastern Algeria)—cited with approval by Sanūsī—spelled out that a person who fasts, prays, and goes on the Hajj pilgrimage nevertheless cannot be counted as a Muslim if it transpires that he has no understanding of the basic principles of the creed, if—for example—he is unsure what the "two professions" mean, and is vague on the difference between a god and a messenger and whether Muhammad was a human or a demigod.[24]

5
Logic

Sanūsī's aversion to "imitation" (*taqlīd*) was, as shown in the foregoing chapters, a major theme in his creedal writings. His first—and major—theological work, which later came to be known as *The Long Creed*, was originally titled "The Creed of the People of Monotheism" (*'Aqīdat ahl al-tawḥīd*), and in both the creed itself and Sanūsī's own commentary, he gave the rhyming subordinate title "Which by the grace of God the Exalted affords escape from the darkness of ignorance and imitation (*taqlīd*)." "Imitation" for Sanūsī—and for Ashʿarī theologians more generally—was regularly contrasted with *naẓar*, i.e., reasoning or ratiocination. In the introduction to his *The Middle Creed*, Sanūsī wrote:

> This is a short compendium the understanding of which will raise—God willing—the legally responsible person from the station of imitation, concerning whose sufficiency for faith (*īmān*) there is disagreement, to correct reasoning (*al-naẓar al-saḥīḥ*), concerning whose sufficiency there is a consensus. (W 87)

For early Islamic theologians, this "reasoning" tended to be informal, analogical, and distinct from the Aristotelian and Stoic logic introduced through the Greco-Arabic translations of the eighth, ninth, and tenth centuries. Beginning with al-Ghazālī (d.1111), however, theologians increasingly adopted and adapted Greek-inspired formal logic. The "reasoning" that leads beyond unreflective and imitative creedal commitment came increasingly to be understood in terms of logical definition and syllogistic inference.

Al-Sanūsī. Khaled El-Rouayheb, Oxford University Press.
 DOI: 10.1093/oso/9780197835630.003.0005

By Sanūsī's time, this process was complete. His explication of "reasoning" was shot through with logical terminology:

> Reasoning (*naẓar*) is to posit something known or to organize two or more knowns, in such a manner that they lead to what is sought . . . If these items lead to the knowledge of a single entity (*mufrad*), then it is called a definition or explicative phrase. If it leads to an assent, and this is to know the relation of one item to another, by way of affirmation or negation, it is called an argument or proof. The example of the first is your saying in explicating the human, "It is the rational animal". The example of the second is your saying, in showing that the world—i.e., what is other than God—is originated, "The world is changing and everything that changes is originated", for organizing these two known [premises] in a specific manner, i.e., with an affirmative minor and a universal major, leads the one who understands their truth by demonstration to the knowledge that the world is originated, for the minor premise is subsumed under the judgment in the major premise. (K 126–7)

In light of the importance for Sanūsī of "reasoning" in that sense, it is hardly surprising that he took a special interest in logic. As mentioned in Chapter 2, he wrote three works in that discipline that are extant: (i) his own *Epitome* of logic and a commentary thereon; (ii) a commentary on the *Introduction* originally by al-Abharī (d.1265) but slightly reworked by the Cairo-based scholar al-Biqāʿī (d.1480); (iii) and a lengthy but incomplete commentary on the advanced *Epitome* of the Tunisian scholar Ibn ʿArafa (d.1401). (He may have started writing other works on logic, though these were presumably left in a fragmentary state when he died and have not survived.) All three works, but especially the first, were widely copied, studied, and cited throughout Islamic Africa in later centuries, down to the beginning of the twentieth century. The current chapter will offer a closer look at his logical writings, especially the extraordinarily influential *Epitome*.

1 Background

The Greek logic that was translated into Arabic was, of course, primarily that of Aristotle, though supplemented with Porphyry's *Isagoge* and later Greek commentators who augmented Aristotle's term logic with the basics of Stoic propositional logic. This Greek tradition of logic underwent two important transformations before it reached Sanūsī.

First, Avicenna (d.1037) had treated the Aristotelian corpus with the brilliance and self-confidence of an autodidact genius, modifying received doctrines in forceful ways. For example, he articulated an influential view of logic as dealing with second-order concepts insofar as these are relevant to the acquisition of new conceptual and propositional knowledge, rejected the Aristotelian *Categories* as extra-logical, introduced numerous modifications and distinctions in modal logic, and greatly expanded the treatment of the logic of conditionals and disjunctions.[1]

A second transformation occurred with the writings of later logicians such as Fakhr al-Dīn al-Rāzī (d.1210) and Afḍal al-Dīn al-Khūnajī (d.1248). Avicenna's writings were a point of departure for such figures, but his views were subjected to searching, critical reflection, and logic came to be decisively divorced from the Aristotelian Organon, becoming instead an entirely formal discipline that studied the content-neutral rules for the acquisition of new conceptual knowledge through definitions and descriptions, and the acquisition of new propositional knowledge through inference. The fourth figure of the syllogism was recognized, the discussion of modal and conditional logic was expanded, while the treatment of "the matter of the syllogism," i.e., demonstration, topics, rhetoric, poetics, and sophistical fallacies, was greatly reduced.[2]

It is this later, post-Avicennian tradition of logic that Sanūsī inherited. It found its way to the Maghreb in the thirteenth and fourteenth centuries, mainly via Egypt where Khūnajī had settled and died, and where some of his students and associates had been active. Khūnajī's short but highly compressed and demanding handbook of logic *The Sentences* came to be widely studied in the Maghreb, as evinced by the numerous commentaries written on it by local scholars, for example, Muḥammad al-Sharīf al-Tilimsānī (d.1370), Ibn Qunfudh al-Qusanṭīnī (d.1406), Saʿīd al-ʿUqbānī (d.1408), Ibn Marzūq al-Ḥafīd (d.1439), and Ibrāhīm al-Zawāwī (d.1453).[3]

Like Ashʿarism, the post-Avicennian logical tradition developed in different ways in the Maghreb and in the eastern Islamic world. Khūnajī and his immediate successors in the thirteenth century had exhibited a particular interest in formal implications: in the relative strengths of the more than dozen modality propositions that they recognized; in the contradictories, converses, and contrapositives of these modality propositions; in the immediate implications of conditionals and disjunctions; and in the modal and hypothetical syllogistic. In Khūnajī's summa *The Disclosure of Secrets*, almost three-quarters of the work is dedicated to working out such formal implications. Eastern Islamic logicians in the fourteenth and fifteenth centuries shifted the focus to other topics such as: the subject-matter of logic; the definition of knowledge and its division into conception and assent; the extra-mental existence of universals; the nature of predication; the parts of the proposition; whether the antecedent and consequent of a conditional are propositions; whether particulars can serve as predicates; and the liar paradox. The shift of emphasis is abundantly clear in the commentary literature on the most commonly used handbooks in the Islamic East: *The Epistle for Shams al-Dīn* by al-Kātibī (d.1276), *The Dawning of Lights* by al-Urmawī (d.1283), and *The Emendation of Logic* by al-Taftāzānī (d.1390). Most of the attention of later eastern Islamic commentators and glossators on these handbooks was given over to the early parts dealing with preliminary, linguistic, and philosophical topics, while the later parts dealing with formal implications received relatively little attention.[4]

In the Islamic West, on the other hand, the focus of Khūnajī and his circle continued throughout the fourteenth and fifteenth centuries. The North African commentary literature on Khūnajī's *The Sentences* retained the primary interest in formal implications, i.e., the contradictories, converses, and contrapositives of categorical and modality propositions; the immediate implications of conditionals and disjunctions; and the categorical, modal, and hypothetical syllogistic. For example, the commentary of al-Sharīf al-Tilimsānī on *The Sentences* devoted around two-thirds of the total to the treatment of these issues. By comparison, a commentary of comparable length by Tilimsānī's Persian contemporary Quṭb al-Dīn al-Rāzī (d.1365) on Kātibī's *The Epistle for Shams al-Dīn* only devoted around a third of the total work to these formal implications. When it came to introductory issues, linguistic preliminaries, the five universals, and definition, the emphases were reversed. Quṭb al-Dīn devoted around a third of his work to such topics, whereas Tilimsānī only devoted around one-sixth.[5]

It is not easy to say with confidence why the eastern and western Islamic logical traditions evolved distinct emphases. But it would be surprising if part of the answer did not involve two developments that primarily affected the Islamic East in the fourteenth and fifteenth centuries. One was the explosion of interest in the field of semantics-rhetoric in the tradition of al-Sakkākī (d.1229) and al-Khaṭīb al-Qazwīnī (d.1338). The other was the previously mentioned philosophical turn of kalam theology in the wake of Fakhr al-Dīn al-Rāzī. Most Eastern logicians of the fourteenth and fifteenth centuries also contributed to the disciplines of semantics-rhetoric and philosophical theology, and many of the issues that they delved into were treated in those other disciplines as well, for example the definition of knowledge;

its division into conception and assent; the ontological status of universals; the theory of linguistic reference; the nature of predication; and the analysis of assents and propositions. By contrast, in the Islamic West, the Sakkākī/Qazwīnī tradition of semantics-rhetoric and the philosophical turn in kalam, though not entirely unknown, were not as rapidly and deeply assimilated as they came to be in the Islamic East.[6] The Maghrebi logicians active in the fourteenth and fifteenth centuries tended to contribute to the disciplines of law and creedal theology, not to semantics-rhetoric and metaphysics. It is unlikely that this was entirely unrelated to the fact that they retained a focus on formal implications. The syllogistic would presumably have been the aspect of logic that was most relevant to scholars whose other interests were extrapolating legal rules from the acknowledged principles of the law or constructing a creedal theology based on rational proofs that would help believers overcome unreflective conformism with respect to the articles of faith.[7]

Whatever the reason may be for the distinctly North African emphasis on the formal aspects of logic, it will be seen in the following section that Sanūsī shared it.

2 *The Epitome of Logic*: An overview

Sanūsī's *Epitome*, and his own commentary on it, is his most widely studied work on logic. It is far and away the most influential non-introductory work on logic ever produced in Islamic Africa, and it elicited numerous commentaries, glosses, and versifications in later centuries by North and West African scholars.[8]

Sanūsī's handbook is furthermore unusual in having been written by a figure widely revered, in his own lifetime and by posterity, as an ascetic and a saint. The tone throughout is very different from what one encounters in other premodern Arabic manuals of logic. In the introduction to his own commentary, Sanūsī wrote:

> This is a work in which I have intended to comment on my *Epitome* in the science of logic, in a manner marked by brevity, avoiding prolixity, and confining myself to what is important, as opposed to additions that inhibit the orientation toward the otherworldly ends of God's law, perplex the mind, and cause confusion in the necessary exercise of reason. I ask of God that He benefit with it [i.e., the commentary] and the original [i.e., the *Epitome*] the intelligent and the stupid, the strong and the weak, and preserve all from officiousness, vanity, and self-importance, and from obscuring the truth and regarding others with contempt. (MM 2)

A couple of pages later, Sanūsī returned to the theme:

> After the student assimilates what is needed [from the science of logic] . . . he should turn away from what is unnecessary and not waste a precious portion of his life. Rather, after learning the instrumental-rational sciences, he should preoccupy himself with the religious sciences, both teaching and continuing to learn, with a pure intention directed toward the Hereafter and the pleasure of the Lord most Exalted and High. He should guard as much as possible against officiousness, what is of no importance, and the love of worldly leadership. (MM 5)

In light of such passages, one might expect Sanūsī's *Epitome* to be a primer that presents, in a dogmatic tone, the bare minimum of logic without which a budding Islamic scholar would not make much headway with other disciplines such as law or theology. In other words, one might expect Sanūsī's work to be a short, introductory manual of logic, akin to the popular *Introduction* by Abharī which is presented by its author as covering what all scholars must know about logic, and which avoids any mention of disagreements among logicians and omits modal logic and the more demanding aspects of hypothetical logic.[9] Yet, such expectations are not met.

Sanūsī's work is considerably more wide-ranging and demanding than Abharī's *Introduction*. It mentions and discusses controversies among previous logicians, raises issues which Sanūsī had not seen treated in previous works and which he urged readers to look into, and covers in some detail modality propositions and the logic of conditionals and disjunctions. In range, it is much more comparable to intermediate-level handbooks popular in the Islamic East such as *The Epistle for Shams al-Dīn* by Kātibī and *The Emendation of Logic* by Taftāzānī.

It is thus clear that Sanūsī thought scholars should master logic well beyond the level of short primers. In his more advanced theological works, such as the *Commentary on the Long Creed*, he assumed that his readers would be familiar not just with basic categorical and hypothetical syllogisms but also with the standard modality propositions of post-Avicennian logic. For example, when discussing the theologically controversial issue of whether the blessed will literally see God in paradise, which was affirmed by Ashʿarīs and Māturīdīs but denied by Muʿtazilīs and later Shi'is, Sanūsī mentioned that one argument used by the latter group was the Quranic passage in which God responds to Moses' request to see Him by saying, "You will not see Me" (Q 7:143). Sanūsī replied that since the request was clearly to see God in this life, the denial should also be understood to refer to this life, not the Hereafter. He adduced in support of this response the principle that the contradictory of the modality proposition known as the "temporal" (*waqtiyya*)—one of the more than dozen modality propositions recognized in post-Avicennian Arabic logic—is also temporally qualified. If one says, "Zayd possibly sees the moon at time t," then the contradictory is not "Zayd does not possibly see the moon" but "Zayd does not possibly see the moon at time t" (K 486, 496).

As mentioned above, Sanūsī also wrote a commentary on a redacted version of Abharī's *Introduction*. In that commentary, too, Sanūsī presented the more than dozen modality propositions recognized in post-Avicennian logic, even though the *Introduction* itself does not invite this kind of information. He also greatly expanded the *Introduction*'s rudimentary treatment of the syllogistic in order to cover the basics of modal and wholly hypothetical syllogisms.[10] So, while it is clear that Sanūsī would have disapproved of a scholar becoming narrowly specialized in logic and neglecting the core religious sciences that he considered more central to humanity's calling, it is also clear that he expected Islamic scholars to know a great deal more than the mere basics of the discipline. Sanūsī's view that logic is an instrumental science and not an end in itself was, moreover, widely accepted in the Islamic tradition. Most Islamic Aristotelian-Neoplatonist philosophers would have agreed that logic should not be pursued for its own sake, though for them it was a preliminary to the study of natural philosophy and metaphysics, whereas for Sanūsī it was to the study of the core Islamic religious sciences, especially kalam-theology.[11]

The overarching organization of Sanūsī's *Epitome* conforms to the mainstream post-Avicennian view of logic as dealing with the acquisition of concepts via definitions and descriptions, and the acquisition of propositional knowledge via syllogism. He wrote that his treatment of logic covers four main issues: (i) "explication," i.e., definitions and descriptions; (ii) the principles of explication, i.e., the five universals: genus, species, differentia, proprium, and general accident; (iii) "argument," primarily syllogism; and (iv) the principles of argument, i.e., propositions and their immediate implications. The following is an overview of the contents of the Cairo printing from 1875 of the *Epitome* and Sanūsī's own commentary on it:

a. Preamble and Introduction (pp. 2–5)
b. Explication and its principles
    i. Types of reference (pp. 6–11)
    ii. Singular and complex utterances (pp. 11–3)
    iii. Equivocal, univocal, and analogical terms (pp. 13–4)
    iv. Universal and particular terms (pp. 14–8)

  v. The Five Universals (pp. 18–25)
  vi. Definition and Description (pp. 26–8)
c. Argument and its principles
  i. Propositions. Conditionals. Disjunctions (pp. 28–34)
  ii. Categorical propositions (pp. 34–5)
  iii. Modality propositions (pp. 36–42)
  iv. Quantified, unquantified, and singular propositions. Quantification of the predicate (pp. 42–5)
  v. Essentialist (*ḥaqīqī*), externalist (*khārijī*), and mental (*dhihnī*) readings of categorical propositions (pp. 46–50)
  vi. The universal-affirmative (A), particular-affirmative (I), universal-negative (E), and particular-negative (O) propositions (pp. 50–3)
  vii. Metathetic propositions, for example, "Every non-J is B" (pp. 53–5)
  viii. Quantified hypothetical propositions, for example, "Always, If p then q" (pp. 56–8)
  ix. Contradiction (pp. 58–69)
  x. Conversion and Contraposition (pp. 69–82)
  xi. Immediate implications of hypotheticals (pp. 82–8)
  xii. Combinatorial syllogisms (pp. 88–111), including the Aristotelian categorical syllogisms and the wholly hypothetical syllogisms recognized in the post-Avicennian tradition.
  xiii. Reiterative syllogisms: modus ponens, modus tollens, and disjunctive syllogism (pp. 111–4).

A comparison with other widely used Arabic handbooks of logic reveals, not just commonalities in overall organization and coverage but also some significant differences. In tone, as already mentioned, it is quite distinct. Not only are the introduction's warnings against excessive interest in logic, intellectual vanity, and officiousness unusual, but the examples Sanūsī adduced are also often explicitly creedal. For example, when introducing the modality proposition known as the "temporal-possible" (*waqtiyya mumkina*), Sanūsī wrote:

> This is like our saying, "Every human is possibly alive at the time of the separation of the soul from him." In other words, it is not rationally impossible that God the Exalted should extend life even after one's soul has departed, for the intertwining of the soul [with the body] has no effect on one's life. Rather, the Lord customarily brings about life in bodies when souls are intertwined with them and brings about death when the souls are departed from them. And had He willed, something else would have come about. He extends life to souls after they depart from bodies . . . And He has created life in many inanimate entities without souls as a miracle or wonder. (MM 39)

As an example of a false modality proposition in which the modal operator does not correspond to the modal matter, Sanūsī gave the following: "The believer necessarily enjoys everlasting life in paradise." This is a false necessity proposition, Sanūsī declared, because:

> A believer enjoying everlasting bliss or not [enjoying it] are both possible, without any necessity or impossibility. For no one has any right over God the Sufficient and Exalted by virtue of faith or obedience. Rather, everlasting bliss is one of the contingents that it pleases God to bring about, without anyone else meriting this or obliging Him. Those who say that the modality proposition [i.e., "The believer necessarily enjoys everlasting life in paradise"] is true are the Mu'tazilīs, may God humble them, due to their believing that one rationally earns a right, by virtue of faith and obedience, from God who is Exalted far above what the unjust say! (MM 39–40.)

Most of the logic handbooks in common use in medieval Islamic education were popular across sectarian boundaries. Abharī's *Introduction*, Kātibī's *The Epistle for Shams al-Dīn*, and Taftāzānī's

The Emendation of Logic were studied, commented upon, and annotated in both Sunni and Shi'i circles in later centuries. Unsurprisingly, the same is not true of Sanūsī's *Commentary on the Epitome*, which only seems to have been regularly studied in later Ash'arī circles in Islamic Africa, the Levant, and western Arabia.

In matters of content, too, Sanūsī's handbook stands out on a number of points. For example, like Khūnajī's *Sentences* but unlike any of the more popular handbooks in the eastern Islamic world, it includes a discussion of propositions in which the predicate is quantified (*al-munḥarifāt*), for example, "Every J is every B" or "Every J is some B." Though it introduces the standard post-Avicennian modality propositions and discusses their contradictories, converses, and contrapositives, it does not include a discussion of modal syllogisms, on the grounds that this topic is too demanding for the reader and of little use, while adding that someone who has mastered the preceding sections on the conversion and contraposition of modality propositions should be able to proceed without much difficulty to the discussions of modal syllogisms in lengthier works. (Sanūsī's commentary on Ibn 'Arafa's *Epitome* includes such a detailed discussion of modal syllogisms.) Sanūsī's handbook also has no discussion of the subject-matter of logic, the matter of the syllogism (i.e., demonstration, dialectic, rhetoric, poetics, sophistry), or of induction and analogy. On the other hand, it includes a relatively lengthy section on the immediate implications (*lawāzim*) of "hypotheticals," i.e., conditionals and disjunctions, a section that will be discussed in greater detail below. By comparison, standard eastern Islamic handbooks devoted little or no attention to this topic. The retaining of interest in the immediate implications of hypothetical propositions in the western Islamic world, and the loss of interest in the same topic in the eastern Islamic world, is one of the more striking differences between the two traditions of Arabic logic in later centuries.

Even though Sanūsī's work has no discussion of the modal syllogism, it still devotes just over a half (approximately 51 percent) of the total to formal implications: contradiction, conversion, contraposition, the immediate implications of hypothetical propositions, and the formal syllogism. This is significantly higher than in commentaries on intermediate-level handbooks on logic by his Persian contemporaries. For example, Qāḍī Mīr Ḥusayn al-Maybudī (d.1504) devoted only around 32 percent of his commentary on Kātibī's *The Epistle for Shams al-Dīn* to such formal topics, despite covering the modal syllogisms, while devoting around 43 percent to preliminary matters, the five universals, and definition.[12] Aḥmad ibn Yaḥyá al-Ḥafīd al-Harawī (d.1510) devoted approximately 28 percent of his commentary on Taftāzānī's *The Emendation of Logic* to formal implications, including the modal syllogisms, and around 39 percent to preliminary matters, the five universals, and definition.[13] (The corresponding figures for Sanūsī are around 51 percent to formal implications and around 23 percent to introductory matters, the five universals, and definition.) The most influential work on logic written in the Persianate world in Sanūsī's lifetime was the commentary by Jalāl al-Dīn al-Dawānī (d.1502) on Taftāzānī's *The Emendation of Logic*. Dawānī's incomplete commentary did not cover the formal implications of propositions at all, this fact not preventing it from being extensively studied and glossed in later times in the Islamic East.[14] It is clear that, for Sanūsī, logic was still a discipline primarily concerned with working out the formal implications of propositions. The same cannot be said of his contemporaries in the Persianate world.

3 The *Commentary on the Epitome*: A closer look

In the present section, I provide a deeper dive into four topics covered in Sanūsī's *Commentary on the Epitome*. Three of these were treated by Sanūsī in a conspicuously detailed manner when compared to other handbooks then current in the eastern Islamic world: the quantification of the predicate, the "externalist" and "essentialist" readings of categorical propositions, and the immediate implications of conditionals and disjunctions. The fourth is Sanūsī's discussion of modal logic, which is less distinctive when compared to mainstream post-Avicennian logic but covers a topic that has received the lion's share of attention from modern scholarship, ever since the pathbreaking studies of Nicholas Rescher in the 1960s and 70s and of Tony Street in the early decades of the 2000s.[15]

Deviant propositions

Categorical propositions in Aristotelian-inspired logic consist of a subject, a predicate, and a copula linking the two, for example "Humans are mortal." Propositions can be quantified, as in "Some humans are literate" or "Every human is mortal." They can also be affirmative or negative, yielding the four quantified propositions of Aristotelian logic:

Universal-affirmative:	"Every J is B"
Particular-affirmative:	"Some J is B"
Universal-negative:	"No J is B"
Particular-negative:	"Some J is not B"

Quantifiers were standardly prefixed to the subject term. Cases in which the predicate is quantified were known, since the time of Avicenna, as "deviant" (*munḥarifa*).[16] As mentioned in the previous section, Sanūsī—in line with Khūnajī's *Sentences* but unlike the standard handbooks on logic used in the eastern Islamic world—included a discussion of such propositions. But he provided what he saw as a corrective to Khūnajī's account. Like Avicenna, he thought that cases in which a quantifier is prefixed to a singular subject or singular predicate, for example, "Every Jane Austen . . . " should also be counted as "deviant." (It is worth pointing out that such a proposition does not say that "Every person called Jane Austen is human," for "person called Jane Austen" is a universal term that can have numerous instances; the sense of the proposition is rather that "Every instance of the particular person Jane Austen [1775–1817] is human.") In general, "deviant" propositions are formally false, according to Sanūsī, under the following circumstances:

(i) A singular term in an affirmative proposition is quantified, for example, "Every Jane Austen is human." This means that the negations of such propositions are true: "It is not the case that every Jane Austen is human."
(ii) The predicate is a universal term and is universally quantified in an affirmative proposition, such as "Zayd is every human" or "Every human is every rational animal." Again, this means that the negations of such propositions must be true: "It is not the case that Zayd is every human" and "It is not the case that every human is every rational animal."

In all other cases, the truth or falsity of such propositions depends on the matter, i.e., the specific content of the terms.

Externalist and essentialist readings of propositions

Post-Avicennian logicians recognized two different readings of standard categorical propositions. On the so-called externalist reading, "Every J is B" should be understood as saying that every J in the extra-mental world is B. If there is no J in the extra-mental world, then the proposition is false. On this account, the proposition "Every unicorn is an animal" is false, for example. On the so-called essentialist reading, "Every J is B" should be understood as saying that all J's, should they exist, would be B. On the latter reading, one might truthfully say that all unicorns are animals.

Sanūsī dealt with the relative strengths of the two readings at considerable length, well beyond what was usual in other intermediate-level Arabic handbooks on logic. Two propositions can be related in one of four ways: They can be (i) equivalent in the sense that they have the same truth values, such as "No human is immortal" and "No immortal is human"; (ii) one can be more general and the other more specific, such as "This is an animal" and "This is a human," for if the latter is true then the former is true, but not vice versa; (iii) the truth-values can overlap partially, such as "This is a mammal" and "This is four-footed," for the two propositions can both be true, but each can be true while the other is false: some mammals are not four-footed, and some four-footed animals are not mammals; and (iv) there can be no overlap at all, such as "This is an animal" and "This is a stone." The following is Sanūsī's account of the relations that obtain between the "externalist" and "essentialist" readings of the four quantified categorical propositions of Aristotelian logic:[17]

"Every J is B":
There is partial overlap between the "externalist" and "essentialist" readings. "Every phoenix is a bird" is true on an "essentialist" reading but false on an "externalist" reading. "Every featherless biped is a human" is true on an "externalist" reading but false on an "essentialist" reading, for elves, were they to exist, would be non-human featherless bipeds. "Every human is an animal" is true in both senses.

"Some J is B":
The "essentialist" reading is "more general". In other words, if "Some J is B" is true on an "externalist" reading, then it must be true on an "essentialist" reading as well; but not vice-versa.

"No J is B":
The "externalist" reading is "more general". If "No J is B" is true on an "essentialist" reading, then it must be true on an "externalist" reading as well; but not vice-versa.

"Some J is not B":
There is partial overlap between the two senses. Sanūsī's handbook differs from all the standard eastern Islamic handbooks on this point. The latter handbooks all expound the view that because there is partial overlap between the two senses of "Every J is B", there must be either partial overlap or no overlap at all between the two senses of "Some J is not B", for if there is partial overlap between A and B, then there is either partial overlap or no overlap at all between not-A and not-B.[18] But Sanūsī noted, correctly, that we can rule out that there is no overlap between the essentialist and externalist senses, for "Some animal is not a horse" is true on both readings. So, the logical relation between the two senses must be one of partial overlap. "Some phoenix is not a bird" is false on an "essentialist" reading but true on an "externalist" reading. "Some featherless biped is not a human" is false on an "externalist" reading but true on an "essentialist" reading. "Some animal is not a horse" is true on both readings.

One might capture the two senses and their mutual relations in modern notation as follows:[19]

"Every J is B":
"Externalist": $\exists x(Jx) \,\&\, \forall x(Jx \rightarrow Bx)$
"Essentialist": $\Diamond\exists x(Jx) \,\&\, \Box\forall x\,(Jx \rightarrow Bx)$

"Some J is B":
"Externalist": $\exists x(Jx \,\&\, Bx)$
"Essentialist": $\Diamond\exists x(Jx \,\&\, Bx)$

"No J is B"
"Externalist": $\neg\exists x(Jx \,\&\, Bx)$
"Essentialist": $\neg\Diamond\exists x(Jx \,\&\, Bx)$

"Some J is not B"
"Externalist": $\neg\exists x(Jx) \vee \exists x(Jx \,\&\, \neg Bx)$
"Essentialist": $\Box\neg\exists x(Jx) \vee \Diamond\exists x(Jx \,\&\, \neg Bx)$

Unusually, Sanūsī went on to discuss the logical relations between the essentialist and externalist readings even when the quality and quantity differ.[20] For example, it has just been shown that the essentialist "No J is B" is "more specific" than the externalist "No J is B." This implies that it is also more specific than the externalist "Some J is not B." This is because the externalist "No J is B" is "more specific" than the externalist "Some J is not B," so if the essentialist "No J is B" is "more specific" than the former, it must also be more specific than the latter. Schematically put, if proposition P is "more specific" than Q (in the sense that P entails Q but not vice versa), and if Q is "more specific" than R, then P must be "more specific" than R. Furthermore, the essentialist "No J is B" cannot overlap in truth-value with the externalist "Every J is B" or "Some J is B." This is because the externalist "Every J is B" entails the externalist "Some J is B," and it has been shown above that the externalist "Some J is B" entails the essentialist "Some J is B." But this last proposition is the contradictory of the essentialist "No J is B." So, if the essentialist "No J is B" contradicts what it entailed by the externalist "Every J is B" and "Some J is B," then it must be incompatible with either of these propositions. More schematically, if proposition P is incompatible with Q, and if Q is entailed by R, then P must be incompatible with R (MM 48–9).

Modality propositions

Modality propositions (*muwajjahāt*) were given considerable attention in non-introductory post-Avicennian handbooks.

Though he did not deal with modal syllogisms, Sanūsī nevertheless gave a detailed account of modality propositions, their contradictories, their converses, and their contrapositives. Mainstream post-Avicennian logicians distinguished between "substantial" (*dhātī*) and "descriptional" (*waṣfī*) readings of such propositions, comparable—even if not exactly identical to—the medieval Latin distinction between *de re* and *de dicto* readings. In the "descriptional" reading, a predicate is stated to be true of a subject with a certain modality insofar as a certain description is true of this subject. In this sense, all bachelors are necessarily unmarried, for all bachelors are necessarily unmarried as long as they are described as "bachelors." In the "substantial" reading, the predicate is claimed to be true of the subject with a certain modality as long as that subject exists. In that sense, it is not true that all bachelors are necessarily unmarried, for at least some of the entities referred to by the term "bachelor" are possibly married.

Mainstream post-Avicennian logicians also distinguished systematically between necessity and perpetuity and between one-sided and two-sided modality, for example between possibility ("J is possibly B") and contingency ("J is possibly B and possibly not B"). These distinctions underlay the more than a dozen modality propositions that feature in non-introductory post-Avicennian handbooks.[21] Sanūsī listed nineteen such modality propositions:

Seven necessity propositions:

1. Absolute necessity (e.g., Every J is necessarily B as long as it exists)
2. General conditioned (Every J is necessarily B as long as it is J)
3. Specific conditioned (Every J is necessarily B as long as it is J but not always)
4. Absolute temporal (Every J is necessarily B at specified time t)
5. Temporal (Every J is necessarily B at a specified time t but not always)

6. Absolute spread (Every J is necessarily B at an unspecified time)
7. Spread (Every J is necessarily B at an unspecified time but not always)

Three perpetuity propositions

8. Absolute perpetuity (Every J is always B as long as it exists)
9. General conventional (Every J is always B as long as it is J)
10. Specific conventional (Every J is always B as long as it is J but not always)

Five possibility propositions

11. General possible (Every J is possibly B)
12. Specific possible (Every J is possibly B and possibly not B)
13. Temporal possible (Every J is possibly B at specified time t)
14. Perpetual possible (Every J is possibly B at all times)
15. Possible continuing (Every J is possibly B as long as it is J)

Four absolute propositions

16. General absolute (Every J is B at some time)
17. Non-perpetual existential (Every J is B at some time but not always)
18. Non-necessary existential (Every J is B at some time but not necessarily)
19. Absolute continuing (Every J is B at some time but not always)

Sanūsī presented the contradictories, converses, and contrapositives of these propositions. For example, the contradictory of "Every J is necessarily B" (nr. 1) is "Some J is possibly not

B" (nr. 11), and the contradictory of "Every J is always B" (nr. 8) is "Some J is not B at some time" (nr. 16).

The discussion of modal conversions and contrapositions is quite technical and difficult to summarize in the present context. But it is worth noting that while Sanūsī's *Epitome* follows Khūnajī's *Sentences* closely on this topic, his own commentary sometimes modifies the handbook's position. The *Sentences* and the *Epitome* itself expound a broadly Avicennian account of the modal conversions, whereas Sanūsī's commentary closely follows the later, revisionist account in Kātibī's *The Epistle for Shams al-Dīn* and in the commentary of Ibn Wāṣil (d.1298) on the *Sentences*, both works that he regularly cited. For example, the *Epitome* expounds the position, accepted by Avicenna, that a "general possible" proposition (nr. 6) converts, but in his commentary Sanūsī—following most post-Avicennian logicians—rejected this. It may be true, he argued, that "Every donkey is possibly ridden by Zayd," but if Zayd only ever rides horses, then it is false that "Something ridden by Zayd is possibly a donkey," for all horses are necessarily not donkeys (MM 73). The point is closely related to the position that the extension of the subject-term only includes entities of which it is actually true. Al-Fārābī (d.950) was understood to have had the position that the subject-term includes anything of which it is possibly true; to adopt a term from medieval Latin logic, the subject term is "ampliated" to the possible. On that account, the aforementioned conversion seems evident:

Every [possible] donkey is possibly ridden by Zayd
∴ Something that is [possibly] ridden by Zayd is possibly a donkey

But if the subject term is not ampliated and only extends to what it is *actually* true of, then the inference admits of counterexamples:

Every [actual] donkey is possibly ridden by Zayd
?∴? Something that is [actually] ridden by Zayd is possibly a donkey

Sanūsī preferred to take subject-terms as not ampliated. In defense of this stance, he gave an interesting justification. When the Quran commands that the thief's hand should be cut off, and the fornicator should be whipped, the terms "thief" and "fornicator" do not extend to all possible thieves or all possible fornicators but only to those of whom the terms "thief" and "fornicator" are actually true (MM 34–5). It may be tempting to see Sanūsī's remark as indicative of a broader intellectual development. When logic came to be "naturalized" into Muslim colleges after the eleventh century, it lost its close connection to Aristotelian science and metaphysics and instead forged close connections to law and creedal theology. A non-ampliated reading of subject terms might have seemed more relevant to jurists or kalam theologians, whereas an ampliated reading might have seemed more relevant to an Aristotelian natural philosopher or metaphysician interested in essences or natures, for whom propositions with subjects such as "ridden by Zayd" or "thief" were simply irrelevant.

Though such an overall interpretation is tempting and perhaps contains a germ of truth, the matter is more complicated. As mentioned above, post-Avicennian logicians recognized both "externalist" and "essentialist" readings of categorical propositions. On the "essentialist" reading, "Every J is B" says that every J, were it to exist, would be B. This entails that the extension of the subject-term "J" goes well beyond what is actually J. The statement that a fornicator is liable to be whipped is, on this account, not false if there are no fornicators; it rather stipulates that *if* a person commits fornication, *then* he or she is liable to be whipped. This sense is not exactly equivalent to the ampliated reading. It is not the case that anyone who possibly fornicates is to be whipped. But it does relax the very stringent assumption of existential import in the "externalist" reading. And the "essentialist" reading would have been relevant to both the Aristotelian philosopher and the jurist-theologian.

This brings back the aforementioned discussion of whether a possibility proposition converts. The standard counterexample to the conversion was the following:

Every [actual] donkey is possibly ridden by Zayd	[TRUE]
Something that is [actually] ridden by Zayd is possibly a donkey	[FALSE]

But the latter proposition is only plausibly false on an "externalist" reading. If indeed Zayd only ever rides horses, then it is false on that reading that something ridden by Zayd is possibly a donkey, for horses are necessarily not donkeys. On an "essentialist" reading, however, the proposition seems to be true: Some of what one can coherently suppose is actually ridden by Zayd is not a horse but a donkey.

So, should one conclude that possibility propositions do not convert on an externalist reading but do convert on an essentialist reading? Sanūsī would almost certainly have denied this. In his most advanced work on logic, his commentary on the *Epitome* of Ibn ʿArafa, he apparently endorsed the position that Ibn ʿArafa attributed (correctly) to Khūnajī and Khūnajī's student Ibn Wāṣil. That position, defended in Khūnajī's summa *The Disclosure of Secrets* and in Ibn Wāṣil's *Commentary on the Sentences*, was to deny that a possibility proposition converts when interpreted in an externalist manner, and to suspend judgment on whether it converts when interpreted in an essentialist manner.[22] Their argument was that it is not enough, in order to show that a proposition converts, to give examples of propositions with true converses. Nor is it incumbent on doubters to provide a counterexample. Rather, proponents of the conversion of universal-affirmative possibility propositions ought to provide a proof. And the standard proofs offered for the claim were found wanting by Khūnajī and Ibn Wāṣil.[23]

Their position might be captured by making use of the previously mentioned formalization of essentialist propositions. Is the following a valid entailment?

$$\Diamond\exists x(Jx) \,\&\, \Box\forall x\,(Jx \rightarrow \Diamond Bx) \Rightarrow \Diamond\exists x(Bx \,\&\, \Diamond Jx)$$

On the one hand, this can be proven to be valid in the modern system of modal logic known as S5. But on the other hand, S5 makes certain disputable assumptions, specifically that what is necessary is necessarily necessary and that what is possible is necessarily possible. From the perspective of the contemporary modal system known as T or M, which does not make such assumptions about reiterated modalities, the entailment is not valid.[24] It can be shown that the objections made by Khūnajī and Ibn Wāṣil to the proofs adduced by Avicenna single out as questionable precisely the steps that would be legitimate in S5 and illegitimate in T/M.[25]

The immediate implications of hypotheticals

Arabic logicians divided propositions into categorical (*ḥamlī*) and hypothetical (*sharṭī*), the latter being subdivided into conditionals (*muttaṣilāt*) and disjunctions (*munfaṣilāt*). Disjunctions were further divided into (i) exhaustive (the disjuncts are not both false); (ii) exclusive (the disjuncts are not both true)[26]; and (iii) "strict" (the disjuncts are not both false and not both true). Conditionals were divided into "coincidental" (*ittifāqī*) and "implicative" (*luzūmī*). In the latter—and for Arabic logicians much more significant—case, there is a causal or conceptual relation between antecedent and consequent that underlies the truth of the conditional. In the former case, the conditional is true simply if both antecedent and consequent are true (e.g., "If humans speak then donkeys bray") or, alternatively, if the consequent is true (e.g., "If all the trees of the world were reeds and the seven seas ink, the words of God would not be exhausted"). Similarly, disjunctions were divided into "coincidental" and "oppositional" (ʿinādī).

Sanūsī dealt with the immediate implications of conditionals and disjunctions in much more detail than in Khūnajī's *Sentences* and the intermediate-level handbooks common in the Islamic East.[27] He gathered together into one section principles set forth in various sections of the more advanced summas of the thirteenth century. In his commentary, Sanūsī divided the section into seven lemmas, each setting forth some immediate implications of conditionals or disjunctions. These are the following:

Lemma 1:

1.1: If P then (Q & R) ⇒ If P then Q; If P then R
1.2: If (P & Q) then R ⇏ If P then R; If Q then R
1.3: P & (Q & R) ⇒ P & Q; P & R
1.4: (P & Q) & R ⇒ P & R; Q & R
1.5: P or (Q & R) ⇒ P or Q; P or R
1.6: (P & Q) or R ⇒ P or R; Q or R
1.7: Not both P and (Q & R) ⇏ Not both P and Q; Not both P and R
1.8: Not both (P & Q) and R ⇏ Not both P and R; Not both Q and R

Lemma 2:

2.1: If P then Q ⇒ Not: If P then not-Q
2.2: Not: If P then Q ⇒ If P then not-Q

Lemma 3:

3.1: If P then Q ⇒ Not both P and not-Q
3.2: If P then Q ⇒ Either not-P or Q
3.3: Not both P and Q ⇒ If P then not-Q; If Q then not-P
3.4: Either P or Q ⇒ If not-P then Q; If not-Q then P

Lemma 4:

4: (Either P or Q) & (Not both P and Q) ⇒ If not-P then Q; If not-Q then P; If P then not-Q; If Q then not-P

Lemma 5:

5.1: If P then Q ⇒ Not: not both P and Q

5.2: If P then Q ⇒ Not: Either P or Q

5.3: (Not both P and Q) & (Not: Either P or Q) ⇒ Not: If P then Q; Not: If Q then P

5.4: (Either P or Q) & (Not: not both P and Q) ⇒ Not: If P then Q; Not: If Q then P

5.5: Not: If P then Q ⇏ Not both P and Q

5.6: Not: If P then Q ⇏ Either P or Q

5.7: Not: not both P and Q ⇏ If P then Q

5.8: Not: not both P and Q ⇏ Either P or Q

5.9: Not: either P or Q ⇏ If P then Q

5.10: Not: either P or Q ⇏ Not both P or Q

Lemma 6:

6.1: Not both P and Q ⇒ Either not-P or not-Q

6.2: Either P or Q ⇒ Not both not-P and not-Q

Lemma 7:

7.1: Always: If Some A is B then Q ⇒ Always: If Every A is B then Q

7.2: Always: If P then Every A is B ⇒ Always: If P then Some A is B

7.3: Sometimes not: If Every A is B then Q ⇒ Sometimes not: If Some A is B then Q

7.4: Sometimes not: If P then Some A is B ⇒ Sometimes not: If P then Every A is B

7.5: Sometimes: If Every A is B then Q ⇒ Sometimes: If Some A is B then Q

7.6: Sometimes: If P then Every A is B ⇒ Sometimes: If P then Some A is B

7.7: Never: If Some A is B then Q ⇒ Never: If Every A is B then Q

7.8: Never: If P then Some A is B ⇒ Never: If P then Every A is B

To give a sense of Sanūsī's exposition of these principles, I will give a summary account of 1.1 and 1.2. In presenting 1.1, Sanūsī wrote:

> An implicative affirmative conditional which has a conjunctive consequent entails as many conditionals as there are parts of the consequent. (MM 82)

For example, "If this is a human then it is rational and an animal" implies the two conditionals "If this is human then it is rational" and "If this is human then it is an animal." This is because the part of the consequent is implied by the whole consequent, and the whole consequent is in turn implied by the antecedent. So, the antecedent must imply each part of the consequent. Formally, the proof is as follows:

If this is a human, then it is rational and an animal	(Original proposition)
If this is rational and an animal, then it is rational	(Simplification)
∴ If this is a human then it is rational	(1st figure hypo. syllogism)

According to principle 1.2, the affirmative implicative conditional with a conjunctive antecedent does *not* imply a multiplicity of conditionals, for a whole may imply something without the part of the whole implying that thing. For example, it is true that "If something is rational and an animal then it is a human" but false that "If something is an animal then it is a human."

Sanūsī pointed out that this principle should be qualified. Avicenna and post-Avicennian logicians tended to quantify conditionals, distinguishing between:

Universal-affirmative:	Always, if P then Q
Particular-affirmative:	It may be, if P then Q
Universal-negative:	Never, if P then Q
Particular-affirmative:	It may not be, if P then Q

The introduction of such quantifiers complicates matters. In the case of the particular-affirmative conditional, a conjunctive antecedent does, according to Sanūsī, imply a plurality of conditionals (MM 83). For example, given that "It may be, if P & Q then R," it can be shown that "It may be, if P then R" and "It may be, if Q then R." The proof is as follows:

Always, if P & Q, then P	Simplification
It may be, if P & Q, then R	Original proposition
∴ It may be, if P then R	3rd figure hypothetical syllogism

Sanūsī added that if the particular-affirmative conditional with a conjunctive antecedent (It may be, if P & Q, then R) implies a plurality of conditionals, then a universal-affirmative conditional with a conjunctive antecedent (Always, if P & Q, then R) also implies the same plurality of conditionals. For the universal-affirmative conditional entails the particular-affirmative conditional, so anything entailed by the latter is also entailed by the former. Sanūsī pointed out that therefore the received view that an affirmative conditional with a conjunctive antecedent does not imply a plurality of conditionals should be modified. He wrote:

> What is apparent from the *Sentences* and [the *Epitome* of] Ibn 'Arafa and others is that the conditional unqualifiedly does not entail a plurality of conditionals when its antecedent is conjunctive. This is not so, and the verified position is what we have mentioned. (MM 83)

In her monograph *Arabic Logic from al-Fārābī to Averroes*, Saloua Chatti presents a modern logical interpretation of Avicennian quantified conditionals.[28] On her account, a universal-affirmative conditional can be formalized as follows:

$$\forall_s (P_s \rightarrow Q_s)$$

The idea is to quantify over situations, so the claim is that in all situations, if P is true in that situation, then Q is true in that situation. Because Avicenna and post-Avicennian logicians, unless they explicitly specified otherwise, tended to assume that there *are* situations in which the antecedent is true, one is usually justified in adding such an assumption to the formalization:

$$\exists_s(P_s) \& \forall_s(P_s \rightarrow Q_s)$$

The particular-affirmative conditional can, according to Chatti, be interpreted as follows:

$$\exists_s(P_s \& Q_s)$$

Less formally, there is at least one situation in which P and Q are both true.

On this interpretation, Sanūsī's point is correct. The following are evidently valid consequences:

$$\exists_s(P_s \& Q_s) \& \forall_s((P_s \& Q_s) \rightarrow R_s) \Rightarrow \exists_s(P_s \& R_s) \& \exists_s(Q_s \& R_s)$$
$$\exists_s((P_s \& Q_s) \& R_s) \Rightarrow \exists_s(P_s \& R_s) \& \exists_s(Q_s \& R_s)$$

4 Sanūsī's impact

In terms of the historical impact of his writings, Sanūsī was undoubtedly a major figure in the Islamic tradition of logic. He was not an iconoclastic logician who took radical departures from the received tradition, nor was he, as some modern scholars have suggested, a mere "vulgarizer" or "schoolmaster." He stood somewhere in between those two poles: synthesizing earlier discussions, adjudicating earlier disagreements, and presenting the discipline in a distinct and influential way. His *Epitome of Logic* was studied for centuries in Islamic Africa, most often with Sanūsī's own commentary. The fact that Sanūsī dealt with quantifications of the predicate, essentialist and externalist readings of propositions, and the immediate implications of hypotheticals, far beyond what was usual in the eastern Islamic world, therefore meant that later African-Islamic logicians tended to deal with these topics much more extensively than was usual among their eastern Islamic contemporaries. Conversely, his resolutely formal orientation, and relative neglect of foundational-philosophical questions (the subject matter of logic; the definition of knowledge; the distinction between conception and assent; the nature of predication; etc.) and of the theory of Aristotelian demonstration also meant that later African-Islamic logicians tended to show less interest in such issues than their contemporaries in the Islamic East.

A few decades after Sanūsī's death, ʿAbd al-Raḥmān al-Akhḍarī (d.1546) from the region of Biskra near Constantine in what is today eastern Algeria, composed a very popular didactic poem entitled *The Ornamented Ladder* that was meant as an introduction to logic, with a brief explicatory commentary. The work was considerably less demanding than Sanūsī's *Epitome*, leaving out the modal logic, quantifications of the predicate, the essentialist and externalist readings, as well as anything more than the rudiments of the logic of hypotheticals.[29] It is not an exaggeration to say that Akhḍarī's primer and Sanūsī's intermediate-level handbook together dominated the study of logic in Islamic Africa, and thus in effect defined what the discipline of logic meant in that region, until—and in some circles beyond—the nineteenth century.

6

Proofs for the Existence of God

As shown in earlier chapters, Sanūsī held that believers are dutybound to engage in "reasoning" (*naẓar*) and thus move beyond simply assenting to the articles of faith by emulation of peers and elders. The first objective of this reasoning is to establish that God exists. In his *Long Creed*, Sanūsī wrote:

> The first duty incumbent on the legally mature person, before anything else, is to exercise his thought on what leads, by certain demonstrations and clear proofs, to knowledge of the object of his worship. (K 83)

In other words, one's first duty is to engage in reasoning with the aim of proving or learning an established proof for the existence of God. After the above-cited lemma, Sanūsī continued by denigrating "imitation" and then proceeded to make the case for the existence of God. The same progression is also set out in the *Middle Creed*: (i) the unsatisfactory nature of "imitation," (ii) the necessity of correct reasoning, (iii) understanding the meaning of "necessary," "impossible," and "contingent," (iv) establishing that the world is originated, and (v) establishing that the world has an originator. Sanūsī wrote:

> The first thing you should embark upon in reasoning is to reason about the origination of the world . . . And if the world is originated after its non-existence, it must have an originator. (W 89, 91)

Al-Sanūsī. Khaled El-Rouayheb, Oxford University Press.
 DOI: 10.1093/oso/9780197835630.003.0006

It is to Sanūsī's proofs for the existence of God that I turn in this chapter. The focus will primarily be on the *Commentary on the Long Creed*, Sanūsī's lengthiest discussion of the topic.

1 Background

Proofs for the existence of God had been advanced by Islamic theologians and philosophers for centuries before Sanūsī, of course. Perhaps the most popular argument used by early kalam theologians of the Muʿtazilī and Ashʿarī schools is sometimes referred to as "the proof from accidents."[1] The details of the argument will be given below—Sanūsī used it in all his creedal works. Briefly put, its starting point is the observation that the accidents of bodies come-to-be and pass-away: foals grow, buds bloom, leaves change color, birds change their position in flight, headaches come and go, bodies become less supple with age. Given that the accidents of bodies come-to-be and pass-away, it must be the case that bodies themselves come-to-be and pass-away, for bodies cannot exist without accidents. Given that bodies are originated, they require an originator. An auxiliary argument was often introduced at this point to show that the originator must have choice and will, for bodies are always in one of several possible ways. If the originator of bodies were a unitary, natural force acting without choice and will, then the effect would have to be pre-eternal, simple, and unchanging, which is obviously not the case.

We encountered the rudiments of such an argument in Chapter 4, when dealing with Sanūsī's shorter creedal works. As indicated then, the kalam proof was rejected by the Aristotelian–Neoplatonist philosophers on a number of grounds:

- First, it assumes that the world consists of bodies and their accidents, a physicalist premise unacceptable to Aristotelian–Neoplatonist philosophers. If we hold that the world contains immaterial substances (souls, heavenly intellects, pure essences, Platonic Ideas), then the cosmological proof that bodies are originated does not tell us that the world—typically defined as "what is other than God"—is originated.

- Second, it infers from the origination of bodily accidents that bodies, too, are originated. Historically, this inference was subjected to criticism. Why could it not be that an infinite series of originated accidents are true of a pre-eternal body? In Aristotelian–Neoplatonist cosmology, the stars and planets are pre-eternal, and yet some of their accidents—specifically their spatial positions—are constantly changing as they revolve around the Earth.

- Third, the argument that the originator of the world must have will and choice was also rejected by the Aristotelian–Neoplatonist philosophers. (More precisely, they reinterpreted the terms "will" and "choice" in the case of the First Cause to mean something very different from their everyday senses.) They conceived of the First Cause as an impersonal force that perpetually emanates—and cannot not emanate—one, pre-eternal, simple, and unchanging effect, namely the first heavenly intellect. The theologians' challenge that a first cause without will and choice must create a world that is pre-eternal, simple, and unchanging was thus met by postulating an emanationist scheme in which the first cause *does* emanate an entity—the first intellect—that is pre-eternal, simple, and unchanging. This intellect in turn emanates a second intellect, which in turn emanates a third intellect, and so on.[2] The justification for this emanationist scheme, and exactly how to derive the complexity of the sublunar world from it, were questions that the theologians could and did press against the Aristotelian–Neoplatonist philosophers.

In the Islamic philosophical tradition, the most influential proofs for the existence of God were put forward by Avicenna (d.1037).[3]

Avicenna took his point of departure, not from the coming-to-be and passing-away of accidents and bodies, but from the concepts of contingent and necessary being. A contingent being is such that it needs an extrinsic cause to exist. It seems plain that there are contingent beings. These contingent beings require causes, and the series of causes cannot be circular or infinite but must end in an uncaused cause. Such an uncaused cause is a necessary being—a being whose quiddity or essence is to exist. In some of his writings, Avicenna proposed a slightly different proof that purportedly does not depend on the premise that an infinite series of causes is impossible: Assume that such an infinite series of contingent causes exists; that series, consisting of contingent parts, must itself be contingent and therefore requires a cause outside the series.

There was good reason for Avicenna to start with the notions of contingency and necessity. He believed that the world is pre-eternal, so the kalam argument from accidents—which begins by establishing that the world is originated and, on that basis, establishes a creator—would have held no appeal to him. Nevertheless, many later Islamic theologians who were committed to the origination of the world adopted or adapted Avicenna's proofs. Some later Ashʿarī theologians in the eastern Islamic world jettisoned the kalam proof from accidents and instead adopted versions of Avicenna's two proofs for the existence of an uncaused cause.[4] These proofs could then be conjoined to older kalam arguments for why this uncaused cause must possess choice and will.

Sanūsī was aware of Avicenna's proofs from contingency. Even if he did not read Avicenna's philosophical writings, he would have been exposed to the proofs in the works of later eastern Ashʿarīs, especially *Landmarks of the Principles of Religion* by Fakhr al-Dīn al-Rāzī (d.1210) and *The Dawning of Lights* by al-Bayḍāwī (d.1291), with both of which he was familiar.[5] However, in line with the generally more conservative attitude of North African Ashʿarism, he—and his North African contemporaries—still gave pride of place to proofs that take their point of departure in origination (*ḥudūth*) rather than contingency (*imkān*).[6]

2 First proof

In Sanūsī's *Long Creed*, the first proof for the existence of God is *not* the standard kalam argument from accidents. He began by enjoining the reader to consider his or her own self. The reader exists after not having existed. Everything that exists after not having existed has been brought about by something else. The reader has therefore been brought about by something else. Sanūsī presented the argument in syllogistic form (K 195–6):

> I exist after not having existed
> Everything that exists after not having existed has been brought about by something else
> ∴ I have been brought about by something else

The first (minor) premise has a good claim to be evident and not in need of proof. Sanūsī did, to be sure, discuss a possible objection. One might perhaps say: How can I be sure that I did not exist before being born? Rather than being non-existent, I was "in" my father's loins, and he was "in" his father's loins, and so on ad infinitum. The objection may strike a modern reader as odd. Modern assumptions about personal identity tend to be quite different from those of the kalam tradition. Among early kalam theologians—and more conservative later North African Ashʿarīs—personal identity was not linked to consciousness or an immaterial soul. The prevalent tendency was to identify the self with a body or certain atoms within the body—Sanūsī explicitly equated a person's "self" (*dhāt*) with a "body" (*jirm*).[7] If "I" am certain parts of my body, then it may well be that these parts existed prior to my birth. The assumption about personal identity also accorded with the Quranic account of the primordial covenant established when God drew out all humans from the loins of Adam and asked them, "Am I not your Lord?" (Q 7:172).

Sanūsī's reply to the objection is that, even granting that parts of me preexisted my birth, it is still the case that what is there of me now is much larger than the miniscule clot from which I grew. So, there are undoubtedly parts that exist now and did not exist then. We can simply run the argument on these parts that did not exist in the past and now exist (K 202–5).

As for the second (major) premise, namely that everything that has come into existence has been brought about by an external cause, some theologians held that it, too, is evident. Fakhr al-Dīn al-Rāzī, for example, held that the truth of this premise is inborn: children and even brute animals believe that if something comes to be then it has been caused by something else.[8] Sanūsī rejected this position. One need not concede that all children hold the principle of causality, and even if they do, or most of them do, it does not follow that it is an evident truth, for children do not only believe what is evident; they also engage in basic inferences. As for brute animals, Sanūsī considered it implausible that they have knowledge of universal truths. He seems to have thought that irrational animals may associate pain with a stick, or a sudden sound with danger, but that such an association is made by their estimative faculty. Sanūsī preferred the view that the major premise can be justified through a further proof. Every occurrent is such that it could have occurred a bit earlier or a bit later. The fact that it occurs at one point in time rather than another must therefore be due to a specifying factor (*mukhaṣṣiṣ*) that determines one time of existence over others that are otherwise equally possible. Sanūsī's move here is fully in line with the kalam tradition and is known in the secondary literature as "the argument from particularization."[9]

Up to this point in the argument, Sanūsī has established the two premises of the syllogism:

I exist after not having existed
Everything that exists after not having existed has been brought about by something else
∴ I have been brought about by something else

He then pressed the point that this "something else" that has brought me into existence has either acted (i) by its essence, (ii) by its nature, or (iii) by choice. These options are exhaustive for the following reason: everything that has an effect (*mu'aththir*) is either such that it can refrain from its effect or not. If the former, then it acts from choice. If the latter, then either the effect comes about in conjunction with certain conditions or not. On the first option, the cause acts by nature. (For example, even if fire burns by nature, there are conditions for its efficacy: physical contact, oxygen in the air, the thing it touches not being wet, and so on.) On the second option, the cause acts by essence and hence invariably and unconditionally. (An example might be the emanation of the First Intellect from the First Cause.)

Sanūsī argued that the creator of my own self does not act by nature or by essence (K 205–11). Anything that acts by nature or essence cannot specify one effect rather than several other, equally possible effects. But the creator of my self has specified one effect rather than several other possible effects. After all, I might have been taller or shorter than I actually am, or younger or older, or stouter or thinner, or darker or fairer. So, the creator of my self acts by choice. Again, Sanūsī presented the argument syllogistically:

You are in one of many possible ways
Everything that is in one of many possible ways has been brought about by a voluntary agent
∴ You have been brought about by a voluntary agent

The conclusion of the syllogism is then a premise in another syllogism (in the second syllogistic figure) ruling out that I could have been brought about by a clot or sperm or any other natural entity:

The cause of your self is a voluntary agent
No clot or any similar natural entity is a voluntary agent
∴ The cause of your self is not a clot or any similar natural entity

Sanūsī also appealed to what was often called *ilzām*, i.e., arguing on the basis of premises that your opponent accepts, hoping to derive an absurdity. According to the Aristotelian–Neoplatonist philosophers, a homogenous natural cause should have a homogenous effect, which in complex effects is the sphere. If I am caused by a natural cause such as a clot, then I should have had a spherical shape. The argument is found in Fakhr al-Dīn al-Rāzī's *Landmarks of the Principles of Religion.*[10] It is not particularly compelling, for the philosophers would surely reply that they do not believe the sperm or clot to be homogenous, and that the complex, non-homogenous effect shows that its natural cause is not simple and homogenous.

So far, Sanūsī has established that at least one thing—the reasoner's own self—has come to be after not existing and has been brought about by a cause. He has also argued that this cause must be a voluntary agent because it is a genuine possibility that the effect—the reasoner's self—could have been older or younger, taller or shorter, thinner or stouter, fairer or darker, and so on. No natural cause acting without will and choice brings about one effect instead of other possible effects. In the next step of the argument, Sanūsī urged the reasoner to generalize the conclusion reached about his/her own self to all other bodies in the world. Just as one's own body has been brought about by a voluntary agent, so all other bodies in the world have been brought about by a voluntary agent.

Why can some bodies in the world not be pre-eternal and other bodies originated? The answer, according to Sanūsī, is this: If some bodies were pre-eternal and other bodies originated, then entities of the same type would have different per se features, but this is absurd (K 211–4). Sanūsī's argument has the form of modus tollens:

> If some bodies are pre-eternal and other bodies are originated, then entities of the same type would have different per se features.
> It is not the case that entities of the same type have different per se features.
> ∴ It is not the case that some bodies are pre-eternal and other bodies are originated.

The proof of the conditional premise is as follows: If something is pre-eternal, then it is intrinsically and necessarily pre-eternal. If the pre-eternal were contingently pre-eternal, then it would need a cause that makes it pre-eternal rather than originated, but its having a cause contradicts its pre-eternality. So, parts of the world would have the intrinsically necessary feature of being originated, and other parts of the world would have the intrinsically necessary feature of being pre-eternal.

The proof that the consequent is false is as follows: The body that has just been shown to be originated is relevantly similar (*mumāthila*) to other bodies—all bodies are tokens of the same type. Two tokens of the same type must have the same "per se attributes" (*ṣifāt nafsiyya*). As mentioned in Chapter 4, exactly how to understand "per se attributes" is elusive, for various kalam theologians gave different and sometimes incompatible definitions. In his *Commentary on the Long Creed*, which is the most relevant for the present argument, Sanūsī mentioned in passing that they are attributes that "do not have an existence that is additional to the entity" (*laysa lahā wujūd zā'id 'alá l-dhāt*) and are "not additional to the entity" (*laysa bi-zā'id 'alá l-dhāt*) (K 213, 242). This would correspond to what, in more Aristotelian terminology, would be called "essential attributes."[11] It is clear that two tokens of the same type must have the same essential or per se attributes.

If something is intrinsically and necessarily true of an entity, then it is either a per se attribute of that entity or a logical concomitant (*lāzim*) of such a per se attribute. So, if some body X is necessarily pre-eternal, and some body Y is necessarily originated, then X and Y must differ in their per se attributes. But we are supposing that X and Y are both bodies and hence do not differ in their per se attributes. So, if X is originated, then Y is originated. The conclusion is ambitious: If there is a single physical body that has come to be, then all physical bodies have come to be.

Sanūsī's argument would have been rejected by the Aristotelian–Neoplatonist philosophers. They maintained that some bodies are pre-eternal, while other bodies come-to-be and pass-away. They might have agreed with Sanūsī that it would be absurd that one human being, for example, is pre-eternal while another human being is not. But they would deny that the same absurdity obtains when we compare human beings with, say, heavenly bodies. They would, in other words, deny that human beings and planets are relevantly "similar." The difference between the two perspectives is thus grounded in different visions of the material world. For Sanūsī's argument to go through, we would have to assume that matter is homogenous: If one material body is necessarily originated, then all material bodies are necessarily originated. The Aristotelian–Neoplatonist philosophers, by contrast, saw an all-important distinction between individual material things in the sublunar world and the ethereal heavenly bodies of the supralunar world. The fact that the former are originated does not imply that the latter are originated as well. Sanūsī's aforementioned assumptions about personal identity may have seemed quaint to modern readers, but when it comes to the theory of matter it is likely his opponents' view that seems antiquated. The overthrow of Aristotelian–Neoplatonist physics and cosmology in early-modern Europe, and the attendant resurgence of atomism or corpuscularism, have given renewed strength to the view that matter is homogenous across the universe.[12]

Kalam-style proofs for the existence of God aim to show that all material substances and their attributes are created. One objection is that such proofs do not establish that the entire "world"—defined as what is other than God—is created. To reach such a conclusion, one would have to rule out that there are pre-eternal, non-material substances. Sanūsī wrote that he found earlier kalam theologians' arguments against immaterial substances to be "weak" (K 215). His own position was agnostic on whether there are such substances. But if this was Sanūsī's position, how could he rule out that there are immaterial substances that are pre-eternal? His reply was to appeal to revelation and the consensus of the community. This is not circular, he added, for it is possible to prove the existence of a Creator on the basis of the existence of material substances and material attributes. Once it has been established that there is a Creator with Will, Power, and Knowledge, then it is possible to prove the veracity of a prophet supported by miracles, which in turn allows us to rely on revelation stating that God has created everything else, and hence we conclude that if there are immaterial substances then they, too, are originated (K 215–6).

To sum up: Sanūsī's first proof is an ambitious attempt to start with the assumption that at least one thing—the reasoner's own body—has come to be and has been brought about by an extrinsic cause. Next, he argued that the cause must be a voluntary agent. He then argued that what is true of this one created person must be true of all bodies: all bodies must have come to be as an effect of a voluntary agent. It is important to note that there is nothing in the proof so far to license the conclusion that all bodies have been brought about by the same voluntary agent. For all that has been shown up to now, each body could have been brought about by a different, non-bodily voluntary agent. Sanūsī, at various points in his presentation, helped himself to the assumption that all bodies are caused by the same voluntary agent, God. But, strictly speaking, he was not entitled to that assumption yet. The proof that there is only one creator, only one voluntary agent who is the cause of the entire world, comes later in the *Long Creed*, when Sanūsī proves that there is only one God. The outline of such a proof was given in Chapter 4. I will return to it in Chapter 8 on occasionalism.

3 Sanūsī's first proof and the question of natural causation

Sanūsī's first proof for the existence of God is unusual. It is reminiscent of the argument given by the early Ashʿarī theologians al-Bāqillānī (d.1013) and ʿAbd al-Qāhir al-Baghdādī (d.1037), both of whom noted that individual bodies might have different accidents from the ones they actually have and hence inferred that they have been brought about by a voluntary "particularizer." But both Bāqillānī and Baghdādī adduced the "argument from particularization" *after* having given the standard argument from accidents, i.e., after trying to show that all accidents are originated and that the bodies in which they inhere are therefore also originated.[13] Sanūsī's first proof, in contrast, applied the particularization argument from the outset, without first trying to show that all accidents and all bodies are originated. One simply applies the argument to a single body and then infers—on the basis of the homogeneity of matter—that all bodies have been brought about by a voluntary agent. In Sanūsī's exposition, it is thus clear—in a way that is not clear in Bāqillānī and Baghdādī—that the particularization argument is independent of the argument from accidents.[14]

Modern scholars such as Herbert Davidson and Ayman Shihadeh have characterized Bāqillānī's application of the "argument from particularization" to particular entities as presupposing the denial of natural causation. To that extent, they judge it less effective and sophisticated than a later version of the argument due to al-Juwaynī (d.1085) that applies it to the world as a whole. Juwaynī argued that since the world as a whole could have been smaller or larger, or older or younger, or have less or more constituents, it must have been created by a voluntary agent. By focusing on the generation of the physical world as a whole, Juwaynī was not open to the charge of simply presupposing the highly contentious premise that there is no natural causation.[15]

To appreciate the point, consider the following example: From the perspective of a belief in secondary causation and natural necessity, there is no reason to insist that only a voluntary agent could have brought me about in just one of many possible ways. The answer to why I have the height and weight that I have, and not other heights and weights, is to be found in antecedent natural causes and conditions, for example, my genes and diet. It only appears that there are possible alternatives to my actual height and weight because of the limitations of our knowledge of the workings of nature. If we had full knowledge of the natural causes at play, we would see that all my attributes are necessitated and that it is not a genuine possibility that I have different attributes from the ones I actually have.[16]

By contrast, a crucial step in Juwaynī's argument is the thesis that the world as a whole could have been different from how it actually is. It seems the world as a whole could, for example, have come into existence earlier or later than it did, or be larger or smaller than it is, or have fewer or more components. In this case, it is difficult to see how one can appeal to antecedent natural conditions and forces, for we are considering the world as a whole, and any proposed antecedent natural cause would itself be part of the world that could have been different. So, invoking a voluntary agent to explain why the world is in one of several possible ways may seem less question-begging.

It may indeed be the case that Juwaynī's version of the particularization argument is more difficult to reject by appeal to natural causation. But I do not think that Sanūsī, at least, was guilty of naively begging the question against natural causation. He took himself to be giving an argument against it on the basis of two theses that, even if not as definitive as he thought they were, deserve to be taken seriously:

> (Thesis 1) It is legitimate to ask why a particular originated entity has precisely the accidents it has, rather than other possible accidents.

The thesis would have elicited widespread assent in his intellectual milieu. An indeterministic or probabilistic view of nature with ubiquitous violations of the principle of sufficient reason would have been rejected as absurd by both Islamic philosophers and kalam theologians and would not have been a live option for Sanūsī or his interlocuters.

> (Thesis 2) Natural causation cannot explain why a particular originated entity has precisely the accidents it has, rather than other possible accidents.

This thesis would have been more controversial. But it has some prima facie plausibility. It is arguably far-fetched to deny that I could have been even a few millimeters or micrometers shorter or taller than I am by invoking antecedent secondary causes such as my genes and my diet. Quite apart from the question whether such antecedents can really explain my height down to the exact micrometer, the obvious question is why my genes and diet could not have been just slightly different. Can the necessitarian upholder of natural causation plausibly keep "passing the buck," so to speak, to avoid ultimate appeal to brute chance (which was generally agreed to be unsatisfactory) or divine will? In any case, it is difficult to see why it is Sanūsī rather than his necessitarian opponents who should be judged to be dogmatically begging the question on this issue.[17]

Sanūsī was, to be sure, not endorsing indeterminism and denying that there is an explanation for why I am exactly the height I am. For him, the explanation is God's Will. He was merely insisting that appeal to natural, secondary causes will not provide a satisfactory answer to why I am not a few millimeters or micrometers shorter or taller. Of course, one might respond that appeal to God's Will is a pseudo-explanation that simply invites the further question why God Willed this exact height. But Sanūsī's response to such an objection is clear. God's Will is pre-eternal and uncaused, and hence the question is illegitimate.[18] The demand for a reason or ground (*'illa*) is only legitimate in the case of what is originated and contingent, not what is pre-eternal and uncaused. One may legitimately ask why I am not taller or shorter, but not why God did not Will me to be taller or shorter.

4 Second proof

Sanūsī's second proof is a version of the classic proof from accidents. Though it appears as the second argument in Sanūsī's *Major Creed*, it is the only one that reappears in Sanūsī's *Middle Creed*, *Short Creed*, and *Shortened Short Creed*. The fact that the first proof was left out of the later creeds might suggest that Sanūsī had second thoughts about it as his argument of choice. Even if cogent, it does not establish that all bodies have been brought into existence by the same voluntary agent. And it shows that each body is originated, not that the world as a whole is originated in the sense that past time and past motion are finite.

The second proof begins by noting that all the attributes that inhere in the bodies of the world are originated. It adds the premise that everything whose attributes are originated is itself originated and then concludes that the world is created. The syllogistic presentation is (K 217–8):

The world has attributes all of which are originated
Everything that has attributes all of which are originated is originated
∴ The world is originated.

Sanūsī then gave arguments for the two premises of the syllogism. The proof of the first (minor) premise is another syllogism (K218):

The attributes of the world are changing or changeable
Everything that is changing or changeable is originated
∴ The attributes of the world are originated.

The fact that some attributes of the world are changing is known by sense-perception. Those attributes of the world that are perceived to be unchanging are nevertheless amenable (*qābila*) to change. Sanūsī added that if one were to accept the older kalam position that attributes do not endure from one moment to another, then it would follow that the attributes of the world are constantly going in and out of existence.[19] It appears that he, like most later theologians, wanted to leave this older kalam position open, neither embracing nor rejecting it.

Why should mere changeability imply origination? In other words, why does the mere fact that an attribute *might* change, even though it does not *actually* change, entail that the attribute is originated? Sanūsī answered that change is impossible for what is pre-eternal. It is clear that what is pre-eternal cannot change from non-existence to existence. What is pre-eternal also cannot cease to exist, for in that case its existence would be contingent and would need a cause.

But why should something not be contingent and changeable in itself and yet be pre-eternal due to the pre-eternality of its cause? Sanūsī rejected this possibility on a number of grounds. First, he had already argued, in the first proof for the existence of

God, that a cause must be voluntary and that there are no causes that are operative by nature or essence. If a cause acts by choice, then its effect cannot be pre-eternal, for the intention of bringing something into existence implies that the effect does not already exist.[20] Though there may be something initially plausible about Sanūsī's argument here, it is doubtful if it holds under scrutiny. As will be clear in the following chapter on God's attributes, Sanūsī—and Ashʿarī theologians more generally—held that God and God's core attributes are outside time. This implies that God's Will does not stand in temporal relations to occurrents, and so we cannot say that something exists "before," "at the same time as," or "after" God's Will to create it. In other words, if God's Will is outside time, then an occurrent cannot be said to exist "already" from God's perspective. Sanūsī's argument seems to be based on an equivocation between God's Will being outside of time altogether, which is his considered position, and God's Will existing at all times. The present argument presupposes the second understanding, i.e., that God's Will to create an entity is "in" time and must temporally precede the existence of the entity.

Sanūsī's second argument for why an accident's amenability to change entails origination is that change in what is pre-eternal is inconceivable. If an effect (such as motion) is pre-eternal due to its pre-eternal natural cause and then ceases to exist, then one would have to suppose that either (a) its cause ceases to exist, which is absurd, for one would then ask why the pre-eternal natural cause ceased to exist, leading to an infinite regress, or (b) the cause remains but the effect's contrary (*ḍidd*) comes to be (in this example, rest), which is also absurd, for the contrary (rest) either comes to be while the effect (motion) exists, which implies that two contrary accidents exist at the same time in the same locus, or comes to be after the effect ceases to exist, which implies that the effect of a pre-eternal natural cause ceases to exist for no reason. Furthermore, if the effect is pre-eternal, then it should rule out the coming-to-be of its contrary, rather than that incipient contrary leading to the cessation of the pre-eternal effect (K 218–9). So, one can conclude that mere amenability to change entails that an accident is caused and not pre-eternal.

Having established to his satisfaction that the world has attributes all of which are originated, Sanūsī now turned to the second (major) premise: Everything that has attributes that are originated is originated. He began by claiming that it is known "necessarily" (i.e., evidently) that a body cannot exist without any of its basic four attributes: motion, rest, coming together, and coming apart. In the kalam tradition, these attributes were termed *akwān* and were considered basic because they hold not only of composite bodies but also of atoms.[21] A body or atom cannot be such that it neither moves nor is stationary, for example. In the early kalam tradition, this was held to imply that if both motion and rest are originated, then bodies and atoms must be originated as well.

As some later kalam theologians conceded, the argument is not compelling as it stands. After all, it seems possible for a body to be in motion, and before then at rest, and before then in motion, and before then at rest, and so on infinitely. This would be a scenario in which the body is pre-eternal whereas its basic attributes of motion and rest are originated. More generally, if the originated attributes exist successively without beginning, then we would not have the absurd situation that the pre-eternal substance exists without any attributes at all.

From the eleventh century, most Islamic theologians came to recognize that, for the argument from accidents to go through, one must rule out the possibility of an infinite succession of changing accidents.[22] Sanūsī adduced four such arguments against the possibility of "occurrents without beginning" (*ḥawādith lā awwala lahā*).

The first argument

The first argument is found in Juwaynī's classic handbook *The Guidance* and goes back to the sixth-century Christian philosopher

Philoponus:[23] If there are occurrents without beginning, then an infinite number of occurrents must have come to pass before the present moment. But it is, or so the argument goes, impossible that an infinite number of events has come to pass, for an infinite series cannot be completed or traversed. As Sanūsī wrote:

> If we assume occurrents without beginning, then it follows that an infinite number of celestial movements and instances of animals, one after the other, have concluded. The conjunction of concluding (*farāgh*) and infinity is a conjunction of contradictories and therefore is evidently impossible. (K 226)

To this, Sanūsī anticipated the objection that Islamic theologians themselves accept that the world is post-eternal and that people in paradise, for example, will exist post-eternally even though they will have ever-changing accidents. He countered that there is no symmetry between pre-eternity and post-eternity. The latter is not impossible, for it does not involve a completed traversal of the infinite. Following Juwaynī, he gave the following analogy: If someone were to say, "I will not give you a dirhem on any day unless I give you a dirhem the day before" then such a condition cannot be met—the giving of the dirhem is endlessly deferred. But if someone says, "I will not give you a dirhem on any day unless I give you a dirhem the day after" then this condition can in principle be fulfilled, assuming of course that the giver and receiver are immortal and the giver's money does not run out. (One might imagine such a commitment being made between two people in paradise.) Sanūsī wrote:

> The imparting of motion, for example, by an efficient cause to the heavenly sphere in our present time, or another time, depends on its imparting, prior to this, motions without end, one after the other. The motion in a specific time is an analogue of the dirhem that is promised at a specific time, and the infinite number of motions before it is the analogue of the infinite

> number of dirhems prior to that dirhem. So, the existence of the heavenly sphere in this example would be impossible, just as it is impossible for the promised dirhem to be given to the person in a specific time. Similarly, it would follow that our existence at the present time, and the existence of all animals and plants, are impossible, for we depend on the existence of parents before us without end, and plants depend on seeds before them without end. (K 228–9)

Sanūsī's (and Juwaynī's) point here can be rephrased as follows: an infinite regress of preconditions is vicious, whereas an infinite progression of consequences is not.[24]

One might have expected the claim that an infinite regress of preconditions is vicious to have garnered widespread assent in the medieval period, especially in light of the widely accepted idea that an infinite regress of secondary causes is absurd and must come to an end with a first cause. Yet, Philoponus's argument was resisted by eminent thinkers in late antiquity (Simplicius), medieval Islam (Avicenna, Averroes), and the medieval Latin West (Aquinas).[25] Avicenna, for one, was willing to accept an infinite regress of preconditions, even though he believed that an infinite regress of contingent causes is vicious. He thought he could prove the pre-eternity of the world by independent arguments, and on that basis he concluded that an infinite regress of preconditions is, in fact, traversed.[26] Sanūsī did not directly address Avicenna's arguments for pre-eternity. It is likely that he thought they had been conclusively refuted by Ashʿarī theologians such as Ghazālī and Fakhr al-Dīn al-Rāzī.

The second argument

The second argument against occurrents without beginning is found in Fakhr al-Dīn al-Rāzī's *Landmarks of the Principles of*

Religion with the commentary of Ibn al-Tilimsānī (d.1260), a work that Sanūsī often cited. In Sanūsī's words, the argument goes as follows:

> Every occurrent is preceded by non-existence without beginning, and these non-existences coincide in pre-eternity (*azal*) for there is no order to them. The genus of occurrents is also pre-eternal . . . and that genus only exists within one of its occurrent instances. This instance is therefore in pre-eternity, but its non-existence is also in pre-eternity . . . And so, the existence of something is conjoined to its nonexistence.[27]

Thus stated, the argument seems straightforwardly fallacious. To speak of non-existences, "coinciding in pre-eternity" (*mujtamiʿa fī l-azal*) is to treat pre-eternity as a point in time during which all occurrents are non-existent. Furthermore, it is sophistical to say that if the type "occurrent" is instantiated in pre-eternity, then there is one instance that exists in pre-eternity. The type must be instantiated, but it is not instantiated at all times by the same instance. All that follows is that one instance exists at time t_1, another instance exists at t_2, and yet another instance exists at t_3, and so on. At no point in time does the same instance both exist and not exist. The earlier Ashʿarī theologian Sayf al-Dīn al-Āmidī (d.1231), active in Iraq, Egypt, and Syria, put the point succinctly:

> It does not follow from non-existence preceding every one of the units that it precedes the whole (*jumla*), for a judgment about a unit does not have to be a judgment about the whole.[28]

Sanūsī was aware of this passage, for it is cited in the theological summa of the Tunisian scholar Ibn ʿArafa (d.1401) with which he was familiar.[29] In sticking to his guns, he may have been influenced by the Maghrebi-born, Alexandrian theologian Abū Yaḥyá al-Sharīf (fl.1231) who had argued that a judgment about instances also applies to the totality when dealing with intrinsic or essential attributes. If one cat is an animal, then a hundred or a thousand cats are also animals. Analogously, if one entity is contingent and originated in time, then all entities are contingent and originated in time.[30] The problem with this argument is that it confuses "each and every" with "the whole qua whole." If one cat is essentially an animal, then all cats are animals, but it does not follow that the totality of cats is one more animal. And if one body is originated and preceded by its own non-existence, and this is an essential feature of it, then each body is originated and preceded by its own non-existence. But it does not follow that all bodies considered as one are collectively preceded by the same non-existence.

The third argument

The third argument against "occurrents without beginning" is what has come to be known as "the argument of superposition" or "the argument of application" or "the mapping argument" (*burhān al-taṭbīq*). The argument seems first to have been proposed by Avicenna to rule out a body of infinite extension. If, wrote Avicenna, an infinite body exists, then one may consider an infinite line from an arbitrary point of the body, say A, to the infinite. Call this line AB; it starts at point A and is infinite in the direction of B. Then, take another point between A and B, say C. Now we have another line CB, also infinite in the direction of B.

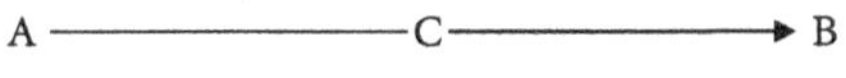

At this stage, we map or superpose the two lines AB and CB unto each other. Either (i) AB is equal to CB or (ii) AB is larger than CB. Either option is absurd. (i) If AB is equal to CB, then the whole is equal to a part of that whole, which is absurd. (ii) If AB is greater than CB, then CB is finite, and AB is greater than this finite line by a finite length, namely the length of line AC. But what is greater than a finite length by a finite length must itself be finite, so AB is finite, though we started by assuming that it is infinite.[31]

Some later Islamic theologians took over this argument and used it to rule out the pre-eternity of the world. Consider the temporal extension from an arbitrary point in time infinitely backward in the direction of the past. Then consider a temporal extension from an earlier point in time infinitely backward to the past. Then superpose the two series: They cannot be equal, for we've assumed that one series is a subset of the other; but if the original temporal series is larger, then the subset is finite and smaller than the original series by a finite amount, and so the original series must be finite as well. The argument came to be presented in influential, later handbooks of Islamic theology as the most dependable argument for the finitude of past time and the origination of the world.[32] In fact, Sanūsī's discussion has a somewhat old-fashioned tone by not giving it pride of place.

Despite its historical popularity, the argument of superposition had its detractors. Aristotelian–Neoplatonist philosophers restricted the applicability of the argument to what exists at the same time, and on that basis rejected it as an argument for the finitude of the past.[33] Even some Islamic theologians expressed doubts. Ibn al-Tilimsānī, an important influence on Sanūsī, rejected the argument on the grounds that it leads to two theologically unacceptable consequences: First, that one could show, by a similar argument, that the future is finite, though Islamic scholars are committed to an infinite afterlife. Second, if one denies that two infinite sets can be unequal, then it seems to follow that what God knows and what God wills—the "attachments" of divine knowledge and divine will—are not infinite, because the set of what God knows is larger than the set of what God wills, for God knows what is necessary, contingent, and impossible, but only wills what is contingent.[34] Pursuing these issues will take us too far from Sanūsī's own writings.

The fourth argument

Sanūsī's fourth argument against occurrents without beginning seems to have been adopted from the Egyptian Ashʿarī theologian al-Muqtaraḥ (d.1216).[35] It goes as follows: Let us assume that there are occurrents without beginning, for example an infinite number of past revolutions of the Moon around the Earth. After each revolution, it would be true to judge that an infinite number of revolutions has passed. We now have two series: one consisting of past revolutions, the other consisting of true judgments. Now, regardless of whether we assume that the series of judgments extends infinitely into the past or comes to an end, an absurdity results. Assuming that the series of judgments comes to an end is clearly absurd, for we are supposing that the number of past revolutions of the Moon around the Earth is infinite, and for each revolution there is a corresponding true judgment. Assuming that the series of judgments extends infinitely into the past also leads to absurdity. The thing judged (*al-maḥkūm ʿalayh*) is prior (*sābiq*) to the judgment (*ḥukm*), so the infinite number of past revolutions of the Moon is prior to the judgment that an infinite number of revolutions has passed. But it is absurd to suppose that one pre-eternal series is prior to another pre-eternal series. Sanūsī wrote:

> It is necessary that each and every instance of a judgment is preceded by occurrents, so that it can judge that they have passed. It follows that the genus of what is judged—which is pre-eternal—precedes (*yasbiqu*) the genus of the judgment, which is pre-eternal as well. And the precedence of one pre-eternal over another pre-eternal is evidently impossible. (K 234)

It seems to me that the argument commits the fallacy of composition. Each individual revolution of the Moon is not pre-eternal, and each subsequent judgment is not pre-eternal. It is the series of past revolutions and the series of past judgments that are assumed to be pre-eternal, not any particular past revolution or past judgment. There seems to be no problem with supposing that one occurrent (a particular revolution of the Moon) precedes another occurrent (the corresponding judgment that a revolution has passed) or even that an infinite number of past revolutions of the Moon has preceded any single judgment. (Each individual revolution of the Moon is also preceded by an infinite number of judgments.) It does not follow from this that the pre-eternal series of revolutions as a whole somehow "precedes" the pre-eternal series of judgments as a whole.

5 Sanūsī's proofs and "the Avicennian turn"

Sanūsī's most extensive discussion of proofs for the existence of God is contained in his *Commentary on the Long Creed.* As seen above, he presented two proofs in that work. The first is an unusual adaptation of the proof offered by the early Ashʿarī theologians Bāqillānī and Baghdādī. It starts from the premise that at least one body—the body of the person who is being enjoined to reason and prove God's existence—has come to be after not existing, and that all bodies that come to be after not existing must have been brought about by something else. The next step is to say that this created body is in one of numerous possible ways: it could have been older or younger, smaller or larger, darker or fairer, heavier or lighter, faster or slower, and so on. This shows, according to Sanūsī, that it has not been brought about by a natural cause but by a voluntary agent. The final step is to argue that since one body is created by a voluntary agent, all bodies must be created by a voluntary agent. The fact that it is the same voluntary agent who has created all bodies is not itself shown in the proof but will be argued later in the work when Sanūsī turned to God's oneness. The proof also does not show that the world as a whole has come into being. For all it shows, there might be an infinite succession of created bodies and accidents extending backward in time.

Sanūsī's second proof is a version of the classic kalam argument from accidents. The starting point is that the attributes in the world are changing or changeable, from which it is inferred that they are originated. It is then argued that the origination of attributes entails the origination of the substances in which they inhere. This step in the proof involves ruling out the possibility that there is an infinite series of originated accidents that are successively true of a pre-eternal substance. Sanūsī gave four, already established arguments against the possibility of "occurrents without beginning." Of these, two seem to be plainly fallacious. The two more substantial arguments are Philoponus's argument that a past infinity cannot be traversed and Avicenna's "argument from superposition" showing that an infinite series of past occurrents would be equal to its own subset, which is taken to be absurd. Even these two arguments, however, were criticized by some medieval philosophers and theologians. Sanūsī did not engage in detail with such criticisms even though he was almost certainly aware of them.

Apart from its unusual first proof, Sanūsī's discussion has two further features that are worth noting. First, is his penchant for regularly casting arguments into explicit syllogistic form. This contrasts with earlier Ash'ari handbooks widely studied in the Maghreb in preceding centuries, such as Juwaynī's *The Guidance* and Salāljī's *The Demonstrative*. The shift in presentation may in part be reflective of Sanūsī's personal enthusiasm for syllogistic logic, but it is also no doubt indicative of the increased tendency to study logic in Islamic scholarly circles after the twelfth century.

A second noteworthy feature is that Sanūsī still gave pride of place to proofs from the origination of attributes and bodies at a time when, especially in the Turco-Persianate world, Ash'ari theologians were often adopting Avicenna's two aforementioned proofs from contingency instead. Strikingly, the most distinctive Avicennian proof, which considers the chain of contingent causes as a whole and argues that it is contingent and in need of a cause, is conspicuously absent from Sanūsī's discussion. Already Ibn al-Tilimsānī, an important influence on Sanūsī, had dismissed the argument in his commentary on Rāzī's *Landmarks of the Principles of Religion*. Why should one concede, Ibn al-Tilimsānī wrote, that the whole series of contingent beings is something over and above the parts and can therefore meaningfully be said to need a cause? After all, we are supposing that each individual contingent being has a cause within the whole series, and the whole is merely a mental consideration (*iʿtibār*) rather than an entity in its own right requiring an additional cause.[36]

It is instructive to compare Sanūsī's proofs with those of his Persian contemporary Jalāl al-Dīn al-Dawānī (d.1502). Dawānī wrote a treatise on proofs for the existence of God that came to be widely studied and glossed in the eastern Islamic world in subsequent centuries.[37] The treatise is organized into two main sections. The first is devoted to variants of Avicenna's proof that considers the series of contingent causes as a whole, and then argues that the series as a whole is contingent and must therefore be caused by a necessary being. The second section discusses variants of Avicenna's other argument from contingency that maintains that an infinite series of contingent causes is absurd and accordingly concludes that there must be a necessary first cause. Dawānī simply ignored the argument from accidents, the argument from particularization, and Philoponus's argument that a past infinity cannot be traversed. All the proofs that he discussed take their point of departure in the Avicennian distinction between contingent and necessary being, not in the origination of bodies or bodily accidents.

Dawānī identified as an Ashʿari, at least in some works, but his Ashʿarism would hardly have been recognizable to someone like Juwaynī in the eleventh century. By contrast, Sanūsī's Ashʿarism was much more continuous with Juwaynī's, though modified by an enthusiasm for syllogistic logic that had been initiated within Ashʿarī circles by Juwaynī's student Ghazālī.

7
The Divine Attributes

When attempting to prove the existence of God, Sanūsī considered the Aristotelian–Neoplatonist philosophers and their upholding of the world's past eternity as the main intellectual challenge. When discussing the divine attributes, he additionally criticized the Christian belief in incarnation, Muslim fideists and literalists whom he thought upheld crassly anthropomorphic conceptions of God, Muʿtazilīs who denied that God has several positive, distinct, and irreducible attributes, and even fellow Ashʿarīs whom he believed had conceded too much to their opponents.

The present chapter will cover some of the major issues in Sanūsī's discussion of the divine attributes. Some subsidiary discussions will be dealt with in the following chapters, specifically Sanūsī's attempt to derive occasionalism from God's Power, Will, and Oneness (Chapter 8) and his polemics against the Muʿtazilī positions that God's Speech is created and that there are objective moral standards that are independent of revelation and place limits on what God can do and decree (Chapter 9).

1 Per se attributes

In Chapters 4 and 6, it was mentioned that the mainstream Ashʿarī tradition tended to distinguish between different kinds of "attribute" (*ṣifa*), one of which is the so-called per se (*nafsiyya*) attribute. As noted there, a precise understanding of the term is hampered by the fact that various kalam theologians gave different and sometimes incompatible definitions. Even Sanūsī himself gave

Al-Sanūsī. Khaled El-Rouayheb, Oxford University Press.
 DOI: 10.1093/oso/9780197835630.003.0007

various and not obviously compatible definitions in various works. Consider the following:

- ". . . reduce to the reality of their bearer" (*rājiʿa ilá ḥaqīqat mawṣūfihā*)
- ". . . what is used to express the entity itself" (*mā yuʿabbar bihi ʿan nafs al-dhāt*)
- ". . . is not added to the entity" (*laysa bi-zāʾid ʿalá l-dhāt*)
- ". . . do not have an existence additional to the entity" (*laysa lahā wujūd zāʾid ʿalá l-dhāt*).[1]

These definitions suggest that "per se attributes" correspond to what in more Aristotelian terminology would be called "essential attributes."[2] But such a translation hardly fits the following definition:

- ". . . Every positive attribute that is additional to the entity and cannot be imagined to be absent while the entity remains" (*kull ṣifa thubūtiyya zāʾida ʿalá l-dhāt lā yaṣiḥḥ tawahhum intifāʾahā maʿa baqāʾ al-dhāt*).[3]

In fact, this last definition seems to fit best the standard, mundane example of a "per se attribute" in earlier kalam literature, namely a body's attribute of occupying space (*taḥayyuz*) which, though not part of the formal definition of "body," and hence "additional," is inseparable from—and intrinsically true of—bodies. This suggests that "per se attributes" correspond to Aristotelian per se accidents.[4]

In Sanūsī's shorter creeds, existence is given as one of the attributes that are necessarily true of God, and in his very popular *Short Creed*, he identified it as a per se divine attribute. This does not, however, seem to have been his considered view. In his commentary on the creedal poem of Jazāʾirī, he maintained that humans have no knowledge of God's essence and therefore of what His per se attributes are (MS 215). Moreover, in his *Commentary on the Short Creed*, he added that it is only with indulgence that existence can be considered an attribute at all (S 142–3, 154–5). His hesitancy echoed that of Juwaynī in his classic *The Guidance* in which it is stated:

> The preferred view is that existence should not be considered one of the attributes, for existence is identical to the entity (*nafs al-dhāt*). It is not like occupying space for an atom, for occupying space is an attribute that is additional to the entity that is the atom, whereas the existence of an atom, in our view, is its self without supposing anything additional.[5]

The mainstream Ashʿarī tradition, from an early period, rejected the view that there are non-existent entities. It accordingly tended to reject the view that existence is an attribute inhering in an entity.[6] In other words, though "exists" can be said of God, it is not a divine attribute but merely an alternative way of saying there is a divine entity or self that has attributes.

2 Negative attributes

Another type of attribute is the "negative" (*salbiyya*). This, like "existence," was standardly presented by Ashʿarīs as truthfully predicated of an entity but not a real attribute inhering in that entity. I will here discuss three such negative attributes.

Pre-eternity

Having established that there is a voluntary agent who has created me, Sanūsī then argued that this voluntary agent must be pre-eternal in the sense of not being preceded by non-existence. To suppose otherwise leads to an infinite regress of voluntary causes, and Sanūsī—in his previously discussed proofs for the existence of God—tried to show that such an infinite regress is absurd.

At this stage, Sanūsī interjected that the Arabic term *qadīm*, which I have hitherto translated as "pre-eternal," can also mean "old." He explained that the latter sense is not legitimately applied to God. God is not "old" in the sense of having existed for a long time. Rather, God is outside time altogether. Time, according to Sanūsī, is either (a) the correlation of one changing thing with another changing thing (*muqāranat mutajaddid li-mutajaddid*), or (b) the movement of the outermost celestial sphere (*sayr al-falak al-aʿẓam*).[7] On the former view, standard among kalam theologians, something is in time if its changes can be correlated with the changes of other things. On the second view, something is in time if its existence is encompassed by the movements of the outermost celestial sphere. On both accounts, God is not a temporal being. Given that God is pre-eternal and immutable, it is impossible that God stands in temporal relations with changing things, whether mundane or celestial. And given that God has created all bodies and their motions, His existence is metaphysically prior to—and not delimited by—the outermost celestial sphere and its movement. Sanūsī used the point to rebut an anticipated objection to the pre-eternity of God:

> If you maintain a pre-eternal being (*qadīm*) without beginning, then it follows that there are successive moments of time without beginning, for what exists can only be understood to be in time. The obtaining of times without beginning is not conceded, for the very reason you adduced to rule out occurrents without beginning. Thus, you tried to avoid an infinite regress but have fallen into it.

Sanūsī answered thus:

> The answer is to deny the conditional [i.e., that if God is pre-eternal then there are moments of time without beginning], for you have just learned that time does not exist before the existence

of the world. So, the statement that "what exists can only be understood to be in time" is false.[8]

Post-eternity

The voluntary agent who has created me is also post-eternal in the sense that the agent's existence is not followed by non-existence. If the agent were amenable to non-existence, then the agent would require a preponderating cause for existing rather than not existing. But it has just been established that the agent is pre-eternal and uncaused.

Sanūsī was willing to use the Avicennian term "necessary of existence" (*wājib al-wujūd*) of God. But the meaning of the phrase for Sanūsī is simply that God is both pre- and post-eternal (M 236), which is very different from what it means within the context of Avicennian metaphysics. For Avicenna, the necessary existent is the one being whose essence and existence coincide.[9] For Sanūsī, the term "necessary of existence" when applied to God means that it can be shown to be rationally necessary that God is pre- and post-eternal. This sense is significant because, as will be seen below, it opens up the possibility of saying that the attributes of God are just as much necessary of existence as God's Self. If one can show—as Sanūsī thought he could—that it is a truth of reason that God's Knowledge is pre- and post-eternal, then it follows that God's Knowledge is "necessarily existent" in the full sense of the term. By contrast, from the perspective of the Avicennian construal of "necessarily existent," a rational proof that God's Knowledge is pre- and post-eternal is insufficient to show that it is necessary of existence in the strict sense, rather than derivatively necessary by virtue of another.

Being unlike generated entities

Given that all bodies are originated, as shown by Sanūsī's proofs for the existence of God, it must be that the voluntary agent who has brought me into existence is not a body. Otherwise, the voluntary agent would also need a preponderating cause, and it has been established that the voluntary agent is eternal. The voluntary agent also cannot be an attribute of a body, for it has been shown that the attributes peculiar to bodies are originated. It follows that the agent cannot inhere in another body in the way, for example, a particular instance of redness inheres in a rose. On this ground, Sanūsī rejected Christian notions of incarnation: It is impossible, he asserted, for two distinct substances to become united in existence; only a particular attribute can become one in existence with a substance; but God is not an attribute and so cannot become one with a human (K 251–3). On this ground too, he maintained that Sufi ecstatic utterances that suggest that the divine indwells in the mystic must either be censured or given a charitable, nonliteral interpretation (K 255–6).

Sanūsī likewise condemned the Muslim groups who believed that God is in the spatial direction of "up" and that He is "above" the celestial throne. The two groups whom he mentioned as having such views were the Karrāmīs and the so-called Ḥashwīs. The former are known to have been active in Khorasan up to the thirteenth century.[10] The second term was sometimes used of the more combative, anti-Ashʿarī followers of the Ḥanbalī school who, as mentioned in Chapter 2, dismissed all natural theology as heretical, insisted that God's eternal Speech consists of Arabic letters and sounds, and rejected any figurative reinterpretation of passages in the Quran and hadith mentioning God's hands, fingers, face, eye, and foot, or God smiling, wondering, and descending to the lower heavens on certain nights of the year.[11] His remarks on the latter group were scathing:

> The Ḥashwīs, who are partisans of the literal, maintain that the Speech of God subsists in Him as letters and sounds, and despite being letters and sounds are nevertheless pre-eternal! These people are an extreme in waywardness and are entangled

> in luxuriant ignorance. Some disputed point may occur to other heretics that does not immediately contravene necessary truths. As for them, they do not heed the necessities of reason . . . They believe that God is a body, sitting on a throne, touching it, and resting on it, then every Friday He moves from His place in the last third of the night to the [lower] heavens, then returns to His place at dawn. (K 365–6)

The group, Sanūsī added, do not admit the basic categories of the necessary, the impossible, and the possible, nor the difference between literal and figurative. They deny the legitimacy of reasoning regarding the principles of religion and believe that God can do the impossible if He so wills.

There is an element of caricature in Sanūsī's description. But the views that he sketched are nevertheless close to the views of radical, anti-Ashʿarī Ḥanbalīs such as Ibn Taymiyya (d.1328) and Ibn Qayyim al-Jawziyya (d.1350), the intellectual forefathers of modern Salafism. There is no evidence that he read their works, nor is there any evidence that such thinkers were influential or widely read in his time in the Maghreb, which by the fifteenth century was overwhelmingly Ashʿarī in creed. Their positions were hardly as crude as Sanūsī made them out to be. Yes, they insisted that God has a face, eyes, hand, fingers, is seated on a throne, and descends to the lower heavens, but they carefully explained that the terms "face," "eyes," "hand," "fingers," "seated," and "descends" must be accepted agnostically and as meaning something very different when applied to God than when applied to created beings. They could and did press the point that even terms such as "knows" and "wills"—which Ashʿarīs were happy to attribute to God—must also mean something very different when applied to God. If so, why interpret "descends" figuratively but not "knows"? One might even turn the tables on the Ashʿarīs and insist that *they* are the anthropomorphists for believing that terms such as "knows" and "wills" can be applied to God in more or less the same sense as they are applied to humans.[12] How would Sanūsī have replied to such an argument? He did not address the challenge directly, but there are indications in his work of how he would have done so.

First, when Sanūsī denied that God is "similar" to created things, he was thinking of the created world as atoms, bodies, and their attributes. The per se attributes of a body include having spatial extension, a shape, a location, and being either in motion or at rest. It is impossible that God should have these attributes, for this would mean that God is also a body and, as such, is originated and brought about by an extrinsic preponderator. It is, by contrast, not a per se attribute of a body to have knowledge, will, power, or speech. If God possesses knowledge and a body possesses knowledge, this does not imply that God is a body or is similar—in a problematic sense—to created things. (I will return to this point later in the chapter.)

Second, Sanūsī adhered to what has been called Ghazālī's "rule of interpretation."[13] A scriptural description of God must be accepted as literal unless that sense is rationally impossible. It is rationally impossible for God to sit, descend, have limbs, or wonder. These terms must therefore be interpreted figuratively or agnostically when applied to God in the Quran and hadith (K 625–7). But it is not rationally impossible for God to know, will, and have power. On the contrary, as seen in Chapter 4, Sanūsī presented arguments to show that such attributes must be literally true of God.

This last point brings out a more fundamental difference between a natural theologian such as Sanūsī and the more fideist Ḥanbalīs. If scriptural testimony is the only ground for attributing existence, knowledge, power, and will to God, then it may be palatable to say that such terms must be understood to mean something very different when applied to God than when applied to humans, i.e., that the terms "exists" and "knows" are equivocal when applied to God and to humans. If, on the other hand, the primary ground for attributing existence, knowledge, power, and will to God is natural reason, then such terms cannot mean something very different when applied to God and when applied to creatures. If one argues, for example, that the fact that the world is in one of many possible ways shows that God has not just Power but also Will, then it is presupposed that the term "will" is used of God in a recognizable, non-idiosyncratic sense not entirely different from the sense it has when applied to humans. Similarly, if one argues that God must have knowledge because it is impossible to have the will to choose one option over other possible options without knowledge, then the term "knowledge" must be used of God in a recognizable, non-idiosyncratic sense. The terms "will" and "knowledge" are, on this account, univocal or analogical when applied to God and to creatures. The same does not apply to descriptions such as "being seated on a throne" or "descending to the lowest heavens," which are only known to be true through revelation and can therefore be interpreted, when applied to God, to mean something very different from their ordinary senses. The point will be discussed further below.

3 Entitative attributes

There was general agreement among Muslim thinkers that God can be described as knowing, willing, powerful, and alive. Understanding such attributions, however, was a much more contentious matter. The Muʿtazilīs upheld what is now sometimes referred to as the doctrine of divine simplicity. God's Knowledge, God's Will, and God's Power cannot, on that account, be distinct attributes additional (*zāʾida*) to God's Self (*dhāt*). One alternative would be to see these descriptions of God as only nominally distinct from God and from each other: the terms "God," "God's Knowledge," "God's Will," and "God's Power" might have different connotations, but their reference is one and the same. Though safeguarding divine simplicity, such a view is, at least at first sight, unappealing. It entails that one cannot strictly say, for example, that God has the power to do what He does not will, or that God has knowledge of what is not within His power, such as truths about what is necessary and impossible. If God, God's Will, God's Power, and God's Knowledge are strictly one and the same, then such statements would seem to be false or, at the very least, would have to be radically reinterpreted.[14]

It is nevertheless not difficult to understand the apprehensions of early Muslim theologians about admitting numerous, distinct, and pre-eternal attributes like God's Power, God's Knowledge, and God's Will. For one thing, it may have seemed uncomfortably close to Christian views of a trinitarian God. Indeed, many Muʿtazilīs accused their Muslim adversaries of committing the same error as the Christians and perhaps even exceeding them in polytheism by admitting not just three but seven or more co-eternal attributes.[15] And Muslim heresiographers routinely interpreted the Christian doctrine of the trinity in terms of attributes: God's Existence is the Father, God's Speech is the Son, and God's Life is the Holy Spirit.[16]

Most later Muʿtazilīs suggested that the divine attributes are "states" (*aḥwāl*), neither existents nor non-existents.[17] God's being knowledgeable, for example, is a different state than God's being powerful or God's being alive. Yet, because states are not existents, there is no commitment to a God with numerous, distinct, and co-eternal existing attributes. The problem with the suggestion is that the theory of the "state" (*ḥāl*), with its postulation of attributes that are neither existent nor non-existent, was predictably controversial and often denounced as nonsensical.

Some Ashʿarī theologians, for example Juwaynī in his widely studied *The Guidance*, accepted the theory of the "state" and therefore accepted that God has states of being powerful, a knower, a willer, alive, and so on. Sanūsī himself vacillated on this topic: In his *Commentary on the Long Creed* he wrote that "the verifiers" among theologians reject "states," but in his later *Commentary on the Middle Creed*, he wrote that he was inclined to accept them, though adding that the issue was not of great doctrinal importance (K 222;

W 265). But Ashʿarī theologians who accepted "states" still insisted that they are grounded in positive attributes inhering in God, like knowledge, will, power, and life. Such attributes were, in the terminology of kalam, the "entitative attributes" (*ṣifāt al-maʿānī*). These were held by mainstream Ashʿarī and Māturīdī theologians to be irreducible to each other or to God's self, and to be distinct from per se, negative, and relational attributes.

Sanūsī gave two main arguments for the Ashʿarī position on the attributes, neither of which was original to him. The first has a broadly analogical structure: When we judge that humans know, we thereby judge that they have the attribute of knowledge, and when we judge that humans will, we thereby judge that they have the attribute of will. And when we ascribe knowledge and will to a person, we are committed to his or her possession of the two different attributes of knowledge and will. This justifies us, or so the argument goes, to make a similar judgment in the case of God. Given that we ascribe knowledge, power, will, and life to God, we are committed to God's possession of the different attributes of knowledge, power, will, and life. This, to use the terminology of kalam theology, is to extrapolate from what is witnessed (*shāhid*) to what is not witnessed (*ghāʾib*).[18] As will be seen shortly, Muʿtazilīs rejected this analogy, on the grounds that there is a relevant difference (*fāriq*) between human and divine knowledge.

Sanūsī's second major argument for entitative attributes is indirect. Let us assume that God's knowledge is not additional but identical to God's self, and that God's Power, Will, and Life are likewise not additional but identical to God's self. This entails that God is identical to God's Knowledge, which is identical to God's Power, which is identical to God's Will, which is identical to God's Life. In Sanūsī's words:

> If these . . . ascriptions were true of God's Self, but without entitative attributes inhering in It, then it follows that the Self is power, will, knowledge, life, and so on.[19]

It is absurd, continued Sanūsī, to suppose that a substance is identical to its attributes. An attribute has a contrary; for example, the contrary of knowledge is ignorance. But a substance does not have a contrary. An attribute logically entails a bearer in which it inheres—knowledge entails a knower, will entails a willer. But a substance does not entail a bearer in which it inheres. Also, some attributes, such as knowledge, logically entail an "attachment"—what the knowledge is about—but other attributes, such as life, do not logically entail an attachment, and the substance does not entail an attachment either. Therefore, the knowledge of God cannot be identical to the life of God or to God Himself.

Having given two arguments in favor of entitative attributes, Sanūsī turned to the standard objections to their existence. One of these was indicated above: Let us suppose that God has several, irreducible, entitative attributes. Such attributes would be pre-eternal, for Muʿtazilīs and Ashʿarīs agree on the principle that what has originated attributes is itself originated. It would follow that there are numerous pre-eternals, but Muslims agree that there is only one pre-eternal being. Sanūsī thought the objection equivocates on the meaning of "one." There is no consensus within the Muslim community that God is one in the sense that God has no attributes, but rather in the sense that the bearer of these attributes is one. There is nothing in revelation, conventional usage of language, or reason to preclude a single being from having several attributes (K 329–30).

A related objection is that positing several pre-eternal attributes implies positing several divinities. This is because "pre-eternity" is the most specific description of God. And it is an uncontroversial principle that if something shares the most specific description of a thing, then it also shares more general descriptions of that thing. If, for example, the most specific description of a cat is that it is an animal that meows, then anything that is an animal that meows also shares more general characteristics of cats, such as being furry, carnivorous, and having retractable claws. So, if anything shares with God the description of being pre-eternal, then it also shares the more general descriptions of being omnipotent, omniscient, the creator of the world, and so on. As mentioned in Chapter 4, Sanūsī's position was that positive attributes cannot themselves bear positive attributes, so he would deny that God's Knowledge, for example, itself has knowledge, power, and will. To rebut the objection, he denied that pre-eternality is the most specific attribute of God. As already established, pre-eternality is a negative attribute whose sense is that there is no beginning to God's existence. The most specific attribute of a being cannot be negative. As for what, then, that most specific positive attribute of God is, Sanūsī remained agnostic, thinking such knowledge beyond the ken of humans (K 331–7).

A third objection to entitative attributes in God can be seen as a response to Sanūsī's first argument that extrapolates from the case of ascribing knowledge to humans to the case of ascribing knowledge to God. Muʿtazilīs could (and historically did) object to the formula that God's being knowing, for example, is grounded in His possessing the attribute of knowledge.[20] The reasoning might work for Jane Doe: Given that she does not know necessarily, it is justifiable to say that her knowing is grounded in an attribute of knowledge inhering in her. But God knows pre-eternally and necessarily, so there is no justification for saying that God's knowing is grounded in an attribute of knowledge inhering in Him. More generally, it is illegitimate to seek a cause or ground (*ʿilla*) for what is necessary.

Sanūsī responded that the Ashʿarī position is that God's state of being knowing, for example, logically entails and is entailed by God's possession of the attribute of knowledge, not that God's being knowing is somehow brought about by that attribute. He wrote:

> By grounding (*taʿlīl*) God's attributes . . . we do not mean anything but co-implication (*talāzum*), i.e., that such-and-such an attribute that is necessary for Him, such as knowledge for example, is co-implied by another attribute that is necessary for Him most

> Exalted that is called a "state", such as being knowledgeable. Its meaning is not that the attribute of knowledge conveyed subsistence to the state of being knowledgeable after it did not subsist. (K321)

Medieval kalam theologians often resorted to slogans such as "God is a knower by virtue of knowledge" (*ʿālim bi-ʿilm*) versus "God is a knower by virtue of His self" (*ʿālim bi-dhātihi*). But such slogans do not take us very far. Sanūsī was very explicit about *not* believing that the attribute of knowledge inhering in God somehow causes or enables God to know. His position was rather as follows: If we do *not* accept "states," then, if we say that God knows, we are in effect saying that God possesses the attribute of knowledge. God's being a knower and God's possessing the attribute of knowledge are one and the same fact, differently expressed, and it is nonsense to affirm one and deny the other. If we *do* accept "states," then God's being a knower is a state and as such distinct from God's possessing the attribute of knowledge. But in that case, Sanūsī held that there is logical co-implication between the former and the latter: If God is in a state of knowing, then God has the entitative attribute of knowledge, and if God has the entitative attribute of knowledge, then God is in a state of knowing.

To say that Ashʿarīs believed that God knows "by means of" possessing the attribute of knowledge is, therefore, either imperspicuous or imprecise. It may be more helpful to bring in the modern philosophical notion of a "truth-maker."[21] Consider the propositions "Socrates is human" and "Socrates is wise." The former proposition, expressing an essential truth, is plausibly made true by Socrates alone. The latter proposition, expressing an accidental truth, is not made true by Socrates alone, but by Socrates and something else, such as the particular attribute—the "trope"—of wisdom inhering in him. Analogously, we may consider the propositions "God knows" and "God wills." Both Ashʿarīs and Muʿtazilīs agreed that these are true, indeed necessarily true, propositions. But for the Muʿtazilīs, the two propositions have exactly the same truth-maker, namely God's Self. For Ashʿarīs, the truth-makers are not exactly the same: In the former proposition, it is God's Self and the particular attribute of Knowledge inhering in It, and in the latter, it is God's Self and the particular attribute of Will inhering in It.

Thus stated, the Muʿtazilī position may seem more plausible at first sight, for modern discussions of truth-makers tend to assume that if a proposition expresses an essential truth about an entity, then its truth-maker is that entity alone (as in the example of "Socrates is human"). The topic cannot be exhaustively explored here. But it seems to me that Sanūsī could have made two responses: First, if the divine attribute of knowledge is inseparable from God, then it is imprecise to say that the truth-maker of the proposition "God knows" is not God "alone" but God and "something else." Second, we do not have insight into God's essence in order to say that "God knows" and "God wills" are essential truths. Indeed, as will be seen in the following section, Sanūsī held that the Aristotelian–Neoplatonist philosophers in effect deny that God knows and wills, and one cannot deny essential truths. Sanūsī would have agreed that "God knows" and "God wills" express *necessary* truths, but not all necessary truths about a subject are made true by that subject alone. "Socrates is created by God" is, for an Islamic theologian, a necessary truth but is not made true by Socrates alone.

4 The Aristotelian–Neoplatonist philosophers on the attributes

Besides the Muʿtazilīs, the doctrine of divine simplicity was also advocated by the Aristotelian–Neoplatonist philosophers. In fact, while most later Muʿtazilī theologians modified the doctrine of divine simplicity by adopting the theory of "states," the Aristotelian–Neoplatonist philosophers rejected the theory of "states" and hence maintained a more uncompromising version of divine simplicity. They were accordingly often accused of really denying that God has any attributes at all. Sanūsī wrote:

> As for the philosophers, they denied all the attributes of God the Exalted and said: He is not described except by means of negation, such as describing Him as "Intellecting Himself", and the meaning of His Intellecting Himself for them is that He is devoid of matter. Or by means of relations, such as calling Him a "Principle". Or by means of a proposition consisting of negation and relation, such as calling Him "Generous", meaning He grants without miserliness. (K 312)

From Sanūsī's perspective, if we deny both entitative attributes and "states," then any true attribution to God would have to be understood as either (i) a different designation of the self/entity, like "exists," which is not really an attribute at all, or (ii) a negative attribute, or (iii) a relational attribute. So, if I say, "God knows," the meaning of "knows" must be reinterpreted to mean something like "exists" (not an attribute at all), or "is not material" (a negation), or "is a cause of" (a relation). If I say, "God wills," the meaning of "wills" must be reinterpreted to mean something like "exists" or "is not compelled by another entity" (a negative relation). For most kalam theologians, such reinterpretations entail stretching the meaning of words such as "knows" and "wills" beyond recognition and, in effect, amount to denying that God can be said to know or will.[22] The accusation is perhaps not charitable, but it is hardly outlandish. It is not particularly controversial to interpret philosophers like Avicenna and Averroes as holding the view that—in the words of Jon McGinnis—"for God to know the world . . . is for God to create the world ... Knowing and creating are identical in God."[23] For a natural theologian like Sanūsī, one can show that God possesses the attribute of Knowledge by arguing (i) that voluntary agency presupposes knowledge, and (ii) that the mind-bogglingly intricate functioning of the effect—nature—shows that its Maker has knowledge (K 278–83). But it would undermine this endeavor if the term "knows," when applied to the Maker, starts meaning things like "is a cause" or "is immaterial."

Relying on Fakhr al-Dīn al-Rāzī's *Landmarks*, Sanūsī presented the following as the Aristotelian-Neoplatonist philosophers' main reason for rejecting attributes that are additional to the divine Self: If there were such divine attributes, then these would—qua attributes—depend for their existence on the divine substance in which they inhere. But if something depends for its existence on the divine self, then it is contingent in itself. If it is contingent in itself, then it requires an effector (*mu'aththir*). In the relevant case, the effector would be the divine self. But in that case, the divine self would both effect the attributes and be amenable to them (*fā'il wa qābil*), which is absurd.[24]

Rāzī's own response to the argument was complex. On the one hand, he rejected the principle that the divine self cannot be both active and passive with respect to the attributes. He adduced the counterexample of the concomitants of a quiddity—for example, the evenness of the number four—which seem to be both effected by the quiddity and yet ascribable to the quiddity. On the other hand, he conceded that the divine attributes depend on the divine self and therefore cannot be said to be necessary in themselves. Rather, they are contingent in themselves but necessitated by another. This need not, he added, contradict their pre-eternality. Rāzī's concession here was widely condemned by later North African Ash'arīs, starting with his commentator Ibn al-Tilimsānī (d.1260) and regularly reiterated down to the nineteenth century. Sanūsī quoted Ibn al- Tilimsānī's severe verdict:

> When Fakhr al-Dīn thought this argument sound, i.e., the philosophers' specious point that dependency, in the sense of being conditioned, necessitates contingency . . . He worried about the counterexample of the divine attributes, and so

> he said at times: This is something to which we seek an answer from God... and at other times he was categorical and expressed something no one did before—we seek refuge in God!—and said: They are contingent in themselves and necessary through the necessity of His Self the Exalted.[25]

Sanūsī believed the argument of the philosophers to be sophistical, based on an equivocation in the term "dependency" (*iftiqār*). Characteristically, he construed the argument as a hypothetical syllogism:

> If there are entitative divine attributes, then they are dependent existents.
> It is not the case that they are dependent existents
> ∴ It is not the case that there are entitative divine attributes

Sanūsī countered by asking what "dependent existent" means. If it means that the attributes are not pre-eternal but have been brought into existence, then he denies the first premise. If "dependent existent" means that the existence of the divine attributes logically entails the existence of the divine self, then he denies the second premise. There is nothing incoherent in claiming that A logically entails B and that A nevertheless exists necessarily. Sanūsī wrote:

> Leave off, then, the terms "dependency" and "contingency" that misleadingly suggest a need for an effector, which has been shown to be impossible. Instead, say: it is impossible to suppose two existents that imply each other such that the mind cannot coherently suppose that both do not exist or that one does not exist. Or say: It is not possible that there be something necessary that is co-implied by another thing that is necessary. Or say: It cannot be that something is necessary unless it is entirely devoid of something else that is necessary. In that case, it would be all too clear that you are making claims that you cannot justify except

by sophistically equivocating and using the misleading term "dependency" of what is conditioned (*tawaqquf*) in general.[26]

Sanūsī's phrasing here might misleadingly suggest that he believed the divine attributes are "other" in relation to the divine self. This is not the case. He adhered to the traditional Ashʿarī doctrine that the attributes are neither "other" nor "identical" in relation to the divine self (K 327–8). This should not distract from the key point he was making here, which is that the Aristotelian–Neoplatonist philosophers confuse logical entailment with metaphysical dependency. An attribute can be said logically to entail a bearer. This does not mean that the attribute cannot necessarily exist pre-eternally and post-eternally. One might equally say that a substance logically implies attributes—after all, an attribute-less substance is arguably as incoherent as a substance-less attribute. Again, this does not mean that the substance cannot necessarily exist pre-eternally and post-eternally.

It was seen in Chapter 4 that Sanūsī, when ruling out that God could be an attribute, adopted an argument that at first sight might seem needlessly complicated. He argued that if God were an attribute, then one could not ascribe knowledge, power, will, and life to God, for an attribute cannot itself be described as knowing, powerful, willing, and alive. He did not adopt the "easy" path of saying that if God were an attribute, then He would "depend" on a substance in which He inheres and would therefore not be necessary of existence. It is possible now to understand that Sanūsī's choice of argument in his more popular works was carefully considered.

5 The seven core attributes

The voluntary agent who, as Sanūsī argued in the previous chapter, has brought me about must have power (*qudra*). Sanūsī presented the argument in the form of a syllogism:

> God has voluntarily brought something about
> Everything that voluntarily brings something about has power
> ∴ God has power

The first (minor) premise has already been proven. The second (major) premise is evidently true, Sanūsī wrote, because:

> The one who voluntarily brings something about is the one of whom it is true that he can do rather than not do, or not do rather than do. This is precisely the meaning of having power. (K 261)

As noted earlier in this chapter, Sanūsī's natural-theological project of proving through reason, without resort to revelation, that God exists and has certain core attributes, began from recognizable understandings of relevant terms such as *qudra* ("power" or "ability"). He clearly did not take himself to be offering a controversial or exotic definition of the term.[27] Note that it would undermine Sanūsī's syllogism if the meaning of the term "power" when applied to God is different from the meaning it bears more generally. In other words, the term "power" in the premise of the syllogism cannot have a different meaning than it does in the conclusion, on pain of committing the fallacy of equivocation:

> God has voluntarily brought something about
> Everything that voluntarily brings something about has "power"
> ∴ God has "power"

With respect to the divine attribute of "will," Sanūsī proceeded in the same manner. Will (*irāda*) is, he wrote, an attribute with which the bearer preponderates the occurrence of what is contingent over its non-occurrence (K 262). If God did not possess the attribute of will, then it would follow that there would be nothing that causes the contingent effect to exist rather than not exist (which is equally possible), nor would the effect exist at a certain time rather than another equally possible time, or have a certain size or location rather than another equally possible size or location. Again, the working definition of "will" offered by Sanūsī is intended to be ordinary and uncontroversial rather than exotic or peculiar.

Though the arguments may have assumed the ordinary senses of terms such as "power" and "will," Sanūsī would go on to argue that only God can be said to have these attributes in the fullest senses of the words. Only God has the ability voluntarily to bring effects into existence, and only God can cause the effect to have one contingent attribute rather than other, equally possible attributes. As will be seen in the following chapter, Sanūsī would not deny outright that humans or brute animals have "power" and "will." But it is God alone who exemplifies these attributes fully. Humans and brute animals can only be said to have "power" and "will" in a looser, attenuated sense.

With this point in mind, it may be helpful to return to an issue that was raised earlier in this chapter. One might wonder whether attributing power, will, and knowledge to God—in the ordinary senses of these terms—does not amount to the heresy of anthropomorphism, of "likening" (*tashbīh*) God to creatures. Both Ḥanbalīs and Islamic Neoplatonists could—and historically did—press the point that terms such as "power," "will," and "knowledge" must mean something very different from their ordinary senses when applied to God. For Sanūsī, and for Ashʿarīs more generally, such worries get things exactly the wrong way round. On the basis of the uncontroversial, everyday senses of the terms "power," "will," and "knowledge," one can conclude through reasoning that only God can be said to have these attributes fully and unqualifiedly. To put it schematically, it is not that power, will, and knowledge are attributed strictly to humans and in an attenuated sense to God; they are rather attributed strictly to God and only in an attenuated sense to humans.

When establishing that God possesses the attributes of Knowledge and Life, Sanūsī did not—in his *Commentary on the Long Creed*—offer definitions of these terms.[28] He seems to have believed that such formal definitions are unnecessary because, on *any* plausible understanding of "knowledge" and "life," they must be true of a voluntary agent.

Earlier Ashʿarīs tried to establish through natural reasoning that God must possess the attributes of Speech, Sight, and Hearing. This is the case with Juwaynī in his *The Guidance* and Salāljī in his *The Demonstrative*, the two standard handbooks of Ashʿarī theology in the Maghreb prior to Sanūsī.[29] Most later Ashʿarīs came to judge as weak such attempts at showing through pure reason that God must possess Speech, Sight, and Hearing, and they therefore preferred the view that such attributes can only be known to be true of God through revelation. As mentioned in Chapter 4, this was also Sanūsī's position (K 288–94). At least at first sight, the fact that these attributes are only known to be true through revelation makes it more difficult to argue that we can start with recognizable senses of these terms and argue that only God exemplifies them fully. Conversely, it seems much more difficult to avoid the conclusion that such attributions are on a par with attributing a "face," "eye," "hand," or "being seated on a throne" to God.

It is clear that most Ashʿarīs would insist that the attribution of "speaking," "seeing," and "hearing" to God is *not* on a par with the attribution of a "hand," "face," "eye," and "being seated on a throne." Sanūsī's own position was that the latter attributions should not be understood in their apparent (*ẓāhir*) senses. They should either be accepted agnostically, as most early Ashʿarīs did, or be reinterpreted figuratively as some later Ashʿarīs such as Juwaynī and Ghazālī advocated. Sanūsī preferred the former option, for he deemed it presumptuous to specify one of many possible non-literal meanings—for example, that God's "hand" means "power"—in the absence of evidence in revelation (K 625–7).

In contrast, Sanūsī did not believe that "speaking," "seeing," and "hearing" should be accepted agnostically or understood figuratively. On the basis of his occasionalism, he argued that "seeing" is not necessarily linked to having eyes, or "hearing" to having ears, or "speaking" to having a throat and tongue. Sight, Hearing, and Speech are therefore not, for Sanūsī, among the "ambiguous" (*mutashābihāt*) attributions in the Quran and hadith (like "sitting," "face," "eye," and "hand") that should not be interpreted literally.

The position that it is not part of the very meaning of terms such as "seeing" and "hearing" that they be linked to eyes and ears, though at first glance implausible, may be defensible upon closer consideration. We seem to be able to make sense of locutions such as "I saw (or heard) in my sleep. . . ." One might, however, say that it is part of the very meaning of "sight" and "hearing" that they involve spatially or temporally extended phenomenal experiences that cannot be attributed to God if God is not in space or time. A defender of Sanūsī's position might perhaps appeal to the existence of "blind-sight," which seems to show that phenomenal experience is not necessary for sight.[30] Pursuing the issue further would take us too far from Sanūsī's writings, though there will be occasion to discuss the attribute of Speech in greater detail in Chapter 9.

6 The eternality and immutability of the divine attributes

Ashʿarī theologians agreed that God does not undergo change. God's core attributes of Power, Will, Knowledge, Life, Speech, Sight, and Hearing are pre- and post-eternal.[31] A fundamental principle for them, used in their standard proofs for the existence of God, is that an entity that has generated attributes must itself be generated. The principle of God's unchangingness does, however, raise some issues, some of which were addressed already in Ghazālī's *Incoherence of the Philosophers*.[32] For example, if God's Power and Will are pre-eternal and unchanging, then why is the effect not pre-eternal as well? In other words, does the fact that the world is not pre-eternal mean that God suddenly changed His mind and willed the world to exist after eons in which He did not will the world to exist? Also, if God's Knowledge is eternal and unchanging, how can He know the changing events of the nether world? It seems, at first sight, that if I am writing on my laptop at this moment, and if God knows this, then when I cease to write, either God's knowledge must change to keep track of the changing fact or cease to be knowledge at all and become false belief.

Sanūsī posed the issue concerning God's knowledge as follows: How can God's knowledge be unitary when knowledge of the past, knowledge of the present, and knowledge of the future are all different? He wrote:

> If you say, how does the position that [God's] knowledge is unitary cohere with the fact that He knows what is and what will be, for knowledge of *what will be* entails that what is known does not yet exist, whereas the knowledge of *what is* entails that it does exist. If the two knowledges are identical, then the object of one of them must be otherwise than it really is. (K 387)

Sanūsī's response was in effect to reject the underlying assumption that God's knowledge is temporal. When God knows that an event occurs at a specific time, the time of occurrence is part of what God knows, not a qualifier of God's knowledge. In other words, there is a crucial distinction between:

(i) God knows timelessly that event E occurs at time t.
(ii) God knows at time t that event E occurs.

On the first—and according to Sanūsī correct—construal of God's knowledge, it is possible to know past, present, and future with the same, unchanging knowledge. Sanūsī quoted Ibn al-Tilimsānī on God's timeless knowledge:

> The Lord most High knows eternally that something exists relative to a certain time, as He knows that it exists relative to a certain

> place, and knows that it did not exist before existing, and if it is one of the things that passes away then He knows that it ceases to exist after existing. His knowledge is not contained within time (*maẓrūfan bi-l-zamān*); rather His Knowledge attaches to the coming-to-be of something in relation to time. The relation to a time is an attribute of the coming-to-be, not a container of the Knowledge. His Knowledge is not temporal so that it can be described as past, present, and future. The misconception comes about because of the relaying by utterance of what this Knowledge attaches to. If the relaying is prior to the event then it [i.e., the event] is called future, and if it is posterior then it is called past, and if conjoined then it is called present. Past, future and present are therefore terms that apply in view of relaying. As for the attachment of Knowledge to its existence in a certain time, this is one and the same.[33]

For example, God knows eternally and unchangingly that I write at time t_1 and sleep at time t_2. There is no need for God's knowledge to change so as to keep track of my ever-changing behavior.

Though Sanūsī did not discuss this, the same answer could be given to the "why not earlier?" objection to the creation of the world. God sempiternally wills the world to come into existence. There is no time "before" the creation of the universe and no implication that God's timeless Will went from one state to another in order to create the world. There may be a sense in which the universe might have been twenty billion years old at the time of my writing this chapter, instead of the actual fourteen billion years. The proper interpretation of this is to say that God may have created more events between the beginning of the universe and my writing this chapter, not that there were eons of empty time before the creation of the world, and that God could have chosen an earlier point in this empty time and created the universe then.

7 Sanūsī and his sources

Compared to his discussions of the proofs for the existence of God and of "imitation" in the principles of religion, Sanūsī's treatment of the divine attributes includes less individually distinctive departures and shows more reliance on earlier authorities. His main guides were the following works, especially the first two:

- The commentary on Fakhr al-Dīn al-Rāzī's *Landmarks* by Ibn al-Tilimsānī (d.1260).
- The commentary on Juwaynī's *Guidance* by al-Muqtaraḥ (d.1216).
- The commentary on Juwaynī's *Guidance* by Ibn Dihāq al-Mālaqī (d.1214).
- The commentary on al-Muqtaraḥ's *Secrets of Reason* by Abū Yaḥyá al-Sharīf al-Sabtī (fl.1231).
- *The Dawning of Lights*, a handbook of logic, metaphysics, and theology by al-Bayḍāwī (d.1291).

The historical importance of Sanūsī's intervention with respect to the divine attributes lies, not in its originality or idiosyncrasy, but in providing a very influential synthesis of such earlier sources. His work served as a starting point for later discussions in Islamic Africa, and there was a clear tendency in subsequent centuries for his own works to be much more widely read than the earlier works on which he had relied.

As mentioned in Chapter 2, Sanūsī's mentioned sources—with the exception of the work by Bayḍāwī—were largely unknown in the Islamic East in his time. Conversely, some of the works that by the fifteenth century were staple handbooks for the study of theology in the Turco-Persianate world were either not referenced at all by Sanūsī or drawn on in an ad hoc, occasional manner: *The Abstract of Kalam* of Naṣīr al-Dīn al-Ṭūsī (d.1274), *The Stations* of al-Ījī (d.1355), and *The Aims* of al-Taftāzānī (d.1390). It is clear that, by Sanūsī's time, the North African and Persianate Ash'arī traditions were distinct; and not just in terms of handbooks used but also in terms of doctrine. For example, Fakhr al-Dīn al-Rāzī's suggestion that the divine attributes are contingent in themselves but necessary by another was passionately rejected by most Maghrebi Ash'arīs, whereas later, Persianate Ash'arīs seem to have been more receptive to the idea.[34]

Another striking feature of Sanūsī's discussion is that he seems to have drawn exclusively on Ash'arī sources. There is no evidence that he read kalam works by Māturīdīs, let alone by authors whom he would have considered heretics or infidels: Mu'tazilīs, Shi'is, anti-Ash'arī Ḥanbalīs, Aristotelian–Neoplatonist philosophers, or Christians. Fakhr al-Dīn al-Rāzī, in the twelfth century, was still reading Aristotelian–Neoplatonist philosophers and Mu'tazilī authors, and he was engaged in oral disputations in Transoxiana with Christians, Mu'tazilīs, Karrāmīs, and Māturīdīs.[35] Rāzī's younger contemporary al-Muqtaraḥ debated Christians in Egypt.[36] The fourteenth-century Persian Ash'arī theologian Ījī rubbed shoulders with Shi'i theologians (who absorbed a great deal of Mu'tazilism) at the Il-Khanid court in Persia.[37] One or two generations later, the theologians Taftāzānī and al-Sayyid al-Sharīf al-Jurjānī (d.1413) in Persia and Central Asia were still reading works by Avicenna and by Shi'i theologians such as Naṣīr al-Dīn al-Ṭūsī and Ibn Muṭahhar al-Ḥillī (d.1325).[38] The Persian Ash'arī scholar Jalāl al-Dīn al-Dawānī (d.1502) read philosophers such as Avicenna and Suhrawardī, as well as the Shī'īs Ṭūsī and Ḥillī and the anti-Ash'arī Ḥanbalī thinker Ibn Taymiyya.[39] All of this is in contrast to Sanūsī who may have read, for example, Avicenna's medical works but who seems to have relied exclusively on Ash'arī authors in matters theological.

Having said this, the somewhat narrow horizon seems not so much to have been an individual failing but a characteristic of many later Ash'arīs in the Maghreb who were victims, so to speak, of their own success. Their contemporary colleagues in the

Islamic East, and their earlier Ashʿarī predecessors in Baghdad and Nishapur, were active in areas where opposing schools of thought were still alive and kicking. By Sanūsī's time, Ashʿarism reigned supreme in the Maghreb, with the exception of a few remote pockets of Ibadi Muslims. The more current threat was likely to be popular ignorance or indifference rather than Aristotelian–Neoplatonist philosophers or non-Ashʿarī theologians.

8
Occasionalism

Occasionalism is the view that nothing besides God has causal power. In other words, all effects—originated substances and their accidents—are directly caused by God. When I touch a fire, the consequent burning sensation is a direct creation of God. The fire itself is causally inert, and my touching it is merely the "occasion" for God's creation of the burning sensation, hence the term "occasionalism," which was coined to describe such a thesis among Western philosophers and theologians in the seventeenth and eighteenth centuries, most famously the French philosopher Nicholas Malebranche (d.1715) and the American Reformed Protestant theologian Jonathan Edwards (d.1758).[1]

The fact that Ashʿarism and Māturīdism are committed to occasionalism is one of the best known facts about these schools of theology. It is also a facet of their teaching that has been virulently criticized in both medieval and modern times.[2] The denial of natural causation was scorned by Aristotelian–Neoplatonist philosophers, and the thesis that God creates all human actions was denounced by Muʿtazilīs and later Shiʿis. Some modern Western scholars and Muslim liberal reformers have also worried whether the commitment to occasionalism promoted "fatalism" and impeded the development of natural science in the Islamic world.[3] Perhaps due to such modern sensitivities, there has been a tendency in contemporary English-language scholarship to deemphasize the importance of the doctrine. It has almost become an academic commonplace in recent years to argue that this or that eminent Islamic theologian—al-Ashʿarī, al-Māturīdī, al-Ghazālī—was not, after all, an occasionalist but can be interpreted to have

Al-Sanūsī. Khaled El-Rouayheb, Oxford University Press.
 DOI: 10.1093/oso/9780197835630.003.0008

allowed some degree of "secondary causality" or at least to have remained agnostic on the issue.[4]

In Sanūsī's case, the theological writings leave little room for serious doubt. He was a fervent occasionalist. As I will show in this chapter, he linked occasionalism to core, non-negotiable theological doctrines, in particular that God is one, that God's Power and Will encompass all that is contingent, and that the extent of God's Power and Will cannot be limited by creatures. The one question is whether Sanūsī remained an occasionalist when writing about non-theological issues, for example medicine. I will argue that he did, and that his doctrinal commitment was not antithetical to an interest in natural science.

1 Power and Will: Their attachments

As was mentioned in passing in previous chapters, most of the core divine attributes—Power, Will, Knowledge, Speech, Sight, and Hearing—logically require an "attachment" (*muta'allaq*), that is, an intentional object to which the attribute is directed. To have power is to have power over something, to will is to will something, to know is to know something, and so on. (The only exception is the divine attribute of Life, which has no attachment.) An important step in Sanūsī's case for occasionalism is the argument that God's Power and Will attach to all that is contingent, i.e., all that is neither necessary nor impossible.

To ward off a potential misunderstanding, it is worth noting that it does not follow from divine attributes logically requiring an intentional object that the object is pre-eternal. As explained at the end of the previous chapter, God Knows and Wills pre-eternally and immutably that I get up at 6 am today. The temporal qualification ("at 6 am today") belongs to what is known and willed, not to God's Knowledge and Will that are timeless. In the following two propositions, what is known—the attachment—is italicized:

(i) God Knows/Wills eternally *that I get up at 6 am on such-and-such a day.*
(ii) God Knows/Wills at 6 am on such-and-such a day *that I get up.*

Only the former reading is theologically acceptable, for the latter makes God's Knowledge and Will within time and ever-changing. The worry that the attachments of God's Knowledge and Will must be pre-eternal and immutable arguably stems from unwittingly confusing the two senses, from assuming that God's Knowledge and Will are within time and that their attachments/objects cannot be separated from them by a temporal gap. As Sanūsī put it, "God's knowledge is not enveloped by time; rather His Knowledge attaches to the coming-to-be of an existent in relation to a time" (K 387).

The attachments of the divine attributes may differ. Knowledge attaches to what is necessary, impossible, and contingent. Power only attaches to what is contingent; in other words, only what is contingent falls under God's Power. Sanūsī's reasoning was that knowledge is an attribute that does not affect what is known, whereas power and will do affect their objects. It is nonsense to suggest that what is necessary or impossible can be affected, which means that they can be known but do not fall under God's Power and Will (S 160).

The point that Ash'arīs recognized limits to God's Power may come as a surprise. They famously placed no *moral* limits on what God may do, nor did they recognize *physical-nomological* limits on what God may do. This has invited statements in the secondary literature to the effect that, according to Ash'arīs, God "can create whatever He wants at whatever time and in whatever chronological order."[5] Such assertions must be qualified to avoid misunderstanding. Ash'arīs overwhelmingly accepted that there are *logical-metaphysical* limits to what is within God's Power. Moreover, the idea that the impossible is not within God's Power is intrinsic to the project of natural theology itself. Ash'arī theologians gave proofs for the existence of God based on the impossibility of effects coming to be without a cause, or of an infinite regress of originated accidents, or of a body being neither in motion nor at rest, and they argued that God must have Power, Will, Knowledge, and Life because it is impossible that an agent who has brought about the world should be devoid of such attributes. It would undermine such arguments if one were to say that, if God so willed, effects could come about without causes, or accidents could exist without inhering in substances, or bodies could be neither in motion nor at rest, or voluntary agents could act without knowledge and life. Already al-Ashʿarī himself was explicit that he acknowledged certain kinds of impossibilities, such as an accident existing without inhering in a body or atom, or two contrary accidents existing in the same locus, or one particular accident inhering in two different loci, or a body not having a spatial location or being neither in motion nor at rest.[6] The idea that God may do the impossible, such as create another God, or have a consort or son, or become a human being, was associated by Sanūsī with fideist and literalist groups opposed to the very enterprise of natural theology. He roundly condemned the view, advanced by Ibn Ḥazm (d.1064), a Spanish Muslim scholar of the literalist (Ẓāhirī) school of law, that God could have had a son had He so wished (S 161).

With respect to God's Will, Sanūsī held that it, too, attaches to all that is possible. This is prima facie surprising. The argument for why God must possess a Will, and not just Power, is precisely that God's Power attaches equally to all that is possible. And so, to account for the fact that one of these possibilities actually comes to pass, we most postulate another divine attribute that "preponderates" among the infinite possible scenarios that fall under God's Power. But then one might have expected divine Will to attach to all that is actual, not to unrealized possibilities. If divine Will attaches to all that is possible, will we not need a further divine attribute that selects (or "preponderates") the realized from the unrealized possibilities?

Sanūsī did not address this worry. But two of the most important sources for his theological works did. The Egyptian Ash'arī theologian al-Muqtaraḥ (d.1216) raised this precise issue in his *Secrets of Reason*, as did his student Ibn al-Tilimsānī (d.1260) in his commentary on Rāzī's *Landmarks*. Their answer was that some possibilities God wills to happen, and other possibilities God wills not to happen. So, all that is within God's Power is willed to happen or not to happen. On this account, divine Will, like divine Power, attaches to all that is possible.[7]

Within the Ash'arī tradition, there were alternatives to this Muqtaraḥ-Ibn al-Tilimsānī-Sanūsī position. One was simply to say that the attachments of God's Will are "more specific" (*akhaṣṣ*) than the attachments of God's Power, i.e., that what God wills is a subset of what falls under God's Power.[8] A related position, which seems to have become common in the later commentary literature that grew around Sanūsī's theological writings, was to make a distinction between the effectual (*tanjīzī*) and apt (*ṣulūḥī*) attachments of God's Will.[9] On this account, all that is within God's Power is apt to be an attachment of God's Will, but only a subset is effectually willed by God. This distinction between effectual and apt attachment should not, however, simply be read back into Sanūsī's writings. He himself did not explicitly distinguish between effectual and apt attachments of God's Will.[10] Furthermore, acknowledging such a distinction would be in tension with the position, for which he argued at length, that the core divine attributes attach to all that they are apt for. He wrote, "Every attribute, from among the attributes that attach, attaches to all that it is apt for" (*kull ṣifa min al-ṣifāt al-muta'alliqa fa-hiya tata'allaq bi-jamī' mā taṣluḥu lahu*) (K 389). It is difficult to understand such a statement if we assume that Sanūsī recognized the distinction between "effectual" and "apt" attachments. If he did, then the statement becomes emptily tautological: "Every divine attribute attaches *aptly* to all that it is apt for," and the ensuing arguments for the claim become superfluous.

Before giving Sanūsī's argument for why the divine attributes must be "general in their attachments" (*'umūm al-ta'alluq*), it may be helpful to clarify what such a thesis involves. The claim is that if Knowledge, for example, is apt to attach to the necessary, impossible, and contingent, then it must be actually attached to all that is necessary, impossible, and contingent. In other words, it cannot be the case that some subset of what is necessary, impossible, and contingent—for example, future contingent events—is potentially known by God but not actually known by God. Similarly, if Power is apt to attach to what is contingent, then it must be actually attached to what is contingent; it cannot be the case that God renounces Power over a certain subset of contingents, for example, human action. And if Will is apt to attach to all that is contingent, then it must be actually attached to all that is contingent, in the sense that everything contingent is either willed to exist or willed not to exist by God. It cannot be the case that some contingent events, for example, sins, plagues, or infant mortality, are exempt from God's Will in the sense that God neither wills them to occur nor wills them not to occur.

Sanūsī anticipated that someone might ask why there could not be an obstacle that prevents God's Power and Will from attaching themselves to something contingent. A concrete example could be that God knows that X will not occur. Could this not be an obstacle that prevents X from falling under God's Power and Will? Sanūsī presented a number of arguments for why this cannot be the case, of which I discuss two:

First, if God's Knowledge that X does not occur is an obstacle preventing X from falling under God's Power and Will, then there would be nothing that falls under God's Power and Will. If God's knowing that something does *not* occur makes it impossible, and hence beyond God's Power and Will, then God's knowing that something occurs makes it necessary and also beyond God's Power and Will. Thus, the occurrence and non-occurrence of all things would be beyond God's Power and Will, and these two attributes would have no attachments at all, which is absurd (K 390).

Second, the fact that, for example, God's Will attaches to all contingents must be true per se (*nafsī*) of It. If the attachment were not per se, then the fact that Will attaches to all contingents, or to some contingents and not others, would require a ground, a preponderating factor that determines the extent of God's Will. But positing such a preponderating factor is absurd. It has been shown that God's Will is pre-eternal, post-eternal, and timelessly immutable. It cannot therefore be determined, affected, or limited by something extraneous. But if it is true per se of the Will that It attaches to all contingents, then one cannot suppose that the attachment to some contingents is absent while the Will remains. Analogously, if occupying space is true per se of a body, then one cannot suppose some bodies ceasing to occupy space while still being bodies. So, if it is true per se of God's Will that It is attached to all contingents, then it cannot be the case that some contingents fall outside God's Will while the Will persists. And it has been shown that the divine Will exists necessarily (K 399–400).

At first sight, one might suspect that there is a sleight of hand in this last argument. Humans have attributes such as power, will, and knowledge. Yet, it seems indisputable that the attachment of these attributes is not general. In the case of humans, it would appear that knowledge, for example, does not attach to all that it is apt for. Humans know some things but are ignorant of other things that they in principle could come to know. If so, then there seems nothing absurd about an attribute being apt to attach to X but not actually attaching to X.

Sanūsī's answer was to deny the unity of human knowledge. My knowledge of one item of knowledge, for example, that I woke up at 6 am this morning, is distinct from my knowledge of another item of knowledge, for example, that I went to bed at 11 pm yesterday. So, each instance of knowledge is attuned to the particular intentional object it has. One cannot therefore say that there is a difference between what that instance of knowledge is apt for and what it actually attaches to. In the case of God, Knowledge is unitary; all that is known by God is known by the same Knowledge. In that case, too, one cannot say that what this Knowledge attaches to falls short of what it is apt for. The same applies to God's Power, Will, and the rest of the divine attributes (K 402–4).

To take stock: Sanūsī's position is that the divine attributes attach to all that they are apt for. Knowledge and Speech attach to the necessary, impossible, and contingent, Power and Will attach to the contingent, and Sight and Hearing attach to what is actual. He has also argued that it is impossible that the attachment of such attributes can be circumscribed in any way. Either divine Power and Will attach to all contingents or they attach to none and cease to be power and will at all. The significance of this conclusion will be clear from the following two sections, which deal with Sanūsī's arguments for why there cannot be another God and why humans lack the power to create their own actions.

2 The proof of God's oneness

Some Ashʿarī theologians had suggested that one might appeal to Scripture to show that God is one. However, the mainstream view, to which Sanūsī adhered, was that the proof for God's oneness must be thoroughly rational, for one cannot prove the authenticity of a prophet's message unless one can show that his supporting miracles were created by God in support of the claim to be a prophet, and this, in turn, presupposes that the miracle was produced by God, not by another being. Sanūsī wrote:

> The one who says that he is a prophet, if he supports his statement by a miracle, the miracle does not support his statement unless it is established that this action [i.e., the miracle] is beyond the power of other beings besides the one who sent him . . . This

> cannot be known unless we know that the miracle, such as raising people from the dead, is not done by something other than God, and this depends on proving oneness. (K 341)

It would, in other words, be insufficient simply to appeal to the sayings of a miracle-worker in support of the claim that there is only one God. One would first need to rule out that the miracle of raising Lazarus from the dead, for example, or the miracle of the Quran, could have been accomplished by trickery, magic, angels (fallen or otherwise), or one of several lesser gods. To rule this out, one must establish, through natural reason, that there is strictly speaking only one being with creative power, that the voluntary agent that Sanūsī has shown (in his proofs for the existence of God) to have brought me about is the very same agent who brought the said miracles—and everything else—about. For Sanūsī, establishing the truth of occasionalism is thus the rational route to showing the truth of monotheism and the Islamic revelation.

Sanūsī proposed several arguments for why there cannot be more than one God, some of which were presented in Chapter 4. One core argument, appearing in all his theological works, appeals to the aforementioned principle that God's Power and Will must be general in their attachments, i.e., they must attach to all contingents. With this principle in mind, it is not difficult to see that there cannot be two or more gods. Suppose that there are two gods: Either the two of them agree that some contingent X occurs, or they disagree. If they disagree, then it clearly follows that the power and will of the two gods cannot both be general in attachment: Either (i) the two neutralize each other, so that some contingent being is beyond both of their powers and wills, which means that their powers and wills are not general in their attachments, which in turn implies—given that attachment to all contingents has been shown to be true per se of divine Power and Will—that the two gods have no power and will at all; or (ii) one overcomes the other, so that the defeated god's power and will do not extend to all contingents, meaning that the defeated god does not have power and will at all, which contradicts the supposition that the defeated entity is a god, or (iii) both powers and wills are efficacious, so X both occurs and does not occur, flouting the principle of non-contradiction (K 416–21; W 359–65).

But could there not be multiple gods that always agree? This too is absurd, according to Sanūsī. Suppose that there are two gods that agree that I wake up at precisely 6am today. Either (i) both gods' power and will are efficacious, or (ii) only one of their powers and wills are efficacious. Both consequences are absurd. The first option leads to causal overdetermination (*taḥṣīl al-ḥāṣil*), i.e., that a single effect has two causes, each of which is sufficient for the effect. The second option is also absurd, for it would mean that only one god's power and will is efficacious, which entails at least two absurdities: (a) that the prevalence of one god's power and will over the other happens for no reason, and (b) that the other god's power and will are inefficacious and do not attach generally to all contingents (K 421–3).

But could multiple gods not have separate spheres of governance? We might suppose, for example, that one governs the skies, another the seas, a third the underworld, and so on. This, Sanūsī argued, will not work either, for a number of reasons. For one, it contravenes the principle that divine Power and Will attach to all contingents. To suppose that a god's power and will are circumscribed to one region of the universe belies this principle. It also cries out for an explanation, i.e., for a preponderating factor that explains why one god's power and will only extend to one part of the universe rather than another, equally possible part. Might one suppose that the delimitation is voluntary? To this, Sanūsī replied that if it is voluntary then it follows that it could be otherwise, so that one god's power and will could extend into the sphere of another god, leading to the aforementioned absurdities if the gods agree or disagree (K 424–7).

In his most widely read work, the *Commentary on the Short Creed*, Sanūsī summed up his argument, thus:

> It has been shown by incontrovertible proof that God's Power and Will must encompass all contingents. If there were another existent who has the power to bring something into existence like our Lord, then it would follow, when the two powers attach to this contingent's coming to be, that it does not exist by means of both powers, for it is impossible to have one effect come about due to two causes. (S 218–9)

One would then have to suppose, Sanūsī continued, that one of the two causes is inert. But if there are two gods, then they are two of a kind, and share all essential and per se attributes. The extent of a god's power and will is determined per se, not through anything extraneous. So, if one of the gods is ineffective in one case, then the other god would be ineffective as well in that case. And if both are ineffective with respect to one contingent thing, then they must be ineffective with respect to all contingent things, implying that nothing ever comes to exist. The above-quoted lemma continues thus:

> It must then be that one of the two causes has no power. But this entails that the other, who is similar to the first in the ability to bring into existence, also has no power. And if it follows that they have no power over this particular contingent, then it follows that they have no power over any contingent, for there is no [relevant] difference. This entails the impossibility of any originated thing coming to be. (S 218–9)

3 The creation of human acts

In Sanūsī's Long, Middle, and Short Creeds, the argument that there cannot be more than one God is followed directly by the claim that humans cannot bring about their own actions. In his *Commentary on the Middle Creed*, Sanūsī wrote:

> The proof from mutual hindrance which proves the impossibility of a second god along with our Lord the Exalted, is the very same proof for the necessity of God being one in His attributes in the sense that it is necessary that He is unique in creating all originated entities without any intermediary, without anything else having any causal efficacy on an effect whatsoever. (W 366)

In other words, the very same logic ruling out that there can be more than one God, also rules out that other creatures, including humans, have causal efficacy. Causal efficacy is directed at contingents, and it has just been shown that all contingents are under God's Power and are either willed to happen by God or willed not to happen by God. If we add the premises that God's Power and Will are sufficient, and that effects cannot have more than one sufficient cause, then it follows inexorably that humans—and more generally all created entities—have no causal efficacy, that all bodily changes and movements are direct effects of God's Power and Will.

As was a commonplace among Ashʿarīs, Sanūsī was keen to distinguish his position from the view, attributed to certain early Islamic figures, that humans have no power and will at all, and that there is simply no difference between voluntary acts (like praying) and involuntary bodily changes (like graying). Sanūsī argued that humans do have power of sorts. This, he maintained, can be shown by the following consideration: The very same bodily movements can be voluntary and involuntary (e.g., trying to catch the attention of a waiter or a spasm). We discern with necessity that there is a difference between the two cases. We also discern that the difference must be grounded in an attribute inhering in the mover in the former case and absent from the mover in the latter case. This attribute (i) presupposes life, for we do not attribute voluntary movement to what is inanimate, (ii) is not identical to life, knowledge, or speech, for these three attributes can be present in involuntary movement, and (iii) is not identical to will, for someone may act voluntarily without consciously willing to do so, as with doing things routinely or while lost in thought (though Sanūsī accepted that many cases of human voluntary action do involve a created will in the agent). It is accompanied by an introspectively apparent sense of capacity or facility. It is therefore justifiable to call the attribute "power" or "ability" (*qudra*). This "ability" is created by God. It is, like all things created by God, causally inefficacious; it is conjoined to (*muqārina*) the movement but does not cause the movement. Differently put, the movement co-occurs with the originated ability but does not result from it (K 450–2).

On this basis, Sanūsī—and Ash'arīs more generally—maintained that they could preserve a meaningful distinction between voluntary and involuntary movements. The former occur in conjunction with the agent's ability (and often also the agent's will), whereas the latter do not. In his *Commentary on the Middle Creed*, Sanūsī offered a clear summation of this view:

> The substances of the world in its entirety are creations of God and are vessels (*aw'iya*) for the effects of His Power, and He creates in every substance whatever He wishes of accidents. For some substances, God creates in it motion or rest or the like, apart from an accident of originated ability attached to it, such as tremorous motion and the like, and the substance is then called "compelled" (*majbūra*). For some substances, God creates the accidents of motion and rest and the like, and He creates with them an accident called "ability" that conjoins the action and attaches to it without any effect on it. Instead, the substance feels an ease and ability with regard to the act. For this reason, the substance in which such an accident is created is called "voluntary" (*mukhtāra*). (W 366–7)

The language Sanūsī used of created, human ability is the same he used of occasional "customary causes" (*asbāb 'ādiyya*) in general. An occasional, customary cause is conjoined temporally to the effect but does not generate the effect. So, when I cut my hand on a sharp knife, the cutting of the skin occurs "with" the contact with the blade, but not "because of" this contact. Similarly, my created ability and created will to get up from my chair and stretch my legs are occasional "customary causes"; they occur "with" the action, but the efficacious power and will that bring about the action belong to God alone. Sanūsī wrote:

> Just as the originated ability has no effect whatsoever on any action, fire has no effect on anything, whether burning, cooking, warming, or the like, neither by its nature nor by a power instilled in it. Rather, God has freely instituted the custom of creating these things [i.e., burning, cooking, warming . . .] along with it [i.e., the fire] (*'indahā*), not by means of it (*bihā*). (S 222)

Readers familiar with the British philosopher David Hume (d.1776) may be reminded of his view of causation. Though the proper interpretation of Hume is a matter of some scholarly debate, one influential understanding is that he sought to reduce mundane instances of causation to regular conjunction, and that he believed there is no hidden force within the cause that brings about the effect, but that the repeated experience of conjunctions of events of one type (hand touches sharp blade) with events of another (hand is cut) results in the involuntary expectation in us that such conjunctions will continue into the future.[11] The model is applicable to my own sense of capacity and will: there is a regular conjunction between my mental states (a sense of capacity, a desire, a belief about means and ends) and my bodily movements, leading to my expectation that such regular conjunctions will recur in the future, but strictly these mental states do not possess a hidden power that produces my bodily movements. I will return to Hume in the following section but will note here that the parallel with an occasionalist account of mundane cause-effect relations is not accidental, for the influence of the occasionalist Malebranche on Hume is well established.[12]

Human will and ability have "attachments," i.e., they logically entail intentional objects at which the will and ability are directed. A will is aimed at *something*, and an ability is an ability to do *something*. Unlike God's Power and Will, however, human ability and will have no effect on their intentional objects. They are, to that extent, like "knowledge," directed at an intentional object but without an effect on it. The fact that human ability and will are directed at something, though without effecting it, grounds religious responsibility. I am held accountable for those bodily movements that are accompanied by my ability (and often also my will), even though my ability and will are inert. This inefficacious attachment of my ability and will to certain bodily movements is called "acquisition" (*kasb*). The Ash'arī concept of "acquisition" was much derided by their opponents, but the core idea is plain: I am not religiously responsible on account of having the creative power of bringing about my actions, nor because I could have done otherwise, but by virtue of my ability and will being directed at my bodily movements. If I kill someone, for example, I am held accountable insofar as my ability and will are directed at—"attached to"—the action. Differently put, agents are responsible for their actions to the extent that these actions are accompanied by a sense of capacity, as opposed to a sense of involuntariness, and—often but not invariably—a conscious intention. Responsibility does not presuppose that the capacity and intention are what brought about the action (K 456–8).

The Ash'arī theory of human action was historically subject to two main objections: (i) that it would be unjust for God to create human actions and then reward or punish humans for these actions, and (ii) that it is nonsense to attribute a "power" or "ability" to humans that has no causal efficacy. Sanūsī addressed the first objection explicitly. As a divine command theorist, he simply rejected the implicit premise that God is subject to a standard of justice that is discernable through natural reason. He wrote:

> They [the theological opponents] say, "If the power of the servant has no effect on the action, then it would not be proper for him to be rewarded or punished."

The proper response to this, he wrote, is:

> He does what He pleases, and "He will not be questioned about what He does" [Quran 21:23]. (K 462–3)

It is wrong, Sanūsī added, to think that a pious deed is a ground (*'illa*) for heavenly reward, or that a sin is a ground for otherworldly punishment. Rather, a pious or sinful deed is a sign or indication (*amāra*) of otherworldly felicity or misery. In other words, there is no necessary connection between a pious deed and otherworldly reward or between a sinful deed and otherworldly punishment. The connection has been freely instituted by God and might well not have existed.

Furthermore, Sanūsī pointed out that alternative accounts of human action run into the same issue with divine justice. After all, Islamic opponents of the Ash'arīs overwhelmingly agreed that God creates all bodily powers, as well as all involuntary desires, and that God foreknows whether an individual will act sinfully or be pious. If that is the case, then an individual can complain that God has created powerful desires in him or her, knowing full well that this will lead to mortal sin and otherworldly punishment. In the words of Sanūsī, such an individual can say:

> O Lord, why did you create an ability for me knowing that I will use it for sin? And why did you create a desire for it? Indeed, why did you create me at all knowing that I will not

> obey? And if you created me, why not let me die young before I reach the age of legal maturity? And if you let me reach legal maturity, why not make me insane [and thus free of legal liability]? (K 467)

The point is that once we start down the road of holding God to account for what He sees fit to do, there is no stopping. Not just the Ash'arī position, but the Mu'tazilī position will be eroded. The question of whether there are rationally discernable standards of justice that apply to God is one that will be taken up again in the following chapter.

The second objection—that one cannot speak of a "power" or "ability" that has no effect—was considered serious enough for a number of earlier Ash'arī theologians to have suggested less uncompromising theories of human action that allow for some sort of human effect. Sanūsī mentioned a few such suggestions, all of which he rejected. One was due to the famous al-Juwaynī (d.1085) who in his major writings defended the standard Ash'arī position but in one ostensibly later work proposed that humans bring about their actions but in ways preordained by God, in the sense that God creates all the preconditions, inclinations, and incentives that lead to the actions.[13] A similar view was defended by Fakhr al-Dīn al-Rāzī (d.1210), though more explicitly linked to an Avicennian-inspired necessitarianism: humans can be seen as causes of their actions, but their capacities, inclinations, and incentives are themselves necessitated by prior causes in a finite causal chain ending with God.[14] Another suggestion was due to al-Shahrastānī (d.1153), author of a theological summa as well as a classic heresiography. Taking his cue from some earlier Ash'arīs, Shahrastānī proposed that human ability has an effect, not on the existence of the action, but on how it is described. The same bodily movements may or may not constitute an act of prayer, for example. Whether they do depends, not just on God's creation of the bodily movement but on the human agent's capacity.[15]

It is worth emphasizing that such suggestions do not in any obvious way address the previous concern about "fairness." If one allows the concern to be legitimate, which Sanūsī did not, then it is difficult to see how it can be allayed by saying, for example, that God allows humans to bring about their actions but only in accordance with divine preordination, or that humans are causes of their actions but that the capacities, drives, and inclinations leading to these actions are themselves entirely determined by previous causes in a thoroughly necessitarian chain leading back to the First Cause, or that human ability and will may affect how we describe an action but that the ability and will are themselves direct creations of God. The suggestions should presumably be seen, not as attempts to deal with the "fairness" objection but as attempts to address the point that it is nonsense to attribute to humans an "ability" that is causally inert.

Sanūsī rejected all such suggested modifications of the principle that human ability or capacity has no effect.[16] As for Juwaynī's one-time suggestion that human ability has an effect with God's permission and in accordance with God's preordination, Sanūsī objected that the created, human ability either has an effect per se or accidentally. If per se, then a particular human action is either an effect of God, in which case what is true per se of human ability is not true of human ability, which is absurd, or of the human agent, in which case what is per se true of God's Power and Will, namely that it has an effect on all contingents, is not true of God's Power and Will, which is also absurd. If human ability does *not* have an effect per se, then it is accidental whether it has an effect or not. This is also absurd. It implies that human ability$_1$, which has an effect, must have some attribute lacked by human ability$_2$ which does not have an effect. This leads to an infinite regress, for we repeat the question concerning this additional attribute possessed by human ability$_1$: Does it have an effect per se or accidentally? (K 443–4).

As for Shahrastānī's suggestion that human ability has an effect on the description of an action, Sanūsī quoted Ibn al-Tilimsānī's response that this is to no avail: The effect that, on this account, is due to human ability is either contingent or not. If contingent, then it falls under God's Power and Will. If not contingent, it cannot be an effect of any ability, human or divine.[17] As an aside, I note that this response arguably misses the point. Consider the case of praying: By definition, praying is impossible unless accompanied by the praying person's intention and sense of not being compelled; going through the physical motions without this intention and sense would just not count as "prayer." It is, therefore, not possible that God simply create prayer without also creating a person's capacity and intention to pray, and this created capacity and will can thus be said to have an effect on the appropriateness of describing the bodily motions as "prayer," even though the bodily motions, as well as the human's capacity and will, are all entirely the creation of God. In other words, a person's capacity and will are devoid of active causal power but are nevertheless necessary conditions without which it is impossible that the effect (prayer) comes to be. This would correspond to what in the medieval Latin tradition was sometimes called sine qua non causality.[18] On this account, the connection between mundane "cause" and a voluntary action is tighter than in standard occasionalist examples such as fire and burning. God usually creates a burning sensation in my hand when I touch fire but could create the burning sensation without such contact. By contrast, it is not possible that God bring about a certain voluntary action like prayer without also bringing about the capacity and intention to pray, for the physical movements without a sense of capacity and intention are, by definition, not "prayer." Therefore, though it is God alone who brings about the physical movements (and the basic contention of occasionalism is thus respected), the agent's accompanying capacity and intention are indispensable conditions for these movements correctly being described as "prayer."

4 Sanūsī and Juwaynī compared

Sanūsī's discussion of the creation of human actions shows some distinct features when compared to Juwaynī's *The Guidance*, the work that up to Sanūsī's time was the standard handbook of advanced theology in the Maghreb. As has been seen above, Sanūsī placed a noticeable emphasis on the doctrine that the attachments of divine power and will must be general, that all contingents fall under God's Power and are either willed to exist by God or willed not to exist by God. On this basis, he argued that there cannot be more than one God and that humans do not have the power to bring about their own actions. The doctrine of the general attachment of God's Power and Will, while acknowledged, is not made front and center in Juwaynī's work, nor in the works of his student al-Ghazālī (d.1111) and the twelfth-century Maghrebi theologians Ibn al-ʿArabī (d.1148) and al-Salāljī (d.1178). Sanūsī's discussion reflects the intervention of the Egyptian theologian al-Muqtaraḥ and his students Ibn al-Tilimsānī and Abū Yaḥyá al-Sharīf (fl.1231). In their works, especially al-Muqtaraḥ's *Secrets of Reason*, the doctrine of the generality of the attachments of divine Power and Will is emphasized and made the linchpin of the subsequent arguments for why there cannot be natural causation and why human ability is inert.[19]

Conversely, there are arguments that loom large in Juwaynī's discussions that are not underlined to the same extent in Sanūsī's work. For example, one traditional argument for the claim that humans cannot bring about their own actions was that humans do not know all there is to know about such actions, and a creator must know all there is to know about the effect.[20] This does not play a conspicuous role in Sanūsī's case. Similarly, Sanūsī did not ground his arguments for occasionalism on the claim, made by Juwaynī and earlier Ashʿarī authorities, that accidents do not persist and must be recreated from one instant to another by God.[21] He seems to have been agnostic about whether this older claim is true. Also, a significant part of Juwaynī's argumentation was to appeal to Quran and hadith in support of the thesis that God is the sole creator.[22] This plays a distinctly less prominent role in Sanūsī's presentation.

Overall, Sanūsī's procedure was first to defend at length a basic position, namely that God's Power and Will attach to all contingents, that all contingents fall under God's Power and are either willed to exist or willed not to exist by God, from which he argued it follows that nothing else, including human power and will, can have any effect on the existence of contingents. The method seems consciously demonstrative in the sense of establishing a fundamental principle and then deducing its logical consequences. Juwaynī's argumentation is, by comparison, more dialectical, involving several skirmishes with the Muʿtazilīs on a range of arguments and issues, with no clear sense of what is a fundamental disagreement and what is a corollary issue. Even stylistically, Juwaynī tended to address the Muʿtazilīs in the second person and to paraphrase their objections and arguments in the second person as well. At the level of form, this difference between the two discussions may reflect the fact that Muʿtazilism was still very much a live presence in Juwaynī's time and place. But it also arguably reflects, at least in part, the increased influence on Sanūsī of formal logic and the ideal of demonstration from first principles.

5 Sanūsī on medicine

In his theological works, Sanūsī's position on natural causation was, as shown above, uncompromisingly rejectionist. It has been suggested that Sanūsī nevertheless departed from his own strict stance in his non-theological works, for example, on medicine.[23] This would be a curious resurrection of the idea that medieval scholars were sometimes committed to "double truth," that what they defended when writing qua theologians need not coincide with what they defended when writing qua philosophers or logicians or physicians.

The issue is complicated by the fact that some works often attributed to Sanūsī may not have been by him. Two works in particular would be relevant to a discussion of occasionalism in Sanūsī's thought if their attribution were secure. One of these is a popular work that circulated with the title *The Tried and Tested Means.* It consists of invocations and incantations that supposedly have certain mundane effects. For example, "If one writes the names of Adam and Eve in apertures in the four corners of one's house, then snakes will leave it."[24] However, the attribution of the work to Sanūsī is doubtful. First, the work is not mentioned in the quite lengthy list of Sanūsī's works given by his student Mallālī, whose hagiography is the most important single source on Sanūsī's life and works. Second, the critical edition by Sabine Dorpmüller utilized nine extant manuscripts, none of which predate the seventeenth century. Third, parts of it are written in a conspicuously less learned and classical register of Arabic than works that are indisputably by Sanūsī. Having said this, there is some overlap between passages in the work and passages quoted from Sanūsī in Mallālī's hagiography, so it is possible that the circulated work had its origins in litanies and invocations written down by Sanūsī for his students and acquaintances, and that these were collected and augmented by later students or scribes in the course of subsequent generations. I will return to the work in Chapter 10.

Another work of doubtful authenticity is a commentary on a supposed hadith attributed to the Prophet Muhammad (though it is not in any of the canonical collections) that says, "The stomach is the home of disease, diet is the chief remedy, and the origin of every disease is indigestion." Again, the work is not mentioned by Mallālī, which should give pause. Furthermore, some extant manuscripts attribute the work to an otherwise unknown scholar by the name of Abū l-Faḍl Qāsim ibn Yaḥyá al-Lamtūnī.[25] It is unlikely that a work by the well-known Sanūsī could have been misattributed to an obscure scholar, and much more likely that a work by a little-known scholar should have been misattributed to the eminent Sanūsī in later centuries.

Happily, it is possible to discuss Sanūsī's approach to natural causation in medicine on the basis of another work whose attribution is not in question. This is his commentary on the celebrated collection of Prophetic hadith by Muslim ibn al-Ḥajjāj (d.875), one of the two most esteemed and authoritative such collections recognized by Sunni Muslims. When discussing a reported saying of the Prophet to the effect that "For every malady there is a cure," Sanūsī took the opportunity to clarify what is meant by saying that a certain medicine cures an illness. He wrote:

> Know that the meaning of this thing being a medicine for this malady is that God the Exalted has instituted the custom that He creates a cure for this illness when one uses this medicine. If He so wished, He would not create a cure when taking the medicine, or He could create the cure without taking the medicine or when taking something else that is not considered a medicine for this illness. It is not that[26] the meaning of its being a cure is that in its nature there is something that repels it [i.e., the malady] or that God creates in it a power or distinctive property that repels this illness . . . as many ignoramuses among the legal scholars believe, let alone the common run of believers. This is a corrupt belief which entails defective creedal commitment, for it has been demonstrated without any doubt in the science of kalam that all contingents must depend on God from the beginning and always, without any intermediary. So, the medicine and other things are alike in not having any effect in repelling this disease, just as food and other things are alike in not having an effect on repelling hunger, and fire and other things are alike in [not causing] burns, and so on. Rather, some contingents are different from others in the sense that God has made them a sign (*'alāma*) that He will create with them something . . . So, the meaning of

> his saying, peace and blessing be upon him, "For every malady there is a cure" is that God has freely chosen it as a sign that He will create the cure if the person who is afflicted with the malady connects to this indicant and God aids him. This is like when you say, "For every spiritual malady there is a cure that provides salvation from it". The meaning is also that it has a sign that God has made to indicate that the malady will be repelled and avoided, not[27] that it provides salvation by itself. The only difference is that religious law has made clear the signs that indicate salvation from these [spiritual] maladies . . . I have reminded the reader of this because I have seen that there are many instances of corrupt beliefs among people on this issue, including their leaders, let alone the commoners.[28]

Sanūsī then quoted a lengthy passage from the commentary on Juwaynī's *Guidance* by the Andalusian scholar Ibn Dihāq (d.1214), according to which belief in natural causation is a form of polytheism (*shirk*). Such beliefs, wrote Ibn Dihāq, are of different kinds. For example, there is the conviction that the motions of the heavenly spheres govern the lower world. There is also the belief in necessary connections based on inherent natures, so that fire burns necessarily and by its very nature. According to Ibn Dihāq, such beliefs, common among the Aristotelian–Neoplatonist philosophers, constitute outright unbelief (*kufr*). Another subtype of belief in natural causation is to hold that God instills in everyday entities causal powers that operate, not necessarily, but with God's permission. Such a view is not outright infidelity but still heretical. Sanūsī interjected here that such a belief was rife among those who had not studied kalam theology, including legal scholars and commoners. A related type of belief in secondary causation was the Mu'tazili position that humans create their own actions by means of a God-given power. Again, Sanūsī interjected that such a belief was also widespread among "imitators" who had not studied kalam. Ibn Dihāq added that there was disagreement concerning whether this third view constitutes outright unbelief or merely heresy, and he himself preferred the former view. Sanūsī did not dissent from such a harsh verdict when reproducing Ibn Dihāq's discussion, and indeed he reiterated it in a similar discussion in the *Commentary on the Middle Creed* (W 406). In some later works, Sanūsī seems to have inclined toward the more mainstream Ashʿari view that the Muʿtazilīs are heretics but not infidels.[29]

The quotation from Ibn Dihāq ended with the following words:

> As for the one who knows that God the Exalted connects some of His actions with others, so that whenever He does this, He voluntarily does that, and [knows] that when He wishes to break this custom, He does so, this is the believer who has escaped from this bane.[30]

There is thus no disconnect or cognitive dissonance between Sanūsī's theological writings and his non-theological writings touching on medicine. Sanūsī did not deny that there are regular patterns in nature, or that it is pragmatic to ascertain these regularities and heed them when engaged in everyday activities and deliberations. He did not enjoin believers to abandon medicine as useless and instead pray for divine intervention when ill. In fact, he saw prayer itself as causally inefficacious. Prayer, uttering the "two confessions" ("There is no god but Allah, and Muhammad is the messenger of Allah"), and avoiding sin are also not "causes" that bring about the state of worldly or otherworldly felicity.

In modern, Anglo-American philosophy of causation, a broad distinction tends to be made between (i) "Humean" or empiricist analyses of causation that avoid postulating hidden powers and reduce causation to an observable and regular correlation between events of certain types, and (ii) non-Humean or "realist" analyses that posit causal powers ("causal oomph") that bring about certain effects.[31] Sanūsī's occasionalism is compatible with the former analysis. More precisely, it is compatible with a "Humean" analysis of everyday, mundane "customary causes," supplemented with a non-Humean or "realist" analysis of divine causation. Sanūsī's occasionalism was thus perfectly compatible with what his student Mallālī noted was a keen interest in medicine and in reading medical works (MQ 73). The assumption that occasionalism precludes an interest in the workings of nature is questionable. By the same logic, one might as well say that occasionalism should have led to a lack of interest in Islamic law or in Sufi supererogatory practices, given that these, too, were held not to bring about otherworldly bliss but rather to be signs that one has been elected, through no merit of one's own, for salvation. I turn to Sufi supererogatory practices in Chapter 10.

9
Some Older Theological Controversies

In this chapter, I discuss Sanūsī's engagement with three older theological controversies. The first is whether the Quran is created, as Muʿtazilīs and Shi'is claimed, or uncreated as was the position of mainstream Sunnism. If uncreated, does this imply that the Arabic Quran with its sounds and letters is uncreated, as Ḥanbalī scholars insisted? Or is God's Speech rather a pre-eternal attribute inhering in God, not consisting of letters and sounds but indicated by created human letters and sounds, such as the Arabic Quran and the Hebrew Bible, as claimed by Ashʿarīs and Māturīdīs?

The second controversy is whether God has obligations toward His creatures and, closely related, whether human reason, prior to and independently of revelation, can know that certain actions are good and others bad, with such moral truths also applying to God and ruling out *a priori* that God does things that are otherwise within His Power. Muʿtazilīs tended to affirm that human reason does have this capacity and that God has certain obligations toward humans, such as compensating them for unmerited suffering and not tasking them with what they cannot do. Ashʿarīs vehemently disagreed that God is under any obligations and that natural reason can know moral truths that impose limits on God's Power and Will.

The second controversy tended to spill over into a further issue. Muʿtazilīs and Shi'is regularly challenged Ashʿarīs to rule out that God lies to us if—as Ashʿarīs claim—God is under no obligations and lying is not known by natural reason to be bad.

Al-Sanūsī. Khaled El-Rouayheb, Oxford University Press.
© Oxford University Press 2026. DOI: 10.1093/oso/9780197835630.003.0009

Sanūsī's interventions on these topics were not particularly original, in the sense that there were precedents for the positions he upheld. But he devoted considerable attention to the issues, and he did so while weighing and adjudicating differences on the details among earlier Ashʿarī authorities. It is naïve to think that such longstanding controversies can ever be put to rest by some compelling argument to which opponents simply cannot respond. But the Ashʿarī case, as presented by Sanūsī, is substantial and should not be set aside patronizingly as the perspective of "faith" as opposed to "reason." Or so I will try to show.

1 God's Speech

The question of the createdness or uncreatedness of the Quran was one of the earliest theological controversies that shook the Muslim community. Starting during the reign of the Abbasid Caliph al-Ma'mūn (r.813–833), and continuing under his immediate successors, there was an attempt to enforce on Islamic religious scholars the doctrine that the Quran is created.[1] Though some scholars supported the policy and happily served as inquisitioners in the major urban centers, the attempt also met with fierce opposition from many jurists and hadith-scholars, the figurehead of whom came to be the eminent Ibn Ḥanbal (d.855) who faced imprisonment and flogging rather than admit that the Quran is created. The incident came to be known in oppositionist circles as the Miḥna ("Tribulation"). The Caliph al-Mutawakkil (r.847–861) abandoned the attempt to impose the doctrine and reversed his predecessors' attitude to Ibn Ḥanbal. The entire incident has been interpreted as a turning point after which, in mainstream Sunni Islam, the class of religious scholars, rather than the political rulers, became the recognized arbiters of correct theological doctrine.

The Miḥna years cemented the existence of two opposing theological factions. On the one hand were the so-called Muʿtazilīs (the term starting to become more commonly used in the aftermath), many of whom had supported al-Ma'mūn's policy and declared their opponents polytheists for believing the Quran to be pre-eternal and uncreated along with God. On the other hand were the religious scholars who revered the Quran as God's uncreated Speech, some of whom—not to be outdone—denounced as infidels those who believe it is created (and even denounced as infidels those who doubt the infidelity of those who believe that it is created). In the generations following the Miḥna, the mainstream, anti-Muʿtazilī camp itself developed in two different directions. The Ḥanbalīs insisted that it is the Arabic Quran with its letters and sounds that is uncreated. The Ashʿarīs and Māturīdīs, by contrast, articulated a view that can be seen as intermediate between the Muʿtazilīs and the Ḥanbalīs, and—as intermediate views often are—was denounced by both sides. The Ashʿarī and Māturīdī position is that a distinction should be made between God's attribute of Speech, which is pre-eternal and uncreated, and the Arabic sounds and letters of the Quran, which are created. God's uncreated Speech is itself not in any human language. Rather, various revelations in different languages (Hebrew, Aramaic, Arabic) are all created expressions of this divine attribute of Speech. This, in broad contours, was also the position of Sanūsī. In what follows, his position and the arguments for it will be presented in greater detail, based primarily on his most extensive treatment of the issue in his *Commentary on the Long Creed*.

The first argument given in the *Long Creed* for God being a Speaker is one given in Juwaynī's *The Guidance*: Given that God is alive, it must be that either the attributes of Sight, Hearing, and Speech are true of Him or that their contraries are true of Him: blindness, deafness, and dumbness. But these attributes of deficiency are impossible of God. So, God must be characterized as seeing, hearing, and speaking. In line with the Egyptian Ashʿarī theologian al-Muqtaraḥ (d.1216), Sanūsī expressed dissatisfaction with this argument. Granted that sight, hearing, and speech are perfections in creatures, it does not follow that they are perfections for God. The ability to feel pleasure and pain are also "perfections" for animals, but no major Islamic theological group attributes the feeling of pleasure and pain to God. The underlying problem is that humans do not have knowledge of God's Self (*dhāt*) to be able to infer what is and what is not a perfection for Him. All we humans know about God is mediated through God's actions: We can tell from God's creation of the world, and the world being in one of many possible ways, that God has the attributes of power, will, knowledge, and life. But the problematic argument under consideration starts by making assumptions about what is a perfection for the divine Self, which is both under-argued and presumptuous.[2]

Instead, Sanūsī preferred—in his main creedal works—to rely on revelation as the ground for attributing Speech to God. This might, at first sight, seem circular—that we are relying on divine Speech to infer that God must be a Speaker. But this is not so, argued Sanūsī. The proof for the truthfulness of a prophet is the miracle, and the miracle may or may not be Speech. Even if the miracle is that the prophet brings forth speech of astounding sublimity, this can be acknowledged even by those who initially are uncommitted to the thesis that God speaks. So, there is no circularity (K 289–91).

As mentioned in Chapter 7, the reliance on revelation to establish the attributes of Speech, Sight, and Hearing does have certain semantic implications. When we establish through natural reason that God exists and has the attributes of Power, Will, Knowledge and Life, then this presupposes that we are ascribing to God "existence," "power," "will," "knowledge," and "life" in recognizable senses of the terms. If I argue, for example, that the Creator of the world must have will because the actual world is one of several possible worlds, then the term "will" must have a recognizable, non-arcane sense when applied to God. And if I say that the Creator must have "knowledge" because this follows from God being a voluntary agent and from the mind-boggling intricacy of creation, then again the term "knowledge" must be used in a way that is close to its ordinary, non-arcane sense and can hardly mean things like "is a cause" or "is immaterial." Such arguments are more difficult to make when it comes to attributes that are only known by revelation to be true of God. If Scripture attributes a "face" and "hands" to God, then Islamic kalam theologians of all stripes tended to say that such terms cannot have their everyday senses but must be accepted agnostically or interpreted figuratively. In saying that Speech, Sight, and Hearing are known to be true of God only through revelation, the risk is that the terms "speech," "sight," and "hearing" also cannot bear their ordinary senses and must be accepted agnostically or interpreted figuratively.

But this was not a consequence that mainstream Ashʿarī theologians were willing to accept. They did not classify "speech," "sight," and "hearing" as among the "ambiguous" (*mutashābihāt*) attributes mentioned in Quran and hadith that should not be taken literally. On the contrary, they went out of their way to argue that the term "speech," when applied to God, is used in a sense that is related to everyday "speech." Though it was not very common for Islamic theologians to be explicit about whether a term is applied of God and creatures univocally, analogically, or equivocally, I think it is fair to say that for mainstream Ashʿarī theologians, including Sanūsī, the terms "hands" and "face" are used equivocally when applied to God and humans, but that the term "speech" is used analogically when applied to God and humans.[3] But affirming such a difference between "speech," on the one hand, and "face" and "hands," on the other, requires some explanation. As will be seen shortly, Ashʿarīs accordingly took pains to show that there is a recognizable, everyday sense of the term "speech" (*kalām*) in which it does not entail being composed of sounds and letters.

In Sanūsī's *Commentary on the Preliminaries*, a shorter and later work, he did give a rational argument for why God must be a Speaker. It is a modified version of Juwaynī's aforementioned argument: Given that God has the attribute of Knowledge, it must be possible for God to have the attribute of Speech, for everything that has knowledge must be such that it can, in principle, speak this knowledge. But if an attribute is possible for God, then it is necessarily true of God, for God does not have contingent attributes. So, God must have the attribute of Speech.[4] On this account, it is immediately clear that the term "speech" is applied non-equivocally to God and to humans. The meaning of "speak" in the premise "Everything that has knowledge must be such that it can, in principle, speak this knowledge" must be the same as in the conclusion "God speaks."

Having established—through revelation or reason—that God has the attribute of Speech, Sanūsī went on to deny that this divine Speech consists of sounds and letters. He took it to be evident that sounds and letters are originated. They are ordered temporally or spatially, and such ordering is incompatible with the assumption that each sound and letter is pre-eternal. Furthermore, the Ḥanbalī view that what is written in the codex, and what is recited by a reciter, is identical to the uncreated Speech of God is absurd. It is tantamount to the idea that the divine, uncreated Speech can come to inhere or dwell in written signs and uttered sounds, just like Christians believe that God's uncreated Logos comes to inhere or dwell in the physical body of Jesus. He wrote:

> The Ḥashwīs, who are partisans of the literal, maintain that the Speech of God subsists in Him as letters and sounds, and despite being letters and sounds are nevertheless pre-eternal! These people are an extreme in waywardness and are entangled in luxuriant ignorance. Some disputed point may occur to other heretics that does not immediately contravene necessary truths. As for them, they do not heed the necessities of reason . . . Among their reprehensible views is that when a reciter recites a verse of the Book of God, what is heard is the Speech that subsists in God the Exalted, and it is thus in the locus of the reciter while not moving from God's Self. And they claim that the letters of the codex are identical to the Speech of God the Exalted without moving from

> His Self either. This is the claim of the Christians who believe that Jesus assumed the divine attribute of Knowledge without it being separated from God. But the Christians specify one creature in this way, and this is Jesus, peace be upon him, whereas these people judge this to happen whenever a reciter recites a verse of the Quran! To judge that the letters and sounds are pre-eternal even though they are renewed and are preceded and succeeded by non-existence, and that one thing is in two separate loci, is to leave the bounds of reason and deny evident truths. (K 365–7)

The correct view, according to Sanūsī, is that what the reciter of the Quran recites, and what the scribe who copies the Quranic codex writes, indicates or signifies (*dālla*) God's uncreated Speech.

Sanūsī—like all Ashʿarīs—tried to show that God's Speech should be thought of as analogous to "soul speech" or "inner speech" (*kalām nafsī*). In the case of human speech, one can draw a distinction between (i) what is said and (ii) the expressions used to say it. The same thing can be expressed in different ways or in different languages. The expressions that are used to say something are in a conventional language, whereas what is in the soul is by nature, not by convention. This shows, according to Ashʿarīs, that "speech" need not consist of sounds and letters. To buttress their position, Ashʿarīs also cited passages from Quran, hadith, and early Arabic poetry to the effect that it accords with revelation and proper Arabic usage to say that there is "inner" speech or speech "in the heart." All this, they argued, supports the contention that "speech" does not inevitably involve conventionally instituted sounds or letters.[5]

The Muʿtazilīs could hardly deny that there is a mundane distinction between linguistic expressions and what is expressed by them. Nor could they deny that there are passages in the Quran, hadith, and early Arabic poetry that use locutions such as "They say within themselves" (Q 58:8). But they tended to identify speech strictly and literally with the conventional linguistic expressions.

What these expressions express is not itself "speech" (at least not in the strict, literal sense) but beliefs and desires or, in the case of God, knowledge and will.[6] To this, Sanūsī responded by arguing that inner speech cannot be reduced to belief/knowledge and desire/will. A linguistic command need not reflect a desire, for I may issue a command simply with the aim of testing a person's obedience. And yet, the command must be in my soul prior to its verbalization in one of the conventional languages I know. In the case of God, Ashʿarīs argued that the distinction between command and will is even clearer, for creatures often disobey God's commands while it is absurd—they claimed—to suggest that mere creatures can defy an omnipotent God's Will. So, "inner speech" is an irreducible attribute of humans and of God.[7] Of course, in the case of humans, the "inner speech" is originated, evanescent, and has finite attachments, whereas in the case of God it is an eternal attribute that attaches to all that is necessary, impossible, and contingent.

The Muʿtazilīs, like the Ḥanbalīs, rejected the very notion of an "inner speech" that does not consist of letters and sounds. But whereas the Ḥanbalīs drew the conclusion that the sounds and letters of the Quran are not created, the Muʿtazilīs insisted that they are created. On the Muʿtazilī view, God simply creates the sounds and letters of the Quran, without the need to postulate an additional Speech inhering in the divine Self. In his *Commentary on the Preliminaries*, Sanūsī addressed the following argument against this position: It implies that Speech, including Commands and Prohibitions, are not strictly God's but that of the loci in which God has created the letters and sounds. An analogy might make the point clearer: God creates the motion of a falling leaf and the graying of a middle-aged person's hair, but it is the leaf that is properly described as "falling," and the hair that is properly described as "graying," not God. Similarly, if God creates commands and prohibitions in a created locus, then it is the locus that is properly described as commanding and prohibiting, not God. This, of course, is absurd. It entails that believers are following the commands and prohibitions of created entities, and that God Himself is neither commanding nor prohibiting. Sanūsī wrote:

> If there is neither command or prohibition, nor promise or warning, subsisting in the Exalted Self, but these exist in created bodies, then believers are worshipping the bodies, for it is these that are commanding and prohibiting. If they [i.e., the Muʿtazilīs] were to reply that what He has created in them indicates the commands, prohibitions, promises, and warnings of God . . . then we reply: The Exalted Self according to them is simply devoid of Speech, so there is no command in It, nor prohibition, statement, promise, or warning. (M 257–8)

One might rephrase Sanūsī's point here as follows: If there is no attribute of Speech inhering in God, then we have to understand that God has created commands, prohibitions, and the like in created loci, just as He creates motion and color in created loci. But this seems to imply that, strictly speaking, the one who commands and prohibits is not God but the created entity in which these letters and sounds are created, presumably the Prophet and the Quranic codex. There are a number of problems with this. First, the generally accepted view is that the Prophet and the Quranic codex convey the commands and declarations of God, not that these commands and declarations are strictly their own, like their hair color or folio size. Second, on occasionalist premises, all speech is the direct creation of God, so it becomes difficult to see in what way the commands of certain people and books are God's, whereas the commands of other people and other books are not God's. Third, it will obviously not do to say that some created commands and declarations correspond to God's commands and declarations if God is devoid of Speech and therefore of commands and declarations.

Some of the issues at stake can be seen in the exegesis of the Quranic passage saying that God spoke to Moses (Q 4:164). The passage should not, Sanūsī wrote, be understood to mean that God suddenly changed from being silent to being a speaker and afterwards became silent again. This would entail that God undergoes change, i.e., that there are originated attributes inhering in God, which in turn would entail that God is Himself originated. Rather, the passage should be understood to say that God enabled Moses in a certain time and place to hear the pre-eternal, uncreated Speech of God that does not consist of sounds and letters (K 379–81). This is like God creating visual impressions of Himself for the blessed in paradise, even though He is not in any spatial location.

According to Sanūsī, the Muʿtazilī interpretation of the Quranic verse would be that God created, in the burning bush, speech addressing Moses. But this would mean that it is the burning bush, not God, that strictly spoke to Moses. Given that God creates all sounds that we hear, there would be nothing that would make this a case of hearing *God's* speech. But the import of the Quranic verse is clearly that Moses had the very unusual experience of hearing the speech of God, not the speech of a burning bush (K 380–4). As an aside, I note that neither of the two major Muʿtazilī Quran exegetes, al-Jishumī (d.1101) and al-Zamakhsharī (d.1141), ascribed speech to the burning bush. The former maintained that God spoke to Moses directly, presumably creating sounds in Moses' ear or head. Such a view is, I think, vulnerable to the aforementioned objection that it is not clear in what sense such created speech can be understood to be God's. The latter exegete idiosyncratically proposed that the Arabic verb *kallama*, usually understood as "spoke," actually derives from *kalm*, meaning "wound," the sense being that God exposed Moses to sore trials.[8]

Sanūsī's view of God's Speech, and his main arguments, should be clear from the foregoing. One problem, which he uncharacteristically left unresolved in his theological writings, is how it can be said that God's Speech is unitary if it encompasses, for example, declarations, commands, prohibitions, promises, and warnings (K 388–9, 404–8). One ninth-century theologian had proposed that there are actually seven divine attributes encompassed by the term "speech": command, prohibition, statement, question, promise, warning, and exclamation. How could one ward off such a position? Some Ashʿarī theologians proposed that it is possible to reduce these seven to two: declarative statement (*khabar*) and bidding (*ṭalab*): Command and prohibition can be reduced to bidding, whereas promise, warning, and question can be reduced to declarative statement. It is possible that these two could, in turn, be reduced to a single attribute of speech. The problem with this suggestion, Sanūsī noted, is that one might then say that, analogously, there could be a single attribute that encompasses power, will, knowledge, and life. If one were to object that there are logical differences between, say, will (which requires an attachment) and life (which does not), then one might equally say that there are logical differences between a declarative statement and a command (the former is not contrary to a prohibition, though the latter is).

Another suggestion was that all subtypes of speech reduce to declarative statement. A command, for example, could be interpreted as a declarative statement about the consequences of an action. The problem with such a suggestion, Sanūsī wrote, is that God need not carry out His warnings and may, if He so wishes, simply forgive sins. On this account, it is not clear how a divine warning or threat can be reduced to a declarative statement about consequences.

In his *Commentary on the Long Creed*, his most detailed treatment of the issue, Sanūsī ended his discussion of God's Speech with no clear solution to how God's Speech can be unitary if it encompasses declarative statements, commands, prohibitions, promises, warnings, questions, and exclamations. He did give a more general argument for why each of the divine attributes is a single attribute, i.e., for why God does not have more than one life, one power, one will, and one knowledge (K 401–2; W 340–3). But the challenge here is not that God may have more than one speech, but that "God's Speech" might be an umbrella term encompassing a few—two, five, or seven—distinct attributes. It appears that Sanūsī did not revisit the issue of the oneness of God's Speech in any of his other works.

2 Are good and bad known by natural reason?

Another older point of contention between Ashʿarīs and Muʿtazilīs traditionally went under the name of "determining good and bad by reason" (*taḥsīn wa taqbīḥ ʿaqlī*). The question was whether human reason, unaided by revelation, knows certain actions to be good or bad. A closely related issue was whether actions have inherent moral value or instead derive their values as "good" and "bad" from divine command.[9]

The classic Muʿtazilī position is that actions have inherent moral values and that in many cases human reason can know these values independently of revelation. Even in cases where it cannot do so, and must rely on revelation, they held that God's commands and prohibitions simply inform us of the independent moral qualities of certain actions (such as the inherent good of prayer, fasting, and the Hajj pilgrimage). For example, unaided human reason can know that lying, theft, and murder are inherently bad. This implies that they would still be bad if God were to decree them. So, God can be known *a priori* not to command lying, theft, and murder. Similarly, Muʿtazilīs believed humans can ascertain, prior to and independently of revelation, that it would be unjust if God were to punish humans for things that are beyond their control, or for transgressing rules of which He did not inform them, or if He were to treat the righteous and sinners in the same way in the afterlife. They also held that God is obliged to grant compensation (*ʿiwaḍ*) to humans for unmerited suffering.[10]

The predominant Ashʿarī position was that God is under no obligations, that actions have no inherent deontic qualities discoverable by natural reason, and that humans are not able to make *a priori* judgments about what God will or will not decree. Rather, God is free to institute whatever precepts He Wills, and such divine precepts determine whether an act is religiously praiseworthy or reprehensible. Such a view is sometimes labeled a "divine command morality." Even more than occasionalism, it is held in disrepute in many modern circles, eliciting terms such as "dangerous," "infantile," "impious," or "less than human."[11] In what follows, I will first attempt to give a charitable (but not entirely uncritical) reconstruction of Sanūsī's position and supporting arguments. In the section that follows, I will then mention some objections to the Ash'arī position and discuss how Sanūsī tried to meet them.

Sanūsī expounded his views on the topic at some length in his two most substantial theological writings, the *Commentary on the Long Creed* and the *Commentary on the Middle Creed*. In both works, he raised the issue in the context of the principle that God can do anything that is contingent, i.e., that is not necessary or impossible. And necessity and impossibility were understood strictly logically, not physically-nomologically or morally. The contrary view, which he associated with the Mu'tazilīs, is that God is under certain obligations to humans. He wrote:

> The Mu'tazilīs . . . have declared it obligatory that God takes into account what is best for His servants and that He is benevolent in the sense that He creates the means in the legally responsible person that make it more likely than not that he will comply, though without actually forcing him. They have also declared it obligatory that God grants the requisite mental powers and abilities to those who are legally responsible and removes obstacles that prevent them from complying. Were God not to do this, they would have a right against Him and may demand their due! God is more Exalted by far than what the unjust say! (K 523)

Sanūsī marshaled several arguments against the Mu'tazilī view. First, God is a voluntary agent. If God were obliged to bring something about, then He would not be a voluntary agent with respect to that thing (K 523). The argument harks back to Sanūsī's position, discussed in the previous chapter on occasionalism, that God's Power and Will attach per se to everything that is contingent and therefore cannot be delimited by any extrinsic factor, such as God knowing that something will not happen or knowing that something will cause more pain than pleasure on aggregate. God's Will is eternal, immutable, and cannot be influenced by anything beyond Itself. If X is contingent, then the only thing precluding God from willing X is that God wills not-X.[12]

Furthermore, Sanūsī added, the source of the obligation (*al-mūjib*) is either pre-eternal or originated. If pre-eternal, then there is a pre-eternal partner of God. (Just like Plato thought that the Forms are eternal and constrain the freedom of the gods.) If originated, then God is subject to change, which is absurd (K 523–4). I briefly note that Sanūsī is arguably too quick here and has not ruled out that the source of the obligation could be God Himself. For example, if one holds that God is inherently "good" or "wise," then one might argue that certain things follow from this, without there being an external source of obligation to which God is subject. The Māturīdī school, which is otherwise close to Ash'arism, emphasizes God's "Wisdom" and takes this to rule out that God could, for example, command humans to do what they cannot do, or not inform them of their duties.[13] Sanūsī did not engage with Māturīdīs, even though they were a major presence in the Sunni world outside the Maghreb in his time, an indication of his somewhat provincial perspective.

A more formidable argument by Sanūsī against the Mu'tazilī view is that if God were obliged to decree what is to the benefit of humans, then there would be no worldly or otherworldly tribulations, no moral obligations, no decrepit old age, no unbelief, and no sin. He wrote:

> If it were obligatory for God to do what is best for His servant, then He would issue no commands or prohibitions, nor would

> He create any tribulation in this world, such as illness and grief, or hunger and destitution, or the torments of death and separation from loved ones ... nor [would He create] in the afterlife the terrors of the grave ... and the innumerable torments of hellfire, for it is obvious that it would be best for servants to be created in Paradise from the beginning without prior tribulations. (W 415)

To this, one might respond that God imposes tests and tribulations to reward humans in the afterlife. But surely, Sanūsī noted, it is within God's Power to grant such rewards without the testing and suffering. Furthermore, God knows the outcome of the tests and tribulations, so why not exempt from obligations those whom He knows will be sinners or unbelievers? Sanūsī wrote:

> There is no doubt that God has the Power to grant all servants the highest stations from the outset, without the tribulations of legal duties and the like. And this would not in any way diminish His dominion ... And there is no doubt that the best for those whom God knows will not believe and will die unbelievers is that He does not impose any obligations on them at all, for the imposition of moral obligations does not benefit them in any way. And if such legal duties are imposed, the best would be for Him to assist them so that they do not commit criminal acts or unbelief, for He has the Power to do so, and He has said, "Had we wished, We would have given every soul its guidance" (Q 32:13). (W 415–6)

Even allowing for God imposing obligations despite knowing that some people will not live up to them, why should God not simply forgive everyone at the end and grant them paradise? Why should God impose eternal damnation when He is not in need of people's obedience in any way? Sanūsī wrote:

> Furthermore, after criminal acts and unbelief have been committed, the best would be for God to forgive and excuse

> everyone. It is not in accord with human customary ways of determining good and bad (*maslak al-nās fīmā yuqabbiḥūnahu wa-yuḥassinūnahu*) for someone who has no need for servants and all their actions, who is not harmed by their disobedience, nor benefits in any way from their obedience, to institute punishment and damnation for all eternity, deprivation of all good, and perpetuation of painful suffering, in return for a disobedience that occurs at one time from a poor servant overcome with passions and incentives of which he cannot divest himself. (W 416)

Furthermore, Sanūsī added, it is also not clear how Muʿtazilī principles can be reconciled with the fact that God allows the Devil (*Iblīs*) to operate across the ages, while causing prophets, saints, and righteous scholars to die. Is one really to believe that this is to the benefit of humans? Sanūsī wrote:

> We say to them: It follows from your position that it is best for His servants that God causes rightly guided and guiding prophets and messengers, goodly scholars, and righteous saints, all to die, while keeping the Devil and his minions who are misled and mislead until the Day of Reckoning. What more incongruous and scandalous consequence can be envisaged? (W 417)

In assessing Sanūsī's arguments here, it should be kept in mind that the premodern Muslim opponents of the Ashʿarīs were overwhelmingly committed to divine omnipotence, divine foreknowledge, and everlasting punishment in hellfire. Modern readers may not be committed to such theses, and some modern Christian thinkers have denied divine omnipotence, divine foreknowledge, and the existence of hell. From such a modern-liberal perspective, Sanūsī's cited objections may even seem eloquent testimonies to why one must abandon the belief in omnipotence, foreknowledge, or hell. But for his premodern opponents, the challenge he expressed must be judged powerful. It is, in fact, a variant of the classic and refractory "problem of evil" advanced, not against theism as such, but against the idea that God's decrees are circumscribed by our ordinary moral intuitions.

Of course, it is naive to think that long-standing theological disputes can be decisively settled by an argument, even a "powerful" one. Mu'tazilīs were not stumped by objections such as Sanūsī's and insisted that it would be rationally abhorrent for God not to put humans to the test and simply grant paradise to all, regardless of merit.[14] Even if the dispute thus remained open, and was not—and likely never will be—resolved by a "master argument," it is clearly tendentious and unhelpful to present Sanūsī and the Ash'arīs as representing "faith" in this controversy and their Mu'tazilī opponents "reason," or to say that "Any unbiased investigation would reveal that most of the Ash'arite criticism was rationally unsound, based on scriptural argument, and that the Mu'tazilites could easily refute it."[15]

Mu'tazilīs are often deemed "rationalists" in ethics because they held that unaided human reason can know the moral qualities of at least some actions, whereas Ash'arīs are often described as denying reason any role in morality. But both characterizations should be qualified. As pointed out by Sophia Vasalou, describing the Mu'tazilīs as "rationalists" tends to elide their theological motivations as well as the extent to which they simply appealed to the "evident" or "necessary" status of their claims about moral truth.[16] (Modern readers should keep in mind that one of the intuitions of the Mu'tazilīs was that prophets and imams must be male because it would be rationally abhorrent to appoint women to such roles.)[17] Their opponents, including Sanūsī, set no store in such appeals to self-evidence. For Sanūsī, the basic, flawed assumption was that one might extrapolate from our natural morality based on all-too-human inclinations, emotions, and customs to what the omnipotent Maker of the universe ought or ought not to do, an assumption he thought reflected presumptuous folly rather than right reason (W 411–4).

Furthermore, simply describing the Ashʿarī position as anti-rationalist is also potentially misleading. As Ayman Shihadeh has noted, an Ashʿarī theologian need not have denied—and many explicitly did not deny—that humans might, through the exercise of reason, discern the societal norms and rules that are conducive to human flourishing in this world. But they refused to concede that natural reason can infer on that basis, and prior to revelation, what precepts God will impose on humans.[18] In other words, there is a logical gap between saying that, for example, theft is not conducive to human flourishing, to saying that God is obliged to legislate against it, or can be known *a priori* to do so, or can be known by natural reason to punish thieves in the afterlife. One can see the relevant distinction in Fakhr al-Dīn al-Rāzī's *Landmarks of the Principles of Religion* and its commentary by Ibn al-Tilimsānī, perhaps the single most important source for Sanūsī's *Commentary on the Long Creed.* Rāzī and Ibn al-Tilimsānī accepted that humans can discern what is of utility (*nafʿ*) and harm (*ḍarr*) for them in this world, and that humans tend to call the former "good" (*ḥasan*) and the latter "bad" (*qabīḥ*). But they refused to concede that humans can infer from such tendencies what God must do.[19]

Sanūsī, too, was careful to state that unaided human reason cannot establish what is good and bad *for God* (*idrāk al-ḥasan wa l-qabīḥ ʿindahu ʿazza wa-jalla*) (K 535). He did not deny that there are "human ways of determining good and bad" (*maslak al-nās fīmā yuqabbiḥūnahu wa-yuḥassinūnahu*) based on emotional and pragmatic considerations (W 416). He did not, in other words, deny that we might have natural knowledge of what by human or societal agreement is called "good" and "bad," but he denied that we can have such natural, *a priori* knowledge of what is good from the perspective of the Creator who has no emotional inclinations or practical needs. What is "good" from the perspective of religious law (*al-ḥasan sharʿan*) is simply what God enjoins, and what is "bad" is simply what God censures (K 536). And it seems to me that there is at least a prima facie case for inverting the standard interpretation of this issue and seeing the Ashʿarīs as representing the hard-headed, unsentimental perspective of mature reason, whereas their theological opponents were swayed by species- and culture-specific prejudices and emotions masquerading as moral insights into the noumenal world.

3 Must God tell us the truth?

The kind of view defended by Sanūsī in the preceding section has historically been subject to a number of criticisms. In the present section, I will go over some of these criticisms, though giving most attention to the one that was commonly raised in the premodern Islamic tradition itself, rather than objections by modern moral philosophers.

One modern worry about divine command theory is that it is somehow linked to religious violence and "fundamentalism."[20] If God's commands might "suspend the ethical," to use a Kierkegaardian expression, then believers might consider themselves religiously obliged to commit morally outrageous acts such as terrorism.[21] Though the worry is understandable, it is important to point out that the modern Islamic groups whose violent actions tend to make headlines and are often loosely described as "jihadi" or "militant" tend to be either Salafi-Sunni or Khomeinist-Shi'i, neither of which adopt the Ashʿarī version of divine command morality. Modern Shiism embraces the Muʿtazilī view of ethical value, this obviously not preventing some of the more radical Shi'i groups from acts of religiously charged violence or mainstream Shi'i scholars from upholding laws about, for example, adultery, apostasy, and calumny of the Prophet that so offend modern liberal sentiments. Salafīs, for their part, tend to reject the discipline of kalam theology entirely, and the medieval thinker who has influenced them most, the Ḥanbalī Ibn Taymiyya (d.1328), saw himself as neither Muʿtazilī nor Ashʿarī on this particular issue but as promoting a view intermediate between the two (and close to the aforementioned Māturīdī position).[22]

A standard, modern philosophical criticism of divine command morality is that it makes it meaningless to say that God is "good."[23] If what God decrees is by definition "good," no matter what He decrees and does, then the term loses its normal sense and becomes an empty designation, as if a dictator were to force his subjects to describe his regime as "democratic" despite not having free elections, political parties, free press, an independent judiciary, and so on. In premodern Islamic discussions, the issue tended not to be phrased in terms of God being "good." One reason is surely that, unlike the case of the Gospels, there is little authority in the Quran and hadith for using the name "good" (*khayr*) of God. It is not one of the core attributes recognized in the kalam theological tradition, nor is it one of the 99 divine names that play a prominent role in popular Islamic piety. But the point could be, and was, expressed in terms of "justice," and "The Just" (*al-ʿadl*) *is* one of the divine names. Sanūsī, in a short treatise in which he explained the meaning and import of the divine names, glossed the term thus:

> The Just is the one who does no injustice (*ẓulm*) or wrong (*jawr*) in whatever He does, regardless of whether this appeals to creatures or not, for His dominion is general over everything else. No command is addressed to Him, nor prohibition. Rather He is the one who commands and prohibits.[24]

Does this explication void the term "Just" of any recognizable meaning? Arguably not. It is true that God is not "Just" in the same sense as humans, for whom—as Sanūsī went on to write—being "just" means obedience to The Just. But there is surely a sense in which someone who commits no wrong or injustice is "just," even if this is simply because His decrees and acts define what "justice" is. There has been much philosophical discussion in recent decades about Wittgenstein's alleged claim that the standard bars in Paris, that in his time still determined what a "meter" is, cannot themselves be said to be a meter long. As a number of scholars have noted, it is far from obvious that this is so.[25]

A related modern criticism is that the "divine command theory" makes morality "arbitrary."[26] Had God commanded it, torturing babies (a recurrent example in the literature) would have been "good" and preventing it would have been "bad." It is doubtful, however, whether this is an effective argument against the Ashʿarī view. Ashʿarīs explicitly "bit the bullet" and accepted that God might have reversed (*ʿakasa*) His decrees and commanded what He in fact prohibits and prohibited what He in fact commands, so if God had decreed torturing babies then that would have been religiously praiseworthy. (Jewish, Christian, and Muslim theists who scoff at this might want to recall God's command to Abraham that he sacrifice his son.)

Sanūsī responded to a related objection, which is that Ashʿarīs reduce God's decrees and actions to "futility" (*ʿabath*) and "inanity" (*safah*). He was clearly not perturbed. The normal senses of such terms are, he wrote, that one acts without knowledge and with no cognizance of consequences. This is not true of God. If one were to stipulate that the terms "futile" and "inane" apply to acts committed without a motive or final cause, then God's acts are futile and inane in that sense (K 533–5). Analogously, Sanūsī might have said that if by "arbitrary" we mean "impulsive" and "incoherent," then God's decrees and actions are not "arbitrary." But if we beg the question and stipulate that a decree or action is "arbitrary" if it does not accord with some independently existing standard of value, then God's decrees and actions are indeed "arbitrary" in that sense.

A much more troublesome problem for Ashʿarīs, and one that their premodern Islamic opponents regularly raised, is the following: If lying is not inherently bad, and if God is under no obligation not to lie to us, then how can we trust revelation at all?[27] Appealing to Quran and hadith to rule out that God lies seems blatantly circular. But it is not at all clear how one can rule out the possibility on purely rational grounds without betraying the principle that lying is not inherently bad and that God may do as He pleases without being accountable to human emotions and prejudices.[28]

In his *Commentary on the Long Creed*, Sanūsī reproduced a number of earlier arguments by Ashʿarī theologians for why it is impossible that God lie (K 567–8). The first argument is that "inner speech" must be in accordance with what one believes to be true. One may, of course, say out loud what one does not really think, but it is not possible to have "inner speech" that does not accord with one's beliefs, i.e., for one's soul to say inwardly, without sounds and letters, what one does not really believe. But God is omniscient and does not have false beliefs, so God's Speech must be true. One problem with this argument, not noted by Sanūsī, is that Ashʿarīs differentiate between God's eternal Speech and the Arabic Quran. So even if this argument works, and God's eternal Speech can be shown to be true, it does not follow that the Arabic Quran is true. One might try bridging the gap by saying that the Arabic Quran must be true because it indicates God's eternal, true Speech. But the question would then be whether one can show that the Arabic Quran really indicates the eternal Speech of God without tacitly presupposing that God does not lie. (I will return to this point shortly.)

A second argument for the claim that it is impossible for God to lie is that if God lies then lying is necessary for God, for God cannot have contingent attributes inhering in Him. But if God lies necessarily, then it is in principle impossible for Him to say what He knows. But this is absurd, for everyone who has knowledge can in principle speak this knowledge. One problem, also not noted by Sanūsī, is that it again seems to equivocate between the eternal Speech of God and the Arabic Quran. If the latter is false, it does not follow that God's eternal Speech is false. It therefore does not follow that God cannot in principle "speak" His Knowledge.

A third argument is that speaking the truth is a perfection, and speaking falsehood an imperfection, and God must be perfect and free from imperfections. This argument, too, seems problematic. How can Ashʿarīs help themselves to the premise that speaking falsehood is an imperfection? As the eminent Persian Ashʿarī theologian al-Ījī (d.1355) wrote, "There does not seem to me to be a difference between the imperfection of a deed and rationally determining the deed to be bad, for to say a deed is imperfect is simply to say that it is rationally bad—it is just the words that are different."[29] It is possible that Sanūsī came to acknowledge the problematic nature of this particular argument, for he did not reiterate it in his *Commentary on the Middle Creed*, though he did repeat the other two.

Some Ashʿarī theologians thought it was not necessary to show the impossibility of God lying, and that they could establish the truth of prophecy and revelation without relying on any of the preceding arguments. In his *Commentary on the Middle Creed*, Sanūsī first presented the overall challenge on behalf of the Muʿtazilīs:

> Even if we were to concede . . . that the miracle is tantamount to an explicit statement from God the Exalted that the claimant to prophethood is truthful, this does not imply his truth unless we can establish the impossibility of God's statements being false. There is no way to do this via revelation, for that would be circular, nor via rational argumentation for the upshot is that lying is bad and is impossible for God the Exalted, but the rational badness of lying is not conceded according to your principles. (W 458)

In response, Sanūsī cited a point made by Juwaynī in *The Guidance*: God's creating a miracle at the hands of a claimant is tantamount to anointing that person a prophet then and there. It is like someone saying, "I hereby appoint you as my representative."

Such a statement is an *inshā'*, i.e., an utterance whose objective is not to state how things are but to bring about a certain state of affairs.[30] In other words, the miracle is equivalent to what the much later English philosopher John Austin (d.1960) would have called a performative speech act.[31] On this account, we can establish that the Prophet Muḥammad is a genuine prophet, and that the Arabic Quran is genuine revelation, independently of whether or not God must tell us the truth. A performative utterance is, by definition, neither true nor false, so the question of the truth or falsity of God's Speech is beside the point. It is in fact possible, Sanūsī wrote, on that basis to rely—without circularity—on the Arabic Quran and hadith to establish that God speaks and is truthful (W 457).

One might object that even if we concede that a miracle is a performative act by God that appoints a person His prophet or messenger, it still does not follow that what this prophet actually propounds is true, especially if we are not sure whether God is misleading us all (including His prophet). On the other hand, one might argue that once it is conceded that a person has been appointed a messenger of God, it follows analytically—from the very meaning of the term "messenger of God"—that what this person propounds is a faithful indication of the true Speech of God. Pursuing this point would take us too far from Sanūsī. But it is worth noting that the opponents of the Ash'arīs may not, despite first appearances, have been in a better position to show that God does not lie or mislead. After all, they could hardly avoid conceding that God often allows horrible things to happen to innocent people for some ultimate good that we cannot discern here and now. For example, God allowed the bubonic plague of the mid-fourteenth century to kill perhaps as much as a third of the populations of Europe and the Middle East within just a few years. How then can we be so sure that God does not lie to us, or allow miracles to be performed by imposters, for some ultimate good that we cannot discern here and now?[32] It is difficult to argue that God telling us a noble lie or allowing imposters to perform miracles in support of their claims to prophecy is somehow more rationally abhorrent than letting millions of innocent people suffer excruciating pain, debilitating diseases, and untimely death.

The foregoing point is not meant to be a knock-down argument against the Muʿtazilīs. Well-established theological traditions have a considerable pool of intelligent adherents who will exercise considerable ingenuity in defending the tenets of that tradition even in the face of what at first sight might seem decisive objections. But this applies to the Ashʿarī tradition as well. There has been a tendency in the modern study of Islamic thought to disparage Ashʿarī positions, especially occasionalism and divine command morality, and to write them off as obscurantism or worse, whereas "reason" has been assumed to be on the side of their opponents. This assumption is ripe for reconsideration, even if one stops short of adopting Sanūsī's own perspective, which was that both reason (*ʿaql*) and revelation (*samʿ*) are firmly on his side, while folly and presumption are on the other.

10
From Knowledge to Works

As mentioned on a number of occasions in previous chapters, Sanūsī was profoundly influenced by the writings of the Egyptian Ashʿarī theologian al-Muqtaraḥ (d.1216) and his students Ibn al-Tilimsānī (d.1260) and Abū Yaḥyá al-Sharīf (fl.1231). He drew regularly on their writings when discussing the core theological issues of God's existence, the divine attributes, occasionalism, divine command morality, and the nature of God's Speech. There are certain aspects of Sanūsī's thought, however, that are distinctive when compared to that earlier Egyptian circle. One is his interest in formal logic, discussed in Chapter 5. Another is Sufism, to which the present chapter is devoted. In both cases, Sanūsī arguably reflected broader historical trends in Islamic history in the thirteenth, fourteenth, and fifteenth centuries, in particular the increased role of the study of logic in Islamic education and the spread and consolidation of Sufi practices and institutions.

Reflections on ethics by premodern Islamic philosophers tended to be rooted in Aristotelian–Neoplatonic psychology and ethics, with virtue being seen as an outcome of the immaterial, rational soul controlling the lower, appetitive, and irascible faculties. This philosophical-ethical tradition was particularly strong in the eastern Islamic world, represented by the influential Persian works of Naṣīr al-Dīn al-Ṭūsī (d.1274) and Jalāl al-Dīn al-Dawānī (d.1502).[1] As will be seen below, Sanūsī's main treatment of ethics is markedly different. It is rooted in a theoretical commitment to occasionalism, i.e., that the only power operative in the world is God's. It then draws out the practical consequences of this commitment by relying on a long-standing Sufi ascetic tradition that focuses,

Al-Sanūsī. Khaled El-Rouayheb, Oxford University Press.
 DOI: 10.1093/oso/9780197835630.003.0010

not on the nature of the soul, its division into faculties, and the cardinal virtues as golden means between extremes, but on "reliance" on God alone, "vigilance" toward one's self and its wiles, "acquiescence" with God's decrees, "sincerity" in one's servitude toward God, and "detachment" from worldly preoccupations, all virtues whose acquisition was thought to require the regular and frequent practice of supererogatory acts of devotion, including litanies, invocations, and supplications. The ethical tradition represented by Ṭūsī and Dawānī was, like its Greek forebear, urbane and "gentlemanly." It valued rational self-control, moderation, and was arguably addressed to the male elite of society, with sections on how to govern one's property, women, children, servants, slaves, and subjects.[2] Sanūsī's Sufi-inflected ethics was, by contrast, otherworldly, renunciatory, introspective, and self-abasing.

1 Occasionalist ethics

In the mid-1470s—the precise year is not known—Sanūsī wrote a commentary on a creedal poem rhyming in the letter L (*lām*) composed by his older contemporary from Algiers Aḥmad al-Zawāwī al-Jazā'irī (d.1479).[3] The two scholars might have met when Sanūsī came to Algiers in his student days and attended the lessons of the eminent Quran exegete and hadith scholar—and Jazā'irī's teacher—'Abd al-Raḥmān al-Tha'ālibī (d.1471). By the mid-1470s, Sanūsī's reputation had already been established by his major creedal works and their commentaries, and it is a testimony to this that Jazā'irī sent his creedal poem to Sanūsī in Tlemcen asking him to write a commentary on it.

Of the 355 lines of the poem, the greater part is dedicated to the Ash'arī creed, but toward the end, Jazā'irī devoted 43 lines to outlining the importance of supplementing knowledge (*'ilm*) with works (*'amal*). In his commentary, Sanūsī marked off these lines as a separate section that includes Sufi discourses (*khiṭābāt taṣawwufiyya*) devoted to the "fruits" of the preceding sections on correct creed, i.e., to purifying the self from bad characteristics so that one may ascend from the status of "believer" (*mu'min*) to that of the "pious" (*muttaqīn*) (MS 22, 462). Sanūsī's commentary on this section, coming to a little over 120 pages in the printed edition, is his most sustained treatment of what one might call "ethics."

A core principle that is adumbrated by Sanūsī at the outset is the necessity of reliance on God alone. This is explicitly linked to the occasionalism that had been expounded in the preceding creedal section. Given that nothing besides God has any causal power, it follows that humans cannot put their reliance on anything else, even their own correct creedal beliefs or their own good works. Correct belief and good works are signs of salvation; they are not causes that force God's hand when dispensing otherworldly judgment. There is no necessary connection between one's present beliefs and works and one's future beliefs and works. All one's sincere avowals and pious deeds are to no avail should God not enable these to continue into the future. Sanūsī wrote:

> There is no partner with Him, the Exalted, in any action, as you have learned previously. It follows that the believer should place no reliance on his knowledge, his works, or his teachers, even if he respects these and heeds them by way of propriety and obedience. Reliance in the heart should only be placed in the Lord, the Blessed and Exalted, for He has the power to change [one's] knowledge into ignorance, illumination into darkness, and good deeds into bad. So, the believer should never relinquish fear of and reliance on his Lord, the Blessed and Exalted, even if he should attain the highest rank of good words and deeds. Nor should he despair of the mercy and guidance of his Lord, Blessed and Exalted, even if he reaches the lowest levels of dreadful lapses . . . The one who knows from what has preceded the inability of creatures, together or individually, to bring anything into existence, whether a benefit or a harm or something else, his

heart will not be attached by way of reliance to any worldly or otherworldly creature, and he will maintain a stance of being in need—in all affairs—of his Lord Who is alone in His Dominion and Governance without any intermediary. (MS 466–7)

The principle of the inward reliance on God alone, which Sanūsī equated with the reality (*ḥaqīqa*) of true faith, should supplement the outward obedience to the religious law (*sharīʿa*). This, he wrote, is the proper understanding of the fifth verse in the opening chapter of the Quran: "You we serve [by outward obedience]; to You we turn for help [by inward reliance and orientation]" (MS 467). There are therefore two pitfalls. One is mere outward obedience and thinking oneself as "earning" salvation through one's own efforts and works. The other is to turn away from outward obedience, forgetting that God has freely instituted it as a "sign," even if not a cause, of ultimate salvation. Sanūsī wrote:

The believer must in all states combine inward reliance (*ḥaqīqa*) and outward obedience (*sharīʿa*). He [al-Jazāʾirī] has urged him [i.e., the reader] to heed the pious ulema and to tread their path by way of adhering to the outward Islamic regulations and heeding the gateways along with which God has freely chosen to create, without intermediary, what pleases Him of benefits and elimination of harm. He [al-Jazāʾirī] then urged him to trust in Him the Exalted, and to rely solely on Him, not on anything else such as good deeds or the like, by way of adhering to the reality of faith (*al-ḥaqīqa al-īmāniyya*) which calls for extending the hand of supplication to God while heeding the legal and customary gateways . . . For these gateways have no effect whatsoever, nor does anything else . . . so reliance on them to obtain any worldly or otherworldly goal is polytheism, just as denying gateways such as acts of obedience and the like which have been instituted as signs for God's benevolence . . . is heresy and defiance of the judgments of God the Exalted. (MS 466–7)

Occasionalism naturally leads to the view that all power is God's, that—as attested in numerous hadith and as has become almost proverbial in everyday Arabic speech—"there is no might and no power except through God." Humans, beset by powerlessness, should acknowledge their own utter dependency on the might and power of God. This entails never feeling secure and self-sufficient. One's sense of utter need for God should be the same—Sanūsī noted—regardless of whether one's personal history has hitherto been one of sin and unbelief or of righteousness and belief.

There is no explicit organizing principle in the relevant section of Jazā'irī's poem and Sanūsī's commentary, though there is a general progression from a discussion of (i) vigilance toward the self, to (ii) the vices that vigilance should combat, to (iii) the virtues that should be cultivated.

Vigilance

One corollary of the basic stance of utter dependence on God is to assume a self-denying attitude, counteracting the self's experienced tendency toward pride and willfulness. In accordance with a long-standing Islamic ascetic and Sufi tradition, Sanūsī enjoined the believer to exercise continuous vigilance (*murāqaba*) toward the self, to treat it as one would treat a warring infidel (*kāfir ḥarbī*). Without such vigilance, both spiritual experience and revelation tell us the self will tend to hinder a person's outward and inward conformity to religious stipulations. It will initially encourage lethargy and indolence preventing the fulfillment of outward duties. If one overcomes this initial resistance and forces the self to comply, it will tend to sully the pure intentions that should accompany outward obedience. Even if that obstacle is also overcome and one obeys the law with proper intention, the self will try to insinuate that the obedience is testimony to one's character, will, and effort, thus promoting smugness. Sanūsī wrote:

> There is no hiding the fact that for the one whose focus is on doing many good deeds and who embarks on this without knowing the wiles of the self and without purifying it of its faults, the harm of the acts will outweigh the benefit. Indeed, the deeds will only increase the corruption and shortcoming. As for the person who first endeavors to know the faults and imperfections of the self, both subtle and overt, and, knowing these, then strives to fight it, while invoking God's help and with a view to obey His command, to erase the blameworthy characteristics, and to replace them with praiseworthy, upright characteristics . . . this is the one who is prudent and proceeds with matters via the proper gateway. (MS 480)

Sanūsī quoted extensively from earlier Sufi manuals, particularly the *Epistle* of al-Qushayrī (d.1072) and *The Trail of Worshippers* widely attributed to al-Ghazālī (d.1111) in medieval times but actually by the twelfth-century Moroccan mystic Abū l-Ḥasan al-Musaffir, to underline the importance of waging war against the self and taming it through constant vigilance and habitually acting in ways that defy its inclinations and wants.[4]

Vices

Obstacles toward reliance on God include arrogance (*kibr*) and vanity (*ʿujb*). The former is defined as seeing oneself superior to others. It is at the root of numerous further vices: being prone to anger and taking offense, being jealous of others, loving honor and fame, being impervious to advice, and expecting special treatment from one's fellows. Its remedies are of various kinds: one might remind oneself of one's origin in a vile blood clot or of God's punishment for arrogance. One might also keep in mind that all creatures are as one, none of them having any intrinsic merit over any other creature, and that whatever merit one enjoys is freely bestowed by God. Sanūsī wrote:

> Contingent entities are all equal in the sense that any accident that is admitted by the lower is admitted by the higher, and there is no precedence for one over the other with respect to its self; rather our Lord the Exalted gives preference to whatever He chooses in any respect He chooses, without anything being more deserving of the preference. (MS 495)

Sanūsī went on to give examples that suggest he was primarily thinking of ranks among individuals. How many believers, he asked, have ended up unbelievers and how many unbelievers have ended up being believers? How many poor people have ended up rich and how many rich have ended up poor? But his point extends to differences between species: Humans have not been given a higher rank than, say, insects because of any intrinsic feature. Rather, they have freely been given precedence by God without any intrinsic merit.

At this stage, Sanūsī anticipated an objection. It is a religiously established virtue to thank God for His grace and blessing (*ni'ma*). Does this not contradict the injunction not to see oneself as superior even to "infidels, dogs, and excrement"? Sanūsī responded that it is precisely the modest person who—seeing God's blessings as unearned—exhibits the virtue of being grateful to God, not those who see their precedence in belief, knowledge, or virtue as somehow earned by their own efforts and exertions. He wrote:

> The arrogant person, because he imagines that there is perfection and superiority in himself, will attribute blessings to that perfection that he imagines is in his self, and deems himself deserving because of it. For example, he will see in himself more readiness in understanding a science and will attribute this to

> what he imagines is his intelligence, or diligence in studying, or reading through the night, or traveling to meet teachers, and the like, as can be seen often in the case of the self-conceited idiots who pursue studies. (MS 496)

By contrast, Sanūsī continued:

> The modest person does not see in himself any essential superiority over anything, even inanimate objects or excrement and the like, given that all contingents are as one with respect to the reach of God's Power and Will. If he sees any blessing by which God favors him over other contingents, such as life, hearing, sight, knowledge, faith and the like, he knows that this is purely due to God's creation, generosity, and favor, and that he does not deserve any of this whatsoever . . . And he knows that there are no contingent beings that are baser than he is, such that he is deserving of the favors whereas they are not. (MS 496)

The view that humans are not inherently superior in value to brute animals and inanimate objects is a radical rejection of the idea, going back to Neoplatonism, of a "great chain of being," an objective scale of perfection in which humans, by virtue of their rationality and immaterial souls, rank higher than, for example, insects but lower than God and perhaps also lower than angels.[5] God's giving a special status to humans is, from this perspective, simply a recognition of humans' objectively higher rank. On this view, it is impossible that God should have given a higher status to insects, for example, than to rational humans.

Within the Islamic tradition, there were Neoplatonic strands that accepted the idea of such a scale of nature. These could—and did—invoke passages from the Quran and hadith, for example, the Quranic passage that says that God breathed His spirit (*rūḥ*) into Adam, or the hadith saying that God created Adam in His image.[6]

Such passages could suggest that humans are inherently superior to other animals by virtue of possessing a divine-like element—reason or an immaterial soul—that is essential to them and makes them objectively closer to divine perfection than brute animals, insects, or inanimate matter.

The Neoplatonic position just sketched was unacceptable to Ashʿarī theologians who, as discussed in Chapter 9, held that there are no intrinsic values inhering in created substances prior to and apart from God's will and command. It is instructive to note how the North African Ashʿarī tradition in which Sanūsī was trained dealt with Quranic passages and hadith reports that might lend support to the view of the inherent superiority of humans. In the Quran-exegesis of the aforementioned ʿAbd al-Raḥmān al-Thaʿālibī, with whom Sanūsī studied in Algiers, the statement that God breathed His spirit into Adam is interpreted as follows: The spirit that was breathed into Adam is God's in the sense that God created it; it is God's spirit in the sense that the world is God's world, or a house can be said to be the builder's house. It is not the case that God granted something of Himself to Adam.[7] As for the hadith stating that God created Adam in His image, the Tunisian scholar Muḥammad al-Ubbī (d.1427), whose commentary on the hadith collection of Muslim ibn al-Ḥajjāj was abridged by Sanūsī, explained at length that God has no image (*ṣūra*), so the meaning would have to be either that God created Adam in Adam's image, or that God created Adam in the image that God freely decided should be considered special, so that "the image of God" is the image that God has freely chosen to be special, just as "the House of God" (the Ka'ba in Mecca) is not literally God's abode but the house that God has freely chosen to occupy a crucial ritual role.[8] In both cases, the suggestion that humans inherently possess divine-like attributes is firmly rejected. Any distinction of value or rank within the created world is purely the effect of God's autonomous and free Will, not a reflection of inherent qualities possessed by certain individuals or species.

The character-trait of "vanity" (*'ujb*) was understood by Sanūsī in the related but somewhat narrower sense of emphasizing in speech or thought the importance of one's acts of obedience. The proper attitude is rather to obey God without reminding oneself or others of the fact that one obeys. People's orientation should be toward the One who is obeyed, not toward enumerating and stressing their own acts of obedience.

A related negative character-trait is covetousness (*ṭama'*). Sanūsī made the surprising claim that covetousness is caused by the self habitually attributing effects to customary causes. In light of previous discussions of occasionalism, it is not surprising that Sanūsī should have impressed on the reader that everyday relations of "cause" and "effect" are really just observable but non-necessary regularities and that God is the only real cause. What is surprising is that he should have written that:

> The cause (*sabab*) from which covetousness is generated (*yatawallad minhu l-ṭama'*) is the self's absorption in attributing effects to customary causes (*istighrāq al-nafs fī isnād al-āthār li-l-asbāb al-'ādiyya*). (MS 517)

It seems at first sight as if Sanūsī was unwittingly doing precisely what he was warning against, namely attributing an effect (covetousness) to a non-divine cause (belief in secondary causation). But on a more charitable reading, his point was that there is a regular and observable conjunction between belief in secondary causation and covetousness, even though strictly speaking there is no necessary connection. This is not inconsistent with occasionalism. Occasionalism does not enjoin people to ignore correlations between phenomena, nor does it deny that it is prudent to take such correlations into account in their everyday practical life. It just insists that such correlations are neither necessary nor autonomous but betray the omnipresence of God's Will and Power.

Freeing oneself from "the worship of customary causes" (*'ubūdiyyat al-asbāb*) will counteract not just covetousness but also the vices of avarice and cowardice. Sanūsī wrote:

> The one who leaves off covetousness by rejecting customary causes and resorts to his Lord, and finds sufficiency in Him from anything else, will find it easy to be generous with money, for it is one of the customary causes that his heart has rejected . . . Likewise, it will be easy for him to sacrifice himself and divest himself of fear when it comes to the rights of God, for he will not be covetous of obtaining life, endurance, or safety from any cause other than his Lord the Exalted and Majestic. (MS 518–9)

Of the bodily ("outer") vices, Sanūsī gave special attention to vices of the tongue, citing well-known hadith and reports from venerable Sufis about the dangers of not reining in one's speech, and how easy it is to say things that lead to otherworldly punishment, either for impious remarks or for indulging in slander (*ghība*) and defamation (*namīma*). People who have difficulty harnessing their tongues should seek solitude (*'uzla*). However, this should only be sought for the proper motive. Avoiding the company of others should not be because one thinks them beneath oneself, for that is arrogance. Nor should it be a way of ensuring that others do not tire of one's company and continue to value it, for this is seeking worldly eminence. Another pitfall is that someone who leads a reclusive life is likely to become esteemed by contemporaries, which again may sully the motives for seeking solitude. If one is aware that the solitude is leading to praise and esteem from one's fellows, then it is better to seek company to a modest extent. The proper motive for solitude should be self-abnegation and considering oneself unworthy of the company of others. In Sanūsī's words, "It is incumbent to see oneself as a snake, a ferocious dog, or an impurity that for shame is to be avoided and whose evils other Muslims are being spared." (MS 532)

Virtues

In a long-standing Sufi tradition, Jazā'irī and Sanūsī emphasized the importance of acquiescence (*riḍá*) with God's decrees and patience (*ṣabr*) in the face of adversity. Sanūsī had no difficulty finding numerous quotes from earlier Sufi authorities in praise of these two traits. What is distinctive about Sanūsī's discussion is his linking explicitly such acknowledged Sufi virtues with Ashʿarī doctrine. Of acquiescence he wrote:

> There is no doubt that this station (*maqām*) is easy for the one who has verified from the previous discussion of the creed that God is not obliged by reason, law, or convention to do or not do anything that is contingent, nor heed what is good or best for any of His creatures. Rather, any favor (*niʿma*) from Him is pure grace (*faḍl*) and any tribulation (*naqma*) from Him is right, good, and just . . . He [i.e., the human] does not deserve anything by way of reward or recompense. (MS 539)

Another acknowledged Sufi virtue is sincerity (*ikhlāṣ*), which Sanūsī—following earlier Sufi authorities such as Qushayrī —defined as being singularly oriented toward God in one's obedience or purifying one's actions from any consideration of creatures. It is closely related to the virtues of asceticism (*zuhd*), i.e., turning away from the world. This involves abandoning worldly matters that cloud one's singular focus on the devotional life. As a much-cited Quranic passage says, "I created jinn and humans only so that they might serve Me. I do not desire any sustenance from them, nor do I ask that they should feed Me. God is the One who gives sustenance, the Possessor of strength, the Firm" (Q 51:56–58). In other words, humans' purpose in life is to serve God, and in doing so they must regard God as their Sustainer (MS 552).

The upshot, Sanūsī wrote, is that one should be content with a modest living, rather than striving for excess that brings worldly anxiety and disappointment and distracts from the all-important devotions incumbent on us in this fleeting life. One's stance toward the world should, therefore, be one of detachment (*tajarrud*) to the extent possible. In Sufi literature, this "detachment" was often said to be from *asbāb*, a term that often means "causes" but in this context is intended in the related sense of "livelihood." Sanūsī was aware that not all would be able to detach themselves fully in that sense. Indeed, he criticized those Sufis who were only able to devote themselves entirely to the religious life by pressuring simple folk for donations or relying on rulers' handouts that might come from illegitimate sources. He wrote:

> The well-directed person is not the one who just detaches himself for devotions, leaves the world and earning a living, and then has his sustenance come to him in an unlawful way, such as overawing others or becoming attached to unjust rulers. Such evils can be seen among those who are detached in our times, especially in rural areas, to such an extent that they have acquired large amounts of money, luxurious clothing, numerous majestic mounts, high-status wives, and resplendent concubines. They start competing with the people of the world for worldly benefits, purely on the basis of false claims, imaginations, folly, and outright ignorance.[9]

It is proper for those who have to earn an honest living—surely the majority—to do so, while avoiding greed (*ḥirṣ*) and yearning (*lahf*) and while considering the source of income a generosity from God rather than an independent mean on which reliance is placed. If the income is tainted in any way, then one should abandon it for another, and if no legitimate source offers itself, one should simply abandon them all and place reliance on God. One should not bemoan one's plight but instead thank God that one has been put in a position of radical "detachment" (MS 553).

Sanūsī may himself have been one of those who had the independent means—possibly inherited income—to live a life of "detachment." As mentioned in Chapter 2, he did not earn his living as a teacher at an endowed madrasa, nor does he seem to have held any kind of judicial position. Mallālī's hagiography reproduces a letter by Sanūsī to the Zayyanid ruler of Tlemcen Abū ʿAbdallah Muḥammad IV (r.1468–1504) in which Sanūsī politely but firmly rejects the ruler's repeated offers of a stipend from a charitable endowment linked to a madrasa. He wrote, among other things:

> May the Commander of the Faithful not worry about us, and may he not strive to grant us anything relating to this-worldly sustenance, for God has granted us sufficiency from this, and the one who is not content with a little of this world will not be satisfied with a lot . . . There is no need for us to take anything, even if it is from a legitimate source, such as a madrasa or the state treasury. If anything were sent to us from such a source, we would not accept it, nor would we feel assured that it is for our otherworldly good. And any income that is not for otherworldly benefit is a temptation and a major trial. Everyone in this world is a passing stranger who has but an instant before the hereafter. (MQ 184)

Love

The overall stress in Jazāʾirī's poem and Sanūsī's commentary is clearly not on what is sometimes referred to as "love mysticism." There is, to be sure, a discussion toward the end of the work of the appropriateness of "love" (*maḥabba*) for God and His Prophet. Sanūsī introduced the theme, by the way, while explicating Jazāʾirī's line enjoining the seeker to invoke God and utter blessings on the

Prophet. Sanūsī linked this injunction to the love for God and His Prophet that entails wishing to repeat the names of these beloveds on a regular basis. He wrote:

> True faith (*al-īmān al-ḥaqīqī*) with certainty engenders in the core of the heart a great love for God the Generous . . . And the love for Him necessitates finding sweet the frequency of invoking Him . . . For all who love something mention that thing frequently. (MS 565)

Love of God, in turn, implies loving His prophet, obeying him, praying for him, and invoking his name.

It is worth asking if the connection between "true faith" and the heart's love for God requires the occasionalist parsing that God customarily creates love for God in conjunction with "true faith." Sanūsī did not address this point. Ashʿarī occasionalists could appeal to regular conjunction, but as has been shown in previous chapters, they also acknowledged rational-logical necessary connections, for example, that an attribute necessarily exists in a substance; that a body necessarily occupies space; and that a voluntary agent is necessarily alive. These kinds of truths would not receive an occasionalist parsing, i.e., it is not simply that God habitually creates an attribute along with its existence in a substance, or a body along with occupying space; or a voluntary agent along with life.[10] Ashʿarīs thus recognized a distinction between what, since Kant, are often called truths known *a priori*, often by virtue of the mere meaning of words (e.g., attributes exist in substances; bodies occupy space; voluntary agents are alive) and truths that are only known to be true *a posteriori*—through observation, experience, or revelation—and that might strictly be otherwise (fire burns; sharp metal edges cut; aspirin alleviates headaches). It is only the later kind that would receive an occasionalist parsing in terms of God's custom. So, it is possible that Sanūsī considered the connection between "true faith" and love for God, or between love for God and finding the invocation of God's name sweet, to be "analytic" necessary truths that follow from the very definition of words such as "true faith" and "love."

Ash'arī Sufism

Despite this brief discussion of love, the emphasis in the work is mostly on self-abnegation: vigilance, fighting the self and its wiles, guarding against vanity, smugness, and covetousness, while emphasizing the contrasting virtues of patience, acquiescence, solitude, sincerity, asceticism, and detachment. Such language is, of course, generic to Sufism. But other Sufi strands tended to supplement it with the language of theophanic ecstasy, vision, and union. This language is almost entirely absent from Sanūsī's discussion. He did quote a line from the eminent mystical poet Ibn al-Fāriḍ (d.1235), who often expressed the more visionary, love-intoxicated dimensions of Sufism, but even in that case the line was introduced to buttress the importance of the seeker's meekness (*dhull*) and servility (*maskana*) when faced with the sheer Beauty and Majesty of the divine beloved (MS 504).

Another current within Sufism that is noticeably absent in Sanūsī's discussion is the speculative, panentheist mysticism of Ibn 'Arabī (d.1240) and his later commentators. The Ibn 'Arabī-inspired (or "Akbari") mystical tradition met with some lukewarmness even from within Sufi circles in the fifteenth-century Levant and North Africa. Sanūsī's influential North African Sufi contemporary Aḥmad Zarrūq (d.1493) was wary of the ideas of Ibn 'Arabī.[11] The Syrian mystic and poetess 'Ā'isha al-Bā'ūniyya (d.1517) also avoided any reference to Ibn 'Arabī and his followers in her manual of Sufism.[12] Sanūsī likewise did not refer to this panentheist and speculative tradition. He instead cited the earlier and more sober Qushayrī, as well as the works of the great Egyptian Shādhilī mystic Ibn 'Aṭā'ullāh al-Iskandarī (d.1309).[13]

The emphasis of these figures was much more ethical than metaphysical.[14] Ghazālī had written in his well-known *Deliverance from Error* that what attracted him to Sufism was its emphasis on works and self-purification, whereas the other major intellectual currents of his time: Aristotelian–Neoplatonic philosophy, Isma'ili Shi'i esotericism, and kalam theology were all theoretical in orientation and compatible with vanity, worldliness, and egotism.[15] As noted by the North African scholar Ibn Khaldūn (d.1406), Sufism at the hands of later speculative-panentheist thinkers became an elaborate theory with distinct metaphysical and epistemological doctrines that one could study and master like any other science (while remaining vain, worldly, and egotistical).[16] These doctrines were often distinct from—and in competition with—Ash'arism, as can be seen in the metaphysical writings of Sanūsī's Persian contemporary Jāmī (d.1492), for whom Ibn 'Arabī-inspired, panentheist Sufism offered a third perspective, distinct from both Aristotelian–Neoplatonic philosophy and kalam theology, on issues such as God's existence, the divine attributes, the relation of essence and existence, the nature of the soul, universals, free will, miracles, the problem of evil, and eschatology.[17] It is important to recognize that there were still other currents of Sufism in later centuries that were more ascetic and practical in orientation, and that saw themselves as drawing out the practical-ethical consequences of Ash'arism rather than providing a theoretical alternative to it.[18]

2 Occasionalism and the benefits of litanies and invocations

As mentioned in Chapter 1, Sanūsī's initiation into Sufism was at the hands of Ibrāhīm al-Tāzī (d.1462) in the town of Oran near Tlemcen. Mallālī's hagiography of Sanūsī gives a description of the initiation, which involved investiture with a robe (*khirqa*), a handshake (*muṣāfaḥa*), an embrace (*mushābaka*), sharing water and dates (*ḍiyāfa*), relaying a particular hadith (*ḥadīth al-raḥma*), having a prayer bead in hand (*subḥa*), and imparting a particular invocation (*talqīn al-dhikr*) (MQ 76–86). In each case, the ritual invoked a tradition going back to venerable Islamic figures and in some cases to the Prophet himself. For example, Tāzī said to Sanūsī: I shake your hand, just like my master X shook my hand, and his master Y shook his hand, and so on. As is clear from these chains, Tāzī's spiritual lineage went back to the widely revered Abū Madyan (d.1198) whose tomb outside Tlemcen had spurred the development of the suburb of 'Ubbād.[19] It is worth noting that the lineage did not go through Abū l-Ḥasan al-Shādhilī (d.1258), the founder of the Shādhilī order that was gaining increased popularity in the Maghreb in the fifteenth century with the activities of Aḥmad al-Jazūlī (d.1465) and Aḥmad Zarrūq (d.1493).[20] Sanūsī was thus initiated into Sufism, but not into any of the major, transregional orders that had consolidated in the thirteenth and fourteenth centuries.

Supererogatory supplications (*ad'iya*), invocations (*adhkār*), litanies (*awrād*), and incantations (*aḥzāb*) played an important part in Maghrebi Sufism and popular culture. The most widely circulated writings by al-Shādhilī were collections of incantations, especially the one known as *The Incantation of the Sea*.[21] The most widely circulating work by al-Jazūlī was an extensive collection of supplications for the Prophet known as *The Indications of Blessings*.[22] The Andalusian scholar Muḥammad al-Sāḥilī al-Mālaqī (d.1353) composed a work entitled *The Aim of the Seeker*, cited by Sanūsī, that discussed the supererogatory invocations appropriate to the various stations of the mystic path, the proper manner of saying them, and their benefits.[23]

When Tāzī initiated Sanūsī, he charged him with regular repetition of the phrase "There is no god but Allah," with saying one hundred times every morning, "God be praised and thanked! God the Great be praised! I seek God's forgiveness," and with reciting four short chapters of the Quran every day and every night (MQ 83).

Sanūsī would presumably have engaged in such supererogatory litanies and recitations for the rest of his life. In turn, he regularly advised his students and companions to utter various other litanies and supplications or recite certain chapters or verses of the Quran on various occasions and for various purposes. Mallālī devoted a short chapter of his hagiography to the litanies that Sanūsī wrote out for his acquaintances (MQ 535–51). Sanūsī advised that, after the dawn prayer, one should repeat three short litanies, each three times. This, he mentioned, was said to be a customary cause (*sabab*) for being in a good state in the afterlife (*ḥusn al-khātima*). Mallālī also quoted Sanūsī as relaying the view that the one who recites Chapter 97 of the Quran after the morning prayer, copies it out, washes off the ink, and then drinks the inky water, will be free from abdominal pains, and if one were to sprinkle this water over the prayer rug then the prayer will be answered. The one who recites the chapter a thousand times will see God in paradise. The one who recites it twenty-one times between noon and the noon prayer will see the Prophet in his or her dreams before death (MQ 545).

All this brings back the issue of occasionalism. Was Sanūsī betraying his professed occasionalism by setting up certain ritual utterances as having salvific efficacy or bringing about dreams of the Prophet? Such an interpretation would, I think, be facile. As has been mentioned in previous sections and chapters, Sanūsī's occasionalism did not commit him to denying observable regularities between phenomena or the prudence of taking these into account in everyday life. It is uncharitable to suppose that occasionalists, whether Islamic, Cartesian, or Reformed Protestant, would say that one should not hold water over a fire to boil it and not use a knife when slaughtering a goat. As mentioned in Chapter 8, Sanūsī did not deny that it is God's custom to bring about a cure from a bodily ailment when one takes a certain medicine. Analogously, he need not have denied that it is God's custom to create bodily or spiritual health when one utters certain litanies or supplications or recites specific passages from the Quran or receives the blessings of a saint.

A term that occurs regularly in Mallālī's chapter is *mujarrab*, i.e., that a certain supplication, litany, invocation, or recitation has been "tried and tested," just as "experience" (*tajriba*)—from the same Arabic root *jrb*—was widely accepted as a fundamental source of natural-scientific and occult knowledge.[24]

As pointed out by Daniel Lav, there is a long tradition of Ash'arīs condoning popular practices such as saint- and shrine veneration, despite what one might have expected from their strict occasionalism, just as there is a long (and in modern times resurgent) tradition of affirming secondary causality and yet condemning saint- and shrine veneration as "polytheism" (*shirk*).[25] Sanūsī—and Ash'aris more generally—would have rejected the idea that visiting a saint or shrine is inherently more polytheistic than seeking out a teacher or a doctor. The saint, the shrine, the teacher, and the medicine are all causally inert, though this does not preclude that there are observable regularities in God's creation that one should heed when pursuing spiritual guidance, learning, and health.

In his most widely studied work, The *Short Creed* and its *Commentary*, Sanūsī included a final section, briefly touched upon in Chapter 4, in which he tried to show that the creedal principles he had outlined could be summed up in the Islamic "two professions": "There is no god but Allah, and Muhammad is Allah's Messenger." He then went on to discuss the benefits and proprieties of repeating especially the first profession: "There is no god but Allah" (*lā ilāha illā llāh*). Citing numerous hadith reports that were considered canonical in Sunnism, he emphasized the importance of repeating the sentence, that it is the most important invocation, that in the final judgment it will outweigh sins one has committed, that the one who utters it sincerely will be spared the terrors of hell, and that it is the key to paradise. Citing somewhat less canonical reports that were nevertheless popular in Sufi circles, he wrote that the one who says it 70,000 times will be spared hellfire, that many early saints would say it 70,000 times *a day*, and that even those who had to earn a living would still manage to say it 12,000 times a day (S 306–17).

Relying on Sufi works, such as the aforementioned *The Aim of the Seeker* by the fourteenth-century Andalusian scholar Muḥammad al-Sāḥilī al-Mālaqī, Sanūsī then outlined the proper manner of uttering "There is no god but Allah" (S 318–28). One should be ritually pure and wear clean clothes when engaged in the invocation, choose a pure spot such as the one usually used for prayer at home, be alone, choose an auspicious time such as between daybreak and morning or just before sunset, and face the Ka'ba. The intention throughout should be to obey the commands of God. One ought to begin by seeking forgiveness and praying for the Prophet and reciting some short chapters of the Quran. Any thought of created entities should be cast out of mind. The point of the profession is precisely that all creatures are as naught, and that, as Sanūsī wrote:

> Benefits and pleasures, or harm and pain, that exist along with some of these creatures—such as food, drink, water, clothes, women, children, money, fire, weapons, lions, snakes, darkness, light, paradise, and hell—is not from these at all, and reliance should not be placed on them or other [created] things. Giving consideration to such things is a great darkness and blindness . . . One should go out of the way to clear the mind, so that the heart is ready for the emanations of pure and brilliant light. (S 324–5)

One should then supplement the first profession with the second, "Muhammad is His messenger."

The benefits of this regular invocation of the profession, Sanūsī noted, are many, and can be divided into two main kinds: (i) pious characteristics and (ii) supernatural powers. The former includes such traits as asceticism, reliance on God, otherworldliness, thankfulness, magnanimity, and a sense of sufficiency with respect to created things. The latter kind includes being able to make do with unusually little food and being able to tell at a glance if food is ritually lawful or somehow tainted. Sanūsī added a story of a saint whose relatives would find money under his prayer mat after he performed his invocations and ritual prayers. However, he pointed out that one should not have such things in mind when engaged in invocations but rather remain entirely focused on pleasing one's Lord. He wrote:

> The relevant reports of supernatural results are too many to recount, but the believer should not intend these in any of his devotions, for otherwise he will fall victim to hidden polytheism and will be deluded—God forbid!—for these are the things from which one should clear one's thoughts when uttering the first profession. One should disregard these things entirely and intend to please one's Lord. (S 333)

3 *The Tried and Tested Means*

Sufi practices that were centered around supererogatory prayers, supplications, and litanies could easily become a full-fledged system of thaumaturgy. It is well attested that in the medieval Maghreb, especially in more rural or unlearned circles, Sufism became intertwined with popular religious practices often loosely called "maraboutism."[26] There must have been a thin line between, on the one hand, asking a saintly person for invocations (*duʿāʾ*) or spiritually uplifting litanies and, on the other hand, treating the saint as a shaman to whom one turns to counteract a magic spell, ensure a male child, or cure an illness. That line has clearly been crossed in the work that in later centuries circulated under the title *The Tried and Tested Means* and was attributed to Sanūsī.[27] There are some continuities between this work and the mentioned chapter of Mallālī's hagiography, and there are even a handful of instances of textual overlap.[28] However, there is a conspicuous difference of emphasis. The chapter in Mallālī's hagiography contains twenty-three reports of litanies and supplications that were purportedly copied from Sanūsī's papers. In the majority of cases (little over a half), the benefits are stated to be otherworldly (good state in the afterlife, seeing the Prophet in dreams, seeing one's status in paradise) or very general (preservation from evil, having prayers answered, obtaining relief when afflicted). In a little less than a third of the cases, the benefit is stated to be worldly but general, for example, one will be protected from enemies, one will not feel in need of others, one's children will turn out as one wishes, etc. In a handful of cases, no explicit benefit is mentioned at all. And in one or two cases only, the benefit is both worldly and very specific: Mallālī quoted Sanūsī as stating that a man who wishes to have a male son should put his hand on the stomach of his wife shortly after it has become clear that she has conceived and say, "O God, grant me from this pregnancy a male child and I will call him Ahmad by way of seeking blessing from Your prophet Muhammad and keeping his name alive." (The Arabic names "Muhammad" and "Ahmad" come from the same root and are often treated as variants of the same name.) The following sentence, which may be a continuation of the quote from Sanūsī or alternatively an interpolation from Mallālī, says that one might also, for the same purpose, visit the tomb of a certain saint called al-Sabtī (MQ 547).

By contrast, *The Tried and Tested Means* is overwhelmingly oriented toward specific mundane aspirations: how to protect oneself against enemies, see distant friends and ask them questions in dreams, cure a headache or sciatica, ensure safety while traveling, protect oneself against thieves and wolves, get rid of fleas, lice, ants, snakes, mice, and scorpions, find out who stole some bread, overcome passionate infatuation, treat sexual dysfunction, make an insufferable guest leave, ease childbirth, get male children, gain favor at court, counteract magic spells, take revenge on the unjust, find a runaway slave, etc. Around two-thirds of the "tested means" are explicitly for such very specific worldly goals.[29] Besides the formulaic invocations and Quranic passages that also appear in Mallālī's chapter, *The Tried and Tested Means* also regularly advises the use of magical combinations of detached letters to obtain a desired outcome.[30] The work has little to do with Sufi ethics, i.e., with the virtues of patience, acquiescence, and complete reliance on God discussed in the previous section. It has—I think justifiably—been placed in an Islamic tradition of "religious magic" and lettrism.[31]

As mentioned in previous chapters, there are good reasons to doubt the attribution of the work to Sanūsī. Neither Mallālī nor other premodern biographers mention it when listing Sanūsī's writings. Furthermore, as Sabine Dorpmüller has shown, manuscripts of the work are late (seventeenth century or later), and there are considerable variations among extant copies, with some manuscripts including additions not attested in others.[32] Such a plasticity of textual transmission does not accord with the transmission of Sanūsī's other works. It is also striking that many passages are written in a conspicuously less learned and classical register of Arabic than works that are indisputably by Sanūsī.

Nevertheless, *The Tried and Tested Means* may well have had its origins in the litanies, invocations, and supplications that Sanūsī wrote at the request of his contemporaries. Given that he was widely revered as a saint in his lifetime, Sanūsī would have been approached by contemporaries for litanies, invocations, and supplications for all sorts of purposes, ranging from a general hope for "blessing" (*baraka*) to very specific religious or mundane goals. It is clear that Mallālī had access to Sanūsī's written responses to such requests, including one from the Zayyanid ruler Abū ʿAbdallāh Muḥammad IV (MQ 539). These writings might have been selectively gathered after Sanūsī's death and then ongoingly supplemented by later scholars, students, or scribes, in the process obtaining a much more worldly and pragmatic orientation.

The mere fact that such a work circulated in later centuries with an attribution to Sanūsī shows that no inconsistency was perceived between Ashʿarism and this kind of thaumaturgy. Indeed, I have argued that there is no strict, logical inconsistency. One might claim that there are "experienced" regular correlations between specific invocations, supplications, and litanies and specific worldly and otherworldly phenomena. At the same time, to say that there is no logical inconsistency is not to say that there is an implication, i.e., that Ashʿarism entails such beliefs. The *Tried and Tested Means* is best seen as representing an independent and powerful strand of premodern North African culture. Ashʿarīs could, logically, have remained aloof from this strand. But they need not have done so, and indeed many—and not just Sanūsī—participated in it actively.

In premodern Maghrebi classifications of the sciences, disciplines such as lettrism, magic squares, astrology, and alchemy were regularly categorized as parts of "natural science" or "natural philosophy."[33] Ashʿarism historically made its peace with such sciences, despite their use of the language of causes and effect, merely insisting that the "causation" reduces to experienced, regular conjunction rather than causal powers and natural necessity. Modern scholars who seek to explain the relative underdevelopment of natural science in the premodern Islamic world—at least compared to early modern Europe—will have to look to other factors than Ashʿarism.

11
Sanūsī's Legacy

When Sanūsī died in 1490, he was already widely revered in Tlemcen and the surrounding region as a saint. The Andalusian scholar al-Balawī, whose description of Sanūsī's last days and funeral were cited at the beginning of Chapter 2, described Sanūsī as a "saint" (*walī*), a term he did not use of any of the other eminent scholars of Tlemcen whose classes he attended and whose certificates he sought. A Moroccan scholar writing in the mid-sixteenth century looked back at the rivalry that had obtained between Sanūsī and Ibn Zakrī. He noted that people in his time esteemed Ibn Zakrī for the breadth of his knowledge, his wide-ranging reputation among peers, and the respect accorded to him by rulers, whereas they esteemed Sanūsī for his verification (*taḥqīq*), saintliness (*wilāya*), asceticism (*zuhd*), and otherworldliness (*tajarrud*).[1] The contrast was thus drawn clearly. On the one hand was Ibn Zakrī, the star pupil of the most eminent teachers of Tlemcen of the previous generation, who became Mufti of the city in his early forties and enjoyed an intimate relationship thereafter with the Zayyanid rulers. On the other hand was Sanūsī, who held no official position, lived a retiring life, eschewed close relations with the state, and rejected gifts from the rulers. As mentioned in the previous chapter, Mallālī's hagiography reproduces a letter by Sanūsī to the Zayyanid ruler of Tlemcen Abū ʿAbdallah Muḥammad IV (r.1468–1504) in which Sanūsī politely but firmly rejected the ruler's repeated offers of a stipend from a charitable endowment linked to a madrasa. Sanūsī thus lived up to the prevalent cultural script for medieval Islamic saintliness, whereas Ibn Zakrī did not. Saints were expected to refuse state positions,

Al-Sanūsī. Khaled El-Rouayheb, Oxford University Press.
 DOI: 10.1093/oso/9780197835630.003.0011

reject efforts by the temporal ruler to draw them to court life, and refuse money from state officials outright or at least distribute all such money immediately to the deserving poor. Ibn Zakrī dedicated his commentary on the *Creed* of the Kurdish-born, Cairene scholar Ibn al-Ḥājib (d.1249) to the ruler of Tlemcen Abū ʿAbbās Aḥmad I (r.1431–1462).[2] Sanūsī, by contrast, did not dedicate any work to a temporal ruler. And it seems the moral distance he maintained to the political authorities only cemented his saintly reputation among admirers, including the rulers themselves who, of course, shared the broader cultural expectations of saintliness in their time. According to Mallālī, Abū ʿAbdallah Muḥammad IV, after his repeated attempts at giving Sanūsī a stipend were rebuffed, sent a letter to Sanūsī asking for some written supplications that the Zayyanid ruler could use to "fortify himself against all evils," which Sanūsī duly did.[3] The Sultan later also attended Sanūsī's funeral.

Sanūsī was not, however, merely a saint in the eyes of his contemporaries and posterity. He was also an eminent scholar of exoteric disciplines such as rational theology and logic, whose writings in these fields were studied, commented upon, glossed, versified, translated, paraphrased, and emulated in later centuries. He was, in the words of the aforementioned sixteenth-century scholar, a "verifier": someone who did not just transmit and explicate received doctrine but also uncovered and assessed their evidential grounds. Though Sanūsī's saintly status must have facilitated the reception of his works, this is hardly the whole story. No other scholar in his time and region wrote so extensively on rational theology and logic. His earliest work on theology—the *Long Creed* and its Commentary—was an advanced, tightly argued, and independent-minded work, and it must have been written before Sanūsī had much of a reputation either as a saint or scholar. His interest in logic was unrivalled in his region in his lifetime, and—as I have tried to show in Chapter 5—his contributions to the field cannot reasonably be written off as "popularizations" or "vulgarizations." There is, in short, no reason to believe that his standing as a theologian and logician was dependent on his prior standing as a saint. Rather, it seems that his reputation as a scholar and as a saint mutually reinforced each other, both for contemporaries and for posterity.

1 The spread of Sanūsī's influence

In premodern Islamic scholarly culture, written works on scholastic disciplines such as rational theology and logic were not just supposed to be copied and read in private. Medieval manuals on the acquisition of knowledge repeatedly warned against taking knowledge from books rather than "from the mouths of men."[4] The very fact that the point was stressed suggests that the norm was not always upheld in practice, but it remained the norm nonetheless. Scholars routinely recorded the names of the scholars with whom they had studied a particular work, then those with whom their teachers had studied the work, and so on, all the way back to the author. The practice allows us to trace the diffusion of Sanūsī's works in later times. In what follows, I try to give the reader a sense of this diffusion in Islamic Africa. The account is, it should be emphasized, a preliminary sketch. An entire monograph could be written on the topic, and bio-bibliographic evidence should ideally be supplemented with a careful study of extant manuscripts.

Tlemcen, Fes, Marrakesh, Algiers

When Sanūsī died, his students continued to teach his works in Tlemcen. Two figures in particular seem to have been among his closest and oldest students: Muḥammad ibn Abī Madyan (d.1509) and Bū l-Qāsim al-Zawāwī (d.1516).[5] These scholars also taught some of Sanūsī's younger students, i.e., those who had started studying with Sanūsī but had not finished their education when he died. Such younger students included Mallālī, whose hagiography of Sanūsī is such an important source of biographical information and who went on to write a commentary on Sanūsī's *Short Creed*.[6] Another scholar who may have fallen under this category is Saʿīd al-Manuwī al-Kafīf (d. after 1525), a central figure in later chains of transmission of the works of Sanūsī.[7]

Two factors helped spread the influence of Sanūsī's works in the western Maghreb. First, Tlemcen was a center of learning that attracted students from the wider region. Second, the town underwent a period of turmoil in the early- to mid-sixteenth century, with Morocco, Spain, and the Ottomans in Algiers all vying for control of the city, leading numerous local scholars to emigrate and seek their fortune elsewhere. A Moroccan army briefly captured Tlemcen in 1551, but was soon driven out by the Ottomans, followed by widespread confiscation of the property of pro-Moroccan notables.[8] Several prominent scholars left Tlemcen at this point and settled in Fes or Marrakesh, bringing with them a tradition of teaching Sanūsī's works.

One can see the two factors at play in the record of studies of the Moroccan scholar Aḥmad al-Manjūr (d.1587).[9] He studied the works of Sanūsī in Fes with Muḥammad al-Yassīthanī (d.1552) who, in turn, had studied them with two teachers. The first was Yaḥyá al-Sūsī (d.1521), a scholar from southern Morocco who had studied in Tlemcen with, among others, Sanūsī's aforementioned student Muḥammad ibn Abī Madyan and then settled in Fes. The second was the aforementioned Saʿīd al-Manuwī al-Kafīf with whom Yassīthanī studied when he passed through Tlemcen on his way to and from the Hajj. Manjūr also recorded the coming to Morocco of two eminent scholars from Tlemcen in the wake of the Ottoman conquest of the city in the early 1550s: Muḥammad Shaqrūn al-Wajdījī (d.1576) and Muḥammad Ibn Jallāl (d.1574), the former becoming Mufti of Marrakesh, the latter Mufti of Fes.[10] Both were renowned for their command of rational theology and feature prominently in chains of transmission of Sanūsī's works.

Manjūr went on to teach Sanūsī's works in Fes, and he wrote glosses on Sanūsī's *Commentary on the Long Creed.* His students included the Moroccan Sultan Aḥmad al-Manṣūr (r.1578–1603). A manuscript in the Escorial library in Spain includes a number of Sanūsī's logical and theological works, written by Manjūr and including a certificate (*ijāza*) from him to the Moroccan Sultan.[11] Manjūr's star pupil, though, was the long-lived ʿĪsá al-Suktānī (d.1651) who became Mufti of Marrakesh for more than thirty years.[12] He wrote an especially well-regarded set of glosses on Sanūsī's *Commentary on the Short Creed.* Two of his students became notable contributors to the commentary literature on Sanūsī's works: the short-lived Muḥammad Ma'mūn al-Ḥafṣī al-Qayrawānī (d.1628), who wrote two commentaries, one long and one short, on the *Short Creed,* and al-Ḥasan al-Yūsī (d.1691) who wrote esteemed glosses on Sanūsī's *Commentary on the Long Creed* and on Sanūsī's *Commentary on the Epitome of Logic.*[13]

Tlemcen's reputation as a center of learning declined in the seventeenth century and came to be eclipsed by Morocco to the west and by the dramatic rise of Algiers to the north. One of the last scholars in Tlemcen who is known to have attracted students from beyond the immediate vicinity was the long-lived Saʿīd al-Maqqarī (d.ca.1617), Mufti of Tlemcen for approximately sixty years.[14] He features prominently in later chains of transmission of the works of Sanūsī. His two most well-known students made a career for themselves outside the city. The first is Saʿīd Qaddūra (d.1656) who was born in Algiers, completed his studies in Tlemcen with Saʿīd al-Maqqarī, and then returned to his hometown where he became Mufti and a renowned teacher of theology and logic, writing—among other things—a set of glosses on Sanūsī's *Commentary on the Short Creed.*[15] The other student is Maqqarī's nephew Aḥmad al-Maqqarī (d.1632) who, after completing his studies, went to Morocco for some years and then settled in Egypt where he is known to have taught Sanūsī's creedal works. He, too, wrote a set of glosses on Sanūsī's *Commentary on the Short Creed.*[16]

Cairo

In Cairo, the copying and citing of Sanūsī's works is already attested within a generation of his death. Contributory factors to this early reception must have been that Cairo was on the way for Maghrebi scholars going to—and returning from—the Hajj and that many Egyptians belonged to the Maliki school of law prevalent in the Maghreb. A commentary on *The Short Creed* was written by the Egyptian Maliki scholar ʿAlī al-Manūfī (d.1532), perhaps the earliest engagement with this Creed outside the Maghreb.[17] Aḥmad ibn Turkī (d.1590), another Egyptian Maliki scholar, abridged Sanūsī's commentary on the creedal poem of Aḥmad al-Jazāʾirī.[18] But there is also evidence of some initial resistance to Sanūsī's ideas in Egypt. It is striking that he is not mentioned in the multivolume biographical dictionary of notables of the ninth Islamic century (1397–1494 CE) by the Cairene scholar al-Sakhāwī (d.1497), though a number of other North African contemporaries are mentioned in it. Some prominent sixteenth-century Egyptian scholars such as al-Shaʿrānī (d.1565), Ibn Ḥajar al-Haytamī (d.1574), and Ibn Qāsim al-ʿAbbādī (d.1585), all of whom wrote on theological topics, ignored Sanūsī's views.[19] It is also conspicuous that Sanūsī was not included in the biographical dictionary of Sufis by the Cairene scholar al-Munāwī (d.1622), an omission made all the more conspicuous in light of the inclusion of some of his North African contemporaries such as the Egyptian scholar and judge Zakariyyā al-Anṣārī (d.1519) and the Maghrebi Sufi and scholar Aḥmad Zarrūq (d.1493).[20]

Despite such wariness, the regular and formal teaching of Sanūsī's works in Egyptian madrasas seems to have become established by the early seventeenth century, after which there is a steady stream of Egyptian commentaries and glosses on these works until the end of the nineteenth century. The aforementioned Aḥmad al-Maqqarī, who was born and educated in Tlemcen and then settled and died in Cairo, has already been mentioned, and he is known to have taught Sanūsī's theological works, writing both a set of glosses on Sanūsī's *Commentary on the Short Creed* and a popular versification of it.[21] Commentaries or glosses on the *Short Creed* were also written by Maqqarī's Egyptian contemporary Aḥmad al-Ghunaymī (d.1634) and by the slightly later scholars Dā'ūd al-Raḥmānī (d.1667) and Muḥammad al-Kharashī (d.1690).[22] The trend was consolidated by Maghrebi scholars, such as Yaḥyá al-Shāwī (d.1685), who settled in Cairo and taught Sanūsī's works there, presumably drawn by the spectacular rise to prominence of al-Azhar college in the seventeenth and eighteenth centuries, with a quarter (*riwāq*) dedicated to teachers and students from the Maghreb.[23] In the eighteenth and nineteenth centuries, the evidence is overwhelming that Sanūsī's theological and logical works dominated the teaching of these two disciplines in Cairo. One testimony to this is the sheer number of Egyptian scholars from this period who wrote commentaries or glosses on Sanūsī's works. Another is the fact that many of these works were printed, often more than once, by the early printing presses of Cairo in the second half of the nineteenth century and the first decades of the twentieth.[24] It seems that Sanūsī's works reached the Malay Archipelago via Cairo, where a number of Malay students studied in the eighteenth century before returning home, such as 'Abd al-Ṣamad al-Palimbānī (d.1788) and Muḥammad Arshad al-Banjārī (d.1812).[25]

Tunis

The difference between familiarity with the works of Sanūsī, on the one hand, and these works being regularly taught and studied, on the other, is also relevant for the case of Tunis and its environs. Though it is likely that Sanūsī's works became known in Tunis within a generation or two of his death, there is reason to believe that the tradition of regularly teaching and annotating them went back to Abū 'Abdallah Muḥammad al-Tuwātī (d.1621) who studied in Fes and later settled in Constantine (in what is now eastern Algeria) and then Beja near Tunis.[26] He was an influential teacher of theology and grammar and is known to have taught Sanūsī's creedal works. One of his students in Constantine gained notoriety for denying the faith of the imitator and for adopting an agnostic stance on whether unlearned "commoners" are true believers.[27] A regular stream of Tunisian commentaries and glosses on Sanūsī's works is in evidence starting from the second half of the seventeenth century, by for example Ibrāhīm al-Saraquṣṭī (fl.1670s), Muḥammad al-Hujayj (d.1697), and Muḥammad Zaytūna (d.1726).[28] It is noticeable that Sanūsī's *Commentary on the Middle Creed* came to be particularly popular in Tunis, and it is there that the first printed editions of that work were published, in lithograph format in 1902 and in movable type in 1909.[29] A document on the organization of studies in the Zaytuna Mosque in Tunis from 1912 confirms that Sanūsī's theological and logical works were an established part of the curriculum there.[30]

Sub-Saharan Islamic Africa

Sanūsī's influence in sub-Saharan Africa seems to have been primarily through his *Short Creed*, transmitted both in Arabic and in the orally transmitted Fulfulde adaptation known as *Kabbe*.[31] His theological works were already being studied in Timbuktu by the second half of the sixteenth century, a testimony to the strong economic and cultural ties with Tlemcen before the Moroccan conquest of Timbuktu in 1591. The well-known scholar Aḥmad Bābā al-Timbuktī (d.1627) studied Sanūsī's works when he was a student.[32] He would later abridge Mallālī's hagiography of Sanūsī and devote to Sanūsī the longest entry in his monumental biographical dictionary of later scholars belonging to the Maliki school of law.[33] He also reportedly wrote a commentary on Sanūsī's *Short Creed*, though the attribution may be due to a confusion with a commentary already written by his father and namesake Aḥmad ibn Aḥmad Aqīt al-Timbuktī (d.1583).[34] A slightly later scholar from Timbuktu, Muḥammad Baghyogho al-Wangarī (d.1655), composed a versification of the *Short Creed* that appears to have been popular in later times and elicited commentaries even beyond sub-Saharan Africa.[35]

Testifying to the widespread teaching of Sanūsī's creedal works in the Fulani and Hausa regions of present-day Niger and northern Nigeria, the famous jihadist Usman dan Fodio (d.1817) wrote numerous refutations of the idea, which he associated with the so-called *kabbenkoobe*, i.e., teachers of the aforementioned Fulfulde adaptations of Sanūsī's *Short Creed*, that anyone ignorant of the contents of that creed is not a believer.[36] Despite his misgivings about such a hardline stance on "imitation" in theology, dan Fodio's own exposition of the creed is unmistakably modelled—in terms of both organization and content—on Sanūsī's *Short Creed*, with sections on (i) what is necessary for God, (ii) what is impossible for God, (iii) what is possible for God, (iv) what is necessary for prophets, (v) what is impossible for prophets, (vi) what is possible for prophets, (vii) rational proofs for what is necessarily, impossibly, and possibly true of God, and (viii) rational proofs for what is necessarily, impossibly, and possibly true of prophets.[37]

In Bornu (present-day northeastern Nigeria and Chad) and in the more easterly regions of Kordofan and Sennar (in present-day Sudan), the study of Sanūsī's works is in evidence from the early- to mid-seventeenth century. Scholars from the region who wrote commentaries on the *Short Creed* include ʿAlī ibn Barrī al-Ṣawārdarī (d.1662 or 1663), Muḥammad al-Muḍawwī al-Miṣrī (d.1683), and Muḥammad al-Walī al-Bāghirmī (fl.1688).[38] The later Sudanese scholar Aḥmad ibn ʿĪsá al-Anṣārī (d.1826), who studied in Cairo and was later active in what was then the Funj Sultanate in northern Sudan, wrote a commentary on the *Short Creed* that has been printed several times, including in Nigeria and the Middle East.[39] It has been translated into English with the annotations of the contemporary Palestinian–Jordanian Ash'ari theologian Said Foudah.[40]

2 The limits of Sanūsī's influence

In sum, by the year 1800 the theological works of Sanūsī were regularly studied throughout Islamic Africa. In the words of the Tunisian scholar Maḥmūd Maqdīsh al-Safāqusī (d.1818):

> The people of the entire Maghreb are devoted to his works, just as they are devoted to the Book and to the Sunna of the Prophet, and these works deserve this status. This is true of all whom we have seen in Africa [i.e., Tunis and its environs] and Egypt, and whom we have heard of in the further Maghreb [i.e., Morocco and its environs]. Indeed, if someone were to claim that this is so in all the lands of Sunnism, it would not be far-fetched.[41]

Maqdīsh's extrapolation to all the lands of Sunnism is inaccurate, however. Sanūsī's works were, by the seventeenth and eighteenth centuries, also commonly studied in the Levant and the Hejaz where the scholarly influence of al-Azhar in Cairo was strong.[42] As mentioned earlier, some of Sanūsī's works, especially *The Short Creed*, also became popular in the Malay Archipelago over the course of the eighteenth and nineteenth centuries. But they never became regularly studied in the Sunni regions of the Persianate world, among Indo-Muslims, Central Asians, and Kurds. In the core, Turkish-speaking Ottoman lands, *The Short Creed* came to be known and copied toward the end of the sixteenth century; it was cited by the Bosnian scholars Ḥasan Kāfī Āḳḥiṣārī (d.1616) and Aḥmed Rūmī Āḳḥiṣārī (d.1631), and it is also mentioned approvingly in the great bibliographic compendium *Kashf al-ẓunūn* by the Ottoman scribe Kātib Çelebī (d.1657).[43] There is reason to think that the creed resonated with the concerns of the so-called

Kadizadeli movement that in the seventeenth century campaigned against what it perceived to be public immorality, Sufi excesses (such as music- and dance sessions), and popular ignorance of religious precepts, campaigns that may have dovetailed with a broader concern in the period with consolidating and disseminating the Sunni identity of the Empire.[44] Sanūsī's *Short Creed* was translated into Turkish in the seventeenth century, and extant copies of the translation tend to be bound with other works that are often seen as emblematic of the Ottoman *'ilm-i ḥāl* literature, i.e., literature aimed at imparting basic religious knowledge to the Turkish-speaking Muslims of the Empire in the sixteenth, seventeenth, and eighteenth centuries.[45]

While the Turkish translation of Sanūsī's *Short Creed* was used for a more popular, Turkish-speaking audience, there is no evidence that it came to be regularly and formally studied in the madrasas of the core parts of the Empire, and there is no Ottoman Turkish tradition of commenting or glossing it or other works by Sanūsī. This is hardly surprising given that Sanūsī's radical and uncompromising Ash'arism would not have appealed to Turkish-speaking scholars who overwhelmingly adhered to the Māturīdī school of theology. Ash'arism and Māturīdism usually acknowledged each other as orthodox, and the differences between them may not have been extensive, especially at the more basic level of the *Short Creed*, but they were substantial enough to have emerged at more advanced levels of study. Strikingly, the aforementioned bibliographer Kātib Çelebī seems to have known but not actually seen copies of Sanūsī's longer theological writings and to have been entirely unaware of his logical works, even though they were regularly studied in the main centers of learning in the Ottoman Empire's North African provinces.[46]

Even in North Africa in Maqdīsh's age, there was an undercurrent of tepidity or hostility toward kalam-theology and logic. An influential exponent of such an attitude was the Egyptian scholar Jalāl al-Dīn al-Suyūṭī (d.1505), a well-known opponent of both logic and natural theology who was widely read in later centuries. In the eighteenth century, an example is the Indian-born, Cairene scholar Muḥammad Murtaḍá al-Zabīdī (d.1791). Though still professing respect for Sanūsī as a saintly person, he defended Suyūṭī's hostile stance toward kalam and logic and defended the view that creedal commitments should be based on the Quran and hadith, rather than logical–theological reasoning.[47] From Zabīdī's correspondences and his biographical dictionary of contemporaries, it is clear that there were like-minded scholars in North Africa in his time.[48] The long-reigning Moroccan ruler Sīdī Muḥammad III (r.1757–1790), who corresponded with and patronized Zabīdī, had similar sentiments, and tried—though with limited success—to curtail the study of logic and natural theology in madrasas in his realm.[49]

In the nineteenth century, this undercurrent was strengthened further. New Sufi orders such as the Sammāniyya, Tījāniyya, and Sanūsīyya spread throughout Islamic Africa in this period. Such orders—controversially termed "Neo-Sufi"—tended to express reservations toward the scholastic traditions of law and theology, relying instead on prophetic hadith, on a greatly simplified law and creed, and on the mystical inspiration of Sufi masters.[50] The founder of the Sanūsīyya order, Muḥammad ibn ʿAlī al-Sanūsī (d.1859) hailed from the same Berber tribe as the fifteenth-century Sanūsī, though from an offshoot that had left the environs of Tlemcen in the sixteenth century to settle in Mostaganem on the Algerian coast and that claimed—conveniently—not to be Berbers at all but Sharifs (descendants of the Prophet) who had settled among this Berber tribe. The emphases of the two Sanūsīs were very different. The nineteenth-century scholar was interested in basing Islamic law on *ijtihād*, i.e., directly on Quran and hadith without being bound by the legal precedent of the established schools, and in founding Sufi lodges in rural areas. He showed no interest in kalam and logic. The works he prescribed to his followers included works on prophetic hadith, Sufi theoretical and practical works, and the *Epistle* of Ibn Abī Zayd al-Qayrawānī (d.996), which expounded the basics of law and creed and dated to before the spread of Ash'arism in the Maghreb.[51]

3 The eclipse of Sanūsī's influence

To be sure, the study of Sanūsī's works in North Africa continued throughout the nineteenth century, as shown by the printed commentaries and glosses of the eminent Cairene scholars Ibrāhīm al-Bājūrī (d.1860), Muḥammad 'Illaysh (d.1882), and Ismā'īl al-Ḥāmidī (d.1898). But toward the end of that century, Sanūsī's legacy began to meet new and more formidable opponents. The well-known Egyptian reformist scholar Muḥammad 'Abduh (d.1905) advocated for a sweeping break with the established traditions of law and theology. In his celebrated *The Theology of Monotheism*, he expounded the view that Islamic theology lost its way after al-Ghazālī (d.1111).[52] He—and an increasing number of his contemporaries—began to promote the view that Islamic civilization entered a prolonged period of stagnation or decadence (*inḥiṭāṭ*) after the end of the Abbasid caliphate in 1258, if not before. This historical account was widely disseminated by popular writers such as Jurjī Zaydān (d.1914) and Aḥmad Amīn (d.1954), forming a central part of the self-conception of the intellectual and cultural movement known as the Nahda ("renaissance" or "reawakening") in the late nineteenth and early twentieth centuries. The narrative of decline or decadence appealed both to those of a liberal-modernist bent and to those who sympathized with the purist and fideist ideas associated with Saudi Wahhabism.[53] The former sought to rediscover and reappropriate the legacy of the supposedly more rationalist Islamic philosophers and Mu'tazili theologians of an earlier age.[54] The latter sought inspiration in the works of the iconoclastic Ḥanbali scholar Ibn Taymiyya (d.1328) and his disciple Ibn Qayyim al-Jawziyya (d.1350), two thinkers who had opposed the prevalent tendencies of their time and whose writings—not much read for centuries beyond the small Ḥanbali school of law—were enthusiastically sought out in manuscript libraries and printed by purist reformers.[55] Both trends—the more liberal-modernist and the more purist-fideist—shared a hostility toward Ashʿarism and Sufism. Sanūsī thus became decidedly unfashionable, seen as a leading exponent of the very traditions that the new movements sought to overturn. Though Sanūsī's works continued to be printed with regularity until the 1930s, there is a noticeable decline thereafter that has only been reversed in recent decades. As mentioned in the Introduction to this book, the dramatic demise in Sanūsī's reputation in the Islamic world was mirrored in the negligible interest in him among twentieth-century Western scholars of Islamic thought.[56]

There is, however, reason to believe that the tide has turned somewhat in recent years. A number of broader trends may be relevant to a renewed interest in figures such as Sanūsī. As mentioned in the Introduction, most specialists in Islamic thought have become critical of the grand narrative of the decline of Islamic civilization after the thirteenth century. Furthermore, Sub-Saharan Islamic thought is beginning to receive the attention it deserves from contemporary academics, and it is hardly possible to do so without facing up to the central role played by Sanūsī's creedal works in the region. There has also been a resurgence of Ashʿarism in the Arabic-Islamic world in recent decades, with government support in countries like Morocco, Algeria, Egypt, Syria, Jordan, and the United Arab Emirates where there has been official wariness of Salafism, which is usually opposed to state-sponsored religious establishments, hostile to regional traditions of law, theology, and Sufism, and often—though not invariably—combative and prone to violence. After a hiatus of more than half a century, Sanūsī's works are once again printed with regularity. It should be emphasized that this interest in his works is not antiquarian. Like Thomism, Ashʿarism is still a living intellectual tradition.

Quite apart from these contemporary resonances, there can be no excuse, at least not from an historian's perspective, for ignoring a scholar whose writings were so influential for centuries in large swathes of the Islamic world and who, on the eve of modernity, was widely seen—in Islamic Africa, the Levant, and the Malay Archipelago—as laying out with authority the core beliefs of—and the main arguments for—the Islamic faith.

Notes

Chapter 1

1. Bājūrī, *Ḥāshiya ʿalá l-Sanūsiyya*; ʿIllaysh, *Hidāyat al-murīd li-ʿAqīdat ahl al-tawḥīd.*
2. For a list of later commentaries and glosses on the creed, see R. Wisnovsky, "The Nature and Scope of Arabic Philosophical Commentary," 185–6. I give an account of Sanūsī's reception in Islamic Africa and Turkey in Chapter 11. For the influence of his *Short Creed* in the Malay Archipelago, see Burhanuddin, "The Popularizing of Sunni Doctrine in Southeast Asia" and Jusoh, *The Malay Exposition of al-Sanusi's Umm al-barahin.* For a Berber adaptation, see Van den Boogert, *The Berber Literary Tradition of the Sous.*
3. Macdonald, *Development of Muslim Theology, Jurisprudence and Constitutional Theory*; Tritton, *Muslim Theology.* This overall focus is retained as late as Tilman Nagel's *The History of Islamic Theology from Muhammad to the Present* (German original 1993, English translation 2000).
4. Gardet and Anawati, *Introduction à la théologie musulmane*, 76–8, 169–71.
5. Watt, *Islamic Philosophy and Theology*, 149–58. In a second edition of Watt's book from 1985, the chapter is titled "The Stagnation of Philosophical Theology" and the dates are amended to 1250–1850 (pp. 133–41).
6. Rescher, *The Development of Arabic Logic*, 73–82, 234–5.
7. For a recent study in Arabic of Sanūsī's contribution to hadith studies, see Dakhkhān, *al-Imām al-ʿallāma Muḥammad ibn Yūsuf al-Sanūsī al-Tilimsānī.* Sanūsī's work on the laws of inheritance and the astrolabe are still in manuscript form and have not been printed.

Chapter 2

1. Balawī, *Thabat*, 436–8.
2. Syndicat d'initiative de Tlemcen, *Tlemcen et sa région*, 53–4. For another description of the mausoleum from the French colonial period, see Marcais, *Les monuments arabes de Tlemcen*, 340–1.
3. Lawless and Blake, *Tlemcen*, ch. 5; Lawless, "Tlemcen, Capital City of the ʿAbd al-Wadids."
4. Leo Africanus, *The History and Description of Africa*, vol. II, 668–9.
5. Lawless and Blake, *Tlemcen*, 59. A census from 1866 yielded 21,234 inhabitants, including French settlers (ibid, 78).
6. MQ 372. If Sanūsī was fifty-six (Hijri years) when he died, he would have been born between January 8, 1436, and December 28, 1436. In later sources, Sanūsī is sometimes given the birthdate 832/1428–1429, but given the agreement of two

contemporary witnesses, there is no reason to accept the later account, especially because it seems rooted in a wish to have Sanūsī, like the Prophet Muhammad, be sixty-three (Hijri years) when he died.

7. Despois, Raynal, and Chaker, "Beni Snous."
8. MQ 43; Balawī, *Thabat*, 436.
9. Powers, *Law, Society, and Culture in the Maghrib*, 184–5.
10. MQ 48–50 (Zawāwī), 50–1 (Ṣanhājī), 53 (Sharīf).
11. Ibn Maryam, *al-Bustān*, 237, 245, 304. It is clear that Ibn Maryam, writing in the early seventeenth century, had no information on the three scholars apart from what he could read in Mallālī's hagiography.
12. MQ 70–1. On this scholar, see Provenzali, *el-Bostan*, 167, 485. According to Provenzali, the attributive derives from the trade of crafting saddle cloth (*kunbūsh*).
13. Qalṣādī came to Tlemcen three times: first as a student in the late 1430s and early 1440s, then in 1450–1451 while on his way back to Granada from the Hajj and his studies in the East, and lastly when he left Granada for the East shortly before his death in 1486. The first two sojourns are recorded by Qalṣādī himself; see Qalṣādī, *Riḥlat al-Qalṣādī*, 94–109, 161. The last sojourn is recorded by Mallālī who mentions that he then received a certificate from Qalṣādī at the urgings of Sanūsī (MQ 52). Sanūsī may have received his certificate on this occasion, too, when he was aged fifty or so. Such ceremonial exchanges of certificates (ijāzas) between accomplished scholars were not unusual. But Sanūsī may have received a certificate already during Qalṣādī's second sojourn in 1450–1451, when Qalṣādī was an accomplished scholar and Sanūsī in his mid-teens. We can surely rule out that the certificate was granted during the first of Qalṣādī's sojourns when he was still a student and Sanūsī a small child.
14. Balawī, *Thabat*, 439.
15. Brunschvig, *Deux récits de voyage inédits*, 43–4 (Arabic text), 106–7 (French text and annotations).
16. Ibn Maryam, *al-Bustān*, 38–41; Ibn 'Askar, *Dawḥat al-nāshir*, 120–1. The latter source mentions that Sanūsī was incensed by Ibn Zakrī's claim to have taught him. Ibn Zakrī was around seventy when he died in 1494, so he must have been born around 1425, some ten years before Sanūsī.
17. S 137 (fn.2). The editor's source is Dasūqī, *Ḥāshiya 'alá Sharḥ Umm al-Barāhīn*, 83 (l. 9).
18. A sixth creed, barely two pages long, was also attributed to Sanūsī in later centuries. It came to be known as "The Grandchild" (*al-Ḥafīda*), presumably because it was thought of as an abridgment of *The Shortened Short Creed* and hence twice removed from *The Mother of Proofs*. The work is not mentioned by Mallālī, so the attribution is not certain, and no commentary on it by Sanūsī has come down to us. Another short theological work, this one mentioned by Mallālī, is a commentary on the ninety-nine names of God.
19. There are at least four manuscript copies of the work in the Royal Library in Rabat; see Khaṭṭāb, *Fahāris al-Khizāna al-Ḥasaniyya*, vol. 3, nrs. 359–62.
20. Other than Mallālī, the medieval biographical sources are Timbuktī, *Nayl al-ibtihāj*, 563–71; Ibn Maryam, *al-Bustān*, 237–48; Ibn 'Askar, *Dawḥat al-nāshir*, 121–2. None of these sources mention this work.
21. One oddity is that the author mentions having met Aḥmad Zarrūq in Tlemcen in 846/1442–1443, which is Zarrūq's year of birth (and Sanūsī himself was only six or seven then). Though this is apparently in all extant manuscripts, it may be a slip of the pen for 864/1459–1460, though this is still earlier than 870/1465 when Zarrūq left Fes and came to Tlemcen (where he stayed for three years and studied with local scholars, including Sanūsī, before going on to Cairo and the Hajj). Some

manuscripts state that the work was completed in 865/1461, again before Zarrūq is known to have come to Tlemcen. Sanūsī would have been in his early twenties then, before his major works were written, and yet strangely the scholar from Meknes is supposed to have sent him the work condemning Sufi innovations for approbation. It is also curious that a work completed in 865/1461 should mention that Zarrūq was on his way to Cairo to be a disciple of Abū l-ʿAbbās al-Ḥadramī (d.1490), ten years before Zarrūq actually went to Cairo and met that Sufi master. Other manuscripts give the date of completion as 885/1480, by which time Zarrūq could hardly have been described as a "young man" (*shābb*) intending to go to the Hajj and seek out al-Ḥaḍramī (whom he would have met some ten years earlier). The two other local scholars mentioned by the author of the treatise, a certain Taqī al-Dīn al-Sūsī (or al-Miknāsī) and a certain Abū l-Ḥasan al-Ḥalwī, cannot be identified. Indeed, the author of the treatise to which Sanūsī is supposed to have responded also cannot be identified in biographical sources and the same treatise circulated with an alternative attribution to Abū Muḥammad al-Fishtālī (d.1262). The perhaps most damning anomaly is that the author mentions the mantle of the Prophet as being in the possession of the Ottomans (*Āl ʿUthmān*), though this relic (of dubious authenticity) only came into their possession after their conquest of Egypt in 1517, decades after Sanūsī's death. The wholehearted defense of controversial Sufi practices in the work also seems to be in tension with the more cautious view expressed in other works by Sanūsī. For the work, see Būqlī Ḥasan, *al-Imām ibn Yūsuf al-Sanūsī*, 393–444; and Sanūsī(?), *Nuṣrat al-fuqayyir*.

22. Davies, *Thomas Aquinas's Summa Contra Gentiles*, 7; Taliaferro, "The Project of Natural Theology," 1. As is clear from Re Manning (ed.), *The Oxford Handbook of Natural Theology*, there are other current understandings of the term "natural theology" that understand it to be narrowly concerned with the argument from design. For a clear distinction between the wider and narrower senses of "natural theology," see Paton, *The Modern Predicament*, 20–2.
23. See Trieger, "Origins of Kalām."
24. For up-to-date surveys of Muʿtazilism, see El-Omari, "The Muʿtazilite Movement (I): The Origins of the Muʿtazila"; Bennett, "The Muʿtazilite Movement (II): The Early Muʿtazilites"; and Schmidtke, "The Muʿtazilite Movement (III): The Scholastic Phase."
25. Abrahamov, "Scripturalist and Traditionalist Theology"; Hoover, "Ḥanbalī Theology."
26. Thiele, "Between Cordoba and Nīsābūr"; Rudolph, "Ḥanafī Theological Tradition and Māturīdism."
27. El-Rouayheb, "From Ibn Ḥajar al-Haytamī (d.1566) to Khayr al-Dīn al-Ālūsī (d.1899)," 271–87.
28. A magisterial study of the theology of al-Ashʿarī is Gimaret, *La doctrine d'al-Ashʿarī*.
29. The most detailed accounts of the history of Ashʿarism in the Maghreb are Iḥnānah, *Taṭawwur al-madhhab al-Ashʿarī* and Zahrī, *al-Maṣādir al-Maghribiyya li-l-ʿaqīda al-Ashʿariyya*. A helpful, shorter survey in English is Thiele, "Ashʿarism in the Hafsid Era." See also Bennison, *The Almoravid and Almohad Empires*, 236–7.
30. Watt, *Islamic Creeds*, 69–72.
31. Fromherz, *The Almohads*, 155ff. Fromherz gives a helpful overview of Ibn Tūmart's *Aʿazz mā yuṭlab*, but his assumption that the Ashʿarīs were "literalists" prevents him from seeing the closeness of Ibn Tūmart's creed to Ashʿarism.
32. Juwaynī, *al-Irshād*, 155–64; Ghāzālī, *al-Iqtiṣād*, 109–29.
33. Ibn Tūmart, *Aʿazz mā yuṭlab*, 213–23. See also his shorter *al-Murshida*, widely commented on in later centuries, printed in the same collection (p. 226).
34. Rosenthal, *The Muqaddimah of Ibn Khaldun*, vol. 1, 471.

35. Fierro, *'Abd al-Mu'min*, 92.
36. On the doubtful attribution, see Amharar, "Autour d'un commentaire de la Muršida attribué à al-Sanūsī (m. 895/1490)."
37. Ibn al-'Arabī, *al-Mutawassiṭ fī l-i'tiqād*.
38. Salāljī, *al-'Aqīda al-burhāniyya*. On this work, see Thiele, "Facing the Mahdi's True Belief."
39. Muqtaraḥ, *Sharḥ al-Irshād*; Ibn al-Tilimsānī, *Sharḥ Ma'ālim uṣūl al-dīn*; al-Sharīf, *Abkār al-afkār al-'ulwiyya*.
40. Bayḍāwī, *Ṭawāli' al-anwār*; Ījī, *al-Mawāqif*.
41. Griffel, *Al-Ghazali's Philosophical Theology*, 97–110.
42. For one important exception, see Ibn 'Arafa, *al-Mukhtaṣar al-kalāmī*.
43. Ibn al-Tilimsānī, *Sharḥ Ma'ālim uṣūl al-dīn*, 91.
44. Ibn al-Tilimsānī, *Sharḥ Ma'ālim uṣūl al-dīn*, 516.
45. Ījī, *Jawāhir al-kalām*.
46. On Dawānī, see Pourjavady, *Philosophy in Early Safavid Iran*, 4–16. His Ash'arī affiliations are clearest in his commentary on the Creed of 'Aḍud al-Dīn al-Ījī (d.1355), widely studied and glossed in Ottoman Turkey, Mughal India, and Uzbek Central Asia in later centuries; see Dawānī, *Sharḥ al-'Aqā'id al-'Aḍudiyya*.
47. For example, when Dawānī briefly defended realism about universals by citing a passage from Avicenna, the Shi'i scholar Mīr Abū l-Fatḥ al-Ardabīlī (d.1568) protested that this does not amount to a proof because "we are not bound to believe what is between the covers of [Avicenna's] *The Healing* and *The Pointers*"; see Mīr Abū l-Fatḥ, *Ḥāshiya 'alá Sharḥ al-Tahdhīb*, 114 (lines 9–10). Rob Wisnovsky has remarked that, whereas in the thirteenth century, being a "verifier" tended to mean critically scrutinizing received opinion, for Dawānī it often simply meant agreeing with Avicenna; see Wisnovsky, "Avicennism and Exegetical Practice," 374–5.
48. Dawānī, *Sharḥ al-'Aqā'id al-'Aḍudiyya*, 72; Dawānī, *Risālat Ithbāt al-wājib al-jadīda*, 140–3; Dawānī, *Shawākil al-ḥūr fī sharḥ Hayākil al-nūr*, 313–25.
49. Dawānī, *Sharḥ al-'Aqā'id al-'Aḍudiyya*, 73–5.
50. Dawānī, *Risālat al-Zawrā'*; Dawānī, *Shawākil al-ḥūr*, 295–311.

Chapter 3

1. Gardet and Anawati, *Introduction à la théologie musulmane*, esp. 305–15, 329–30.
2. Cantwell Smith, *The Meaning and End of Religion*, 179; Cantwell Smith, *On Understanding Islam*, 241; van Ess, "The Logical Structure of Islamic Theology," 24–5; van Ess, *The Flowering of Muslim Theology*, 15; Makdisi, "Law and Traditionalism in the Institutions of Learning of Medieval Islam," 75.
3. Taylor, "Averroes: Religious Dialectic and Aristotelian Philosophical Thought," 182–9; Belo, "Averroes (d.1198), The Decisive Treatise," 288; Adamson, *Philosophy in the Islamic World*, 38–9, 43, 76. Adamson shows awareness of the tendentious nature of the accusation.
4. Juwaynī, *al-Irshād*, 3–5.
5. Juwaynī, *al-Irshād*, 6–16.
6. Juwaynī, *al-Irshād*, 17–29.
7. Muqtaraḥ, *Sharḥ al-Irshād*, vol. 1, 463–72.
8. Ghazālī, *al-Iqtiṣād*, 74–9.
9. Bakkī al-Kūmī, *Taḥrīr al-maṭālib*, 86–95.

10. Qalshānī, *Taḥrīr al-maqāla*, 88–9; Ibn Zakrī, *Bughyat al-ṭālib*, 189–92.
11. Frank, "Knowledge and Taqlīd," 48–9. I have slightly modified Frank's translation. For the Arabic text, see R.M. Frank, "Al-Ustādh Abū Isḥāḳ," 135.
12. Baghdādī, *Uṣūl al-dīn*, 255.
13. Subkī, *Ṭabaqāt al-Shāfiʿiyya al-kubrà*, vol. 3, 418–20.
14. Griffel, *Apostasie und Toleranz im Islam*, 208–15.
15. Ibn al-ʿArabī, *al-Mutawassiṭ fī l-iʿtiqād*, 113.
16. Ibn al-ʿArabī, *al-Mutawassiṭ fī l-iʿtiqād*, 113–4.
17. Ibn al-ʿArabī, *al-Mutawassiṭ fī l-iʿtiqād*, 114.
18. Zarrūq, *Ightinām al-fawāʾid*, 208–9.
19. Zarrūq, *Ightinām al-fawāʾid*, 209.
20. Bakkī al-Kūmī, *Taḥrīr al-maṭālib*, 88.
21. Sanūsī, *Sharḥ Wāsiṭat al-sulūk*, 53.
22. Balawī, *Thabat*, 436.
23. K 180. The editor identifies the contemporary scholar referred to here as Sanūsī's rival and townsman Ibn Zakrī. The identification was already made by the Moroccan scholar Aḥmad al-Manjūr (d.1587); see his *Mukhtaṣar Naẓm al-farāʾid*, vol. 1, 552–3.
24. On more general concerns in the medieval Maghreb about gross creedal ignorance and its possible legal implications, see Olson, "The Magian Position."
25. Bencheneb, "al-Sanūsī, Muḥammad b. Yūsuf," 21a; Gardet and Anawati, *Introduction à la théologie musulmane*, 76–8.
26. Manjūr, *Mukhtaṣar Naẓm al-farāʾid*, vol. 1, 585 (verses 262–3 and 276–8). The commentator al-Manjūr takes the words to be aimed at Sanūsī (pp. 588 and 591).
27. Manjūr, *al-Ḥāshiya al-kubrá*, 29.

Chapter 4

1. Frank, "The Ashʿarite Ontology I," 174–7; Frank, "Attribute, attribution, and being," 271–4.
2. Gimaret, in his study of the theology of al-Ashʿarī, variously translates *taʿalluq* and *mutaʿallaq* as "rattachement," "relation," "application," "connexion nécessaire" (Gimaret, *La doctrine d'al-Ashʿarī*, 595). The English terms "correlate" or "intentional object" might also work as translations. The term "dependent" will not work, for Ashʿarī theologians explicitly state that an attribute such as knowledge has a correlate/attachment/intentional object but has no causal influence on it.
3. Ghazālī, *al-Iqtiṣād*, 257.
4. For the Imami Shiʿi view, see Ḥillī, *Kashf al-murād*, 470–1. For the Māturīdī view, see Taftāzānī, *Sharḥ al-ʿAqāʾid al-Nasafiyya*, 164–5.
5. Ḥillī, *Kashf al-murād*, 418.
6. Brown, *Hadith*, 104–6.
7. Ahmed, "Satanic Verses."
8. See SS 201 editor's note (1). See also Suktānī, *al-Tuḥfa al-mufīda*, 122; Foudah, *A Refined Explanation*, 158–9, 168.
9. Muqtaraḥ, *Sharḥ al-Irshād*, vol. 2, 1348.
10. Watt, *Islamic Creeds*, 69–72.
11. Zarrūq, *Ightinām al-fawāʾid*.
12. Ibn Tūmart, *Aʿazz mā yuṭlab*, 226.

13. al-Qāḍī ʿIyāḍ, *al-Iʿlām bi-ḥudūd wa-qawāʿid al-islām*, 33–41.
14. Catechisms that sought to teach ordinary believers the fundamentals of their faith also became increasingly popular in Reformation and Counter-Reformation Europe in the sixteenth and seventeenth centuries, though again it seems to have been unusual to include rational proofs in such catechisms; see Eire, *Reformations*, 591–3; Bireley, *The Refashioning of Catholicism*, 101–4.
15. Watt, *Islamic Philosophy and Theology* (1985 edition), 138–9.
16. This is apparent from the profiles of some of the fifteenth- and sixteenth-centuries North African scholars who were reported to have appreciated or taught Sanūsī's *Short Creed*; see Ibn ʿAskar, *Dawḥat al-nāshir*, 7–14, 30–3, 66–71.
17. Suktānī, *al-Tuḥfa al-mufīda*, 50–1.
18. Horten, *Muhammadanische Glaubenslehre*, 3–4.
19. For a recent and influential protest at the privileging of law above other expressions of Islamic piety, see Ahmed, *What Is Islam?* esp. 117–29.
20. Two of the most well-known Muʿtazilīs, the theologian al-Qāḍī ʿAbd al-Jabbār (d.1025) and the Quranic exegete al-Zamakhsharī (d.1144) adhered, respectively, to the Shāfiʿī and Ḥanafī schools of law; see Subkī, *Ṭabaqāt al-shāfiʿiyya al-kubrá*, vol. 5, 97–8; Qurashī, *al-Jawāhir al-muḍiyya fī ṭabaqāt al-ḥanafiyya*, vol. 3, 447–8.
21. Wilferd Madelung, "The Origins of the Controversy Concerning the Creation of the Koran."
22. Ibn al-Malāḥimī, *al-Fāʾiq fī uṣūl al-dīn*, 515–22.
23. Knysh, *Ibn ʿArabi in the Later Islamic Tradition*, esp. chapter 8.
24. Olson, "The Magian Position." Olson rightly points out that the fatwas and ensuing discussions in the medieval and early-modern Maghreb should lead us to revisit the assumption that Islam emphasizes "orthopraxy" over "orthodoxy." Sanūsī cites the fatwa approvingly in W 346–7.

Chapter 5

1. Strobino, "Ibn Sina's Logic."
2. El-Rouayheb, *The Development of Arabic Logic*, 29–36.
3. El-Rouayheb, *The Development of Arabic Logic*, 121–41.
4. El-Rouayheb, *The Development of Arabic Logic*, 75–80.
5. El-Rouayheb, *The Development of Arabic Logic*, 122.
6. Noted by the historian Ibn Khaldūn (d.1406); see Rosenthal, *The Muqaddimah of Ibn Khaldūn*, vol. 3, 337.
7. El-Rouayheb, *The Development of Arabic Logic*, 121–4.
8. R. Wisnovsky, "The Nature and Scope of Arabic Philosophical Commentary," 168.
9. For an English translation, see Calverley, "Al-Abharī's Īsāghūjī fī l-manṭiq."
10. Sanūsī, *Sharḥ Muqaddimat Īsāghūjī*, pp. 37–9 (the modality propositions), pp. 68–70 (modal syllogisms), pp. 71–98 (wholly hypothetical syllogisms).
11. On the philosophers' view of logic as an instrumental science, see McGinnis, *Avicenna*, 27–35 and, more generally, López-Farjeat, *Classical Islamic Philosophy*, 90–118.
12. Maybudī, *Sharḥ al-Shamsiyya*. Of 182 pages, 80 (pp. 2–81) are devoted to preliminary matters, types of linguistic reference, the five universals, and definition, and 59 pages (pp. 111–70) to contradiction, conversion, contraposition, and the formal syllogism.

13. Ḥafīd al-Taftāzānī, *Sharḥ Tahdhīb al-manṭiq*. Of 216 pages (pp. 17–233), pp. 17–102 are devoted to preliminary matters, linguistic reference, the five universals and definition, and pp. 141–201 to contradiction, conversion, and the formal syllogism. The variable length of editorial footnotes makes these figures a rough estimate.
14. Wisnovsky, "The Nature and Scope of Arabic Philosophical Commentary," 166–7.
15. See, for example, Rescher, *The Development of Arabic Logic*; Rescher, *Temporal Modalities in Arabic Logic*; Rescher and vander Nat, "The Theory of Modal Syllogistic in Medieval Arabic Logic"; Street, "Toward a History of Syllogistic After Avicenna"; Street, "An Outline of Avicenna's Syllogistic"; Street, "Arabic Logic"; Street, "Suhrawardī on Modal Syllogisms"; Street, "Medieval and Modern Interpretations of Avicenna's Modal Syllogistic"; Street, "Afḍal al-Dīn al-Khūnajī (d.1248) on the Conversion of Modal Propositions"; Street, "Kātibī (d.1277), Taḥtānī (d.1365), and the Shamsiyya"; Street, "Al-ʿAllāma al-Ḥillī (d.1325) and the Early Reception of Kātibī's *Shamsiyya*."
16. Ibn Sīnā, *al-Shifāʾ: al-ʿIbāra*, 54–8.
17. El-Rouayheb, "Arabic Logic After Avicenna," 77–8.
18. Rāzī, *Lawāmiʿ al-asrār*, vol. 2, 95; Rāzī, *Sharḥ al-Shamsiyya*, 77; Taftāzānī, *Sharḥ al-Shamsiyya*, 49; Maybudī, *Sharḥ al-Shamsiyya*, 92.
19. Sanūsī was explicit that the subject in an "essentialist" proposition must be possible, thus excluding such constructions as "Every square circle . . . " or "Every married bachelor . . . " (MM, 49–50). This justifies the assumption, in the formalization of essentialist propositions, that the subject possibly exists. Propositions with impossible subjects are recognized by Sanūsī and most later Arabic logicians as "mental" (*dhihnī*) propositions in which the subject is a concept in the mind.
20. MM 48–9. The only previous work I have found that discusses such relations is Quṭb al-Dīn al-Rāzī, *Lawāmiʿ al-asrār*, vol. 2, 96–7. The parallels suggest that this was, directly or indirectly, the source for Sanūsī's account, unless there is a common source that I have not managed to identify.
21. For a convenient introduction to the topic, see Strobino and Thom, "The Logic of Modality." See also, Street (ed. and trans.), *Najm al-Dīn al-Kātibī: The Rules of Logic*, 114–28.
22. Khūnajī, *Kashf al-asrār*, 144–5; Ibn Wāṣil, *Sharḥ al-Jumal*, 130–1.
23. For the discussion of the conversion of affirmative possibility propositions and the closely related issue of the productivity of first-figure syllogisms with possibility minors, see Sanūsī, *Sharḥ Mukhtaṣar Ibn ʿArafa*, fols. 87^b–89^a, 131^b–133^b.
24. Paul Thom was the first to point out that many of the distinctive claims of Avicenna's modal logic presuppose S5; see Thom, "Logic and Metaphysics in Avicenna's Modal Syllogistic." For more on modern systems of modal logic, see Garson, *Modal Logic for Philosophers*, 38–44; Priest, *An Introduction to Non-Classical Logic*, 36–49.
25. El-Rouayheb, "Arabic Logic After Avicenna," 75–9.
26. It may seem odd to classify this as a "disjunction," but it arguably corresponds to one recognizable use of the "Either . . . or . . ." construction (in both English and Arabic) to claim that the disjuncts cannot both be true (though they may both be false).
27. Urmawī's *The Dawning of Lights* does include a detailed account of the topic, but it was an advanced rather than intermediate-level handbook, and there is abundant evidence that the later eastern Islamic tradition focused on the early parts of that handbook, covering the preamble, introduction, linguistic reference, the five universals, and definition.
28. Chatti, *Arabic Logic from al-Farabi to Averroes*, 286–92.
29. El-Rouayheb, *The Development of Arabic Logic*, 137–40.

Chapter 6

1. Davidson, *Proofs for Eternity, Creation and the Existence of God*, 134–43; Shihadeh, "The Existence of God," 205–8. The term "kalam cosmological argument" has become popularized by the contemporary Christian philosopher William Lane Craig; see Craig, *The Kalam Cosmological Argument* and, more recently, Craig and Sinclair, "The Kalam Cosmological Argument." But Craig's modern version does not start by showing that accidents, specifically, are originated.
2. Davidson, *Alfarabi, Avicenna, & Averroes on Intellect*, chs. 3 and 4.
3. Davidson, *Proofs for Eternity*, 281–310; Adamson, *Ibn Sina (Avicenna)*, 68–72.
4. Bayḍāwī, *Ṭawāliʿ al-anwār*, 165–6; Ījī, *al-Mawāqif*, 266 (gives both the older kalam proofs and then Avicenna's proof from contingency, noting that the latter is much more straightforward).
5. Ibn al-Tilimsānī, *Sharḥ Maʿālim uṣūl al-dīn*, 159–70; Bayḍāwī, *Ṭawāliʿ al-anwār*, 165–6.
6. As noted in Olson, "Beyond the Avicennian Turn," 124–32. For Sanūsī's Maghrebi contemporaries, see Bakkī al-Kūmī, *Taḥrīr al-maṭālib*, 43–7; Ibn Zakrī, *Bughyat al-ṭālib*, 195–6; Zarrūq, *Ightinām al-fawāʾid*, 55–8. All gave the standard kalam argument from accidents, though al-Bakkī al-Kūmī also gave Avicenna's proof from contingency—though not the more distinctive version in which one considers the set of contingent beings as a whole.
7. K 85. See more generally Shihadeh, "Classical Ashʿarī Anthropology."
8. K 196-8; Davidson, *Proofs for Eternity*, 158–9.
9. Davidson, *Proofs for Eternity*, 154–212; Shihadeh, "The Existence of God," 209–11.
10. Ibn al-Tilimsānī, *Sharḥ Maʿālim uṣūl al-dīn*, 168–9.
11. This is the translation given in Richard Frank, "The Ashʿarite Ontology I," 216.
12. Wilson, *Epicureanism at the Origins of Modernity*, ch. 1; Osler, *Reconfiguring the World*, ch. 3.
13. Bāqillānī, *Tamhīd*, 41–3 (on proving that the world is originated), 43–4 (the particularization argument for God's existence); Baghdādī, *Uṣūl al-dīn*, 55–60 (proving that attributes are all originated, that bodies cannot exist without attributes, and that bodies are originated), 68–9 (the particularization argument for God's existence).
14. Sanūsī's first proof shows some clear parallels with the proof found in the writings of Ibn Tūmart (d.1130), the founder of the Almohad movement whose *Guidance* was often commented upon in the Maghreb between the twelfth and fifteenth centuries. Ibn Tūmart also argued that every person knows with necessity that s/he is created and must have a creator, and that therefore all physical entities are created and must have a creator; see Ibn Tūmart, *Aʿazz mā yuṭlab*, 214–5; Griffel, "Ibn Tūmart's Rational Proof for God's Existence." Ibn Tūmart's version is much less developed than Sanūsī's, however, and he did not use a "particularization argument" to show that the creator must be a voluntary agent.
15. Davidson, *Proofs for Eternity*, 160–1, Shihadeh, "The Existence of God," 209–10.
16. On this line of thinking, see Richardson, "Avicenna and the Principle of Sufficient Reason."
17. Sanūsī's position that there are no involuntary causes is in line with the "volitional" understanding of causation defended in later centuries by George Berkeley (d.1753), Thomas Reid (d.1796), and Maine De Biran (d.1824) (see Mander, *The Volitional Theory of Causation*). However, most advocates of the volitional theory were not occasionalists but admitted that created souls have real causal powers.

18. The principle that God's decrees and actions are not extraneously determined and have no final cause is reiterated repeatedly in Sanūsī's works; see, e.g., K 528–32.
19. On this assumption, see Frank, "The Ash'arite Ontology I," 197. Later Ash'arī theologians are less committed to this doctrine; see Ibn al-Tilimsānī, *Sharḥ Ma'ālim uṣūl al-dīn*, 134–6; Bayḍāwī, *Ṭawāli' al-anwār*, 104–5.
20. K 200, 219. The argument is already present in Fakhr al-Dīn al-Rāzī; see Ibn al-Tilimsānī, *Sharḥ Ma'ālim uṣūl al-dīn*, 142.
21. Frank, "The Ash'arite ontology I," 203.
22. Davidson, *Proofs for Eternity*, 143–6.
23. On Philoponus's argument, see Davidson, *Proofs for Eternity*, 86–94; Sorabji, *Time, Creation and the Continuum*, 214–24. Muqtaraḥ, in his commentary on Juwaynī's *Irshād*, attributed the argument to Philoponus (Yaḥyá al-Naḥwī); see Muqtaraḥ, *Sharḥ al-Irshād*, vol. 1, 559–60.
24. For a recent philosophical defense of this position, see Pruss, *Infinity, Causation & Paradox*, 27.
25. Davidson, *Proofs for Eternity*, 119–20.
26. McGinnis, *Avicenna*, 200–1.
27. K 230. Cp. Ibn al-Tilimsānī, *Sharḥ Ma'ālim uṣūl al-dīn*, 141.
28. Āmidī, *Abkār al-afkār*, vol. 1, 234.
29. Ibn 'Arafa, *al-Mukhtaṣar al-kalāmī*, 621.
30. See the editor's footnote 2 in Ibn 'Arafa, *al-Mukhtaṣar al-kalāmī*, 621–2. The relevant passage is in Sharīf, *Abkār al-afkār al-'ulwiyya*, 73–4.
31. Avicenna, *The Physics of The Healing*, vol. 2, 325. For a detailed account of Avicenna's use of the argument, see Zarepour, "Avicenna on Mathematical Infinity."
32. Taftāzānī, *Sharḥ al-'Aqā'id al-Nasafiyya*, 60–2; Jurjānī, *Sharḥ al-Mawāqif*, 181–3; Dawānī, *Sharḥ al-'Aqā'id al-'Aḍudiyya*, 49–54; Manjūr, *Mukhtaṣar Naẓm al-farā'id*, 841–6.
33. McGinnis, "Creation and Eternity in Medieval Philosophy," 80–1.
34. I have discussed Ibn al-Tilimsānī and some other medieval Islamic critics of the argument in El-Rouayheb, "The argument of superposition (*burhān al-taṭbīq*) and its critics."
35. Muqtaraḥ, *al-Asrār al-'aqliyya*, 68.
36. Ibn al-Tilimsānī, *Sharḥ Ma'ālim uṣūl al-dīn*, 164.
37. Dawānī, *Risālat ithbāt al-wājib al-qadīma*. Dawānī also wrote a "new" treatise on establishing God's existence and attributes, on which see Bdaiwi, "Philosophia Ottomanica: Jalal al-Din Davani on Establishing the Necessary Being." But the new treatise did not delve as deeply into proofs for the existence of God and was not as intensively annotated and glossed in later centuries.

Chapter 7

1. SS 159; M 235; K 213, 242.
2. This is the translation given in Frank, "The Ash'arite Ontology I," 216.
3. MS 215. In both this work and in his *Commentary on the Short Creed*, Sanūsī also offered the following definition: "a state (*ḥāl*) that is necessary for a substance—as long as the substance is—but is not grounded (*mu'allala*)" (S 154–5). I will discuss "states" below.

4. Breno Zuppolini, "Aristotle on Per Se Accidents"; Strobino, "Per Se, Inseparability, Containment and Implication."
5. Juwaynī, *Irshād*, 31; Muqtaraḥ, *Sharḥ al-Irshād*, vol. 1, 575–80.
6. Frank, "The Ash'arite Ontology I," 174–7; Frank, "Attribute, Attribution, and Being," 271–4. Frank suggests "entity" or "self" for *dhāt*. On this point, Fakhr al-Dīn al-Rāzī departed from mainstream Ash'arism and defended the view that existence is an attribute additional to the self. His position is critically discussed by Ibn al-Tilimsānī, *Sharḥ Ma'ālim uṣūl al-dīn*, 88–91.
7. K 237–9. Sanūsī appears to be following al-Muqtaraḥ, *Sharḥ al-Irshād*, vol. 1, 582–6. For a concise and helpful overview of various accounts of time in medieval Islamic theology and philosophy, including the two mentioned by Sanūsī, see Lammer, "Time and Mind-Dependence in Sayf al-Dīn al-Āmidī's Abkār al-afkār."
8. K 240. The argument is already in Muqtaraḥ, *Sharḥ al-Irshād*, vol. 1, 582–6.
9. Wisnovsky, "Avicenna," 126; Bertolacci, "Ibn Sīnā (d.428/1037): Metaphysics of the Shifā'," 156–7.
10. Zysow, "Karrāmiyya."
11. On the term *Ḥashwī* being used of Ḥanbalīs such as Ibn Taymiyya and Ibn Qayyim al-Jawziyya, see El-Rouayheb, "From Ibn Ḥajar al-Haytamī (d.1566) to Khayr al-Dīn al-Ālūsī (d.1899)," 273.
12. For this line of argument, see Hoover, *Ibn Taymiyya's Theodicy of Perpetual Optimism*, 51–6.
13. Griffel, "Al-Ghazali at His Most Rationalist."
14. Some of the issues with divine simplicity are well raised in Stump, *Aquinas*, 92–130; Muhtaroğlu, "Plantinga and Ash'arites on Divine Simplicity"; and McGinnis, "Simple Is as Simple Does."
15. The late Mu'tazilī theologian Ibn al-Malāḥimī (d.1141) wrote that the received view in his school was to declare as infidels (*takfīr*) those who say that God has pre-eternal attributes (*ṣifāt qadīma*), such as power (*qudra*) and knowledge (*'ilm*), even if they add that these are "neither God nor other than God." This is, of course, the Ash'arī view. He himself demurred from this position, however. See, Ibn al-Malāḥimī, *al-Fā'iq fī uṣūl al-dīn*, 521–2. The later Shī'ī theologian Miqdād al-Suyūrī (d.1423) wrote that the belief that the divine attributes are pre-eternal is infidelity (*kufr*); see Suyūrī, *Irshād al-ṭālibīn*, 222–3.
16. K 250; Ibn Zakrī, *Bughyat al-ṭālib*, 199. Both authors seem to be following Ibn al-Tilimsānī, *Sharḥ Ma'ālim uṣūl al-dīn*, 191–2. Such an interpretation of the trinity is found in the classic heresiography of al-Shahrastānī (d.1153), *Kitāb al-Milal wa l-niḥal*, 172.
17. Thiele, "Abū Hāshim al-Jubbā'ī's (d.321/933) Theory of 'States' (*aḥwāl*)"; Benevich, "The Classical Ash'ari Theory of Aḥwāl."
18. K 313–5. This is the argument found in Juwaynī's *Guidance*; see Muqtaraḥ, *Sharḥ al-Irshād*, vol. 2, 715. Sanūsī is closely following Ibn al-Tilimsānī, *Sharḥ Ma'ālim uṣūl al-dīn*, 282–5.
19. K 316. The argument is found in Muqtaraḥ's *al-Asrār al-'aqliyya*, 116. It is prefigured by Ghazālī; see McGinnis, "Simple Is as Simple Does," 104.
20. Ibn al-Malāḥimī, *al-Fā'iq fī uṣūl al-dīn*, 74.
21. On "truth-makers" see Effingham, *An Introduction to Ontology*, 137–9. For an application of "truth-makers" to the discussion of divine simplicity, see Vallicella, "Divine Simplicity," sect. 5.
22. For similar criticisms of the philosophers, see Ibn al-Malāḥimī, *al-Fā'iq fī uṣūl al-dīn*, 101; Muqtaraḥ, *al-Asrār al-'aqliyya*, 99.
23. McGinnis, "Simple Is as Simple Does," 100. McGinnis is speaking specifically of Avicenna. For a similar view in Averroes, see Taylor, "Averroes," 195.

24. Ibn al-Tilimsānī, *Sharḥ Ma'ālim uṣūl al-dīn*, 289–90.
25. K 327. Cp. Ibn al-Tilimsānī, *Sharḥ Ma'ālim uṣūl al-dīn*, 99. Ibn al-Tilimsānī is also quoted by Ibn Zakrī, *Bughyat al-ṭālib*, 232–3.
26. K 326. The response, in very similar wording, is already in Ibn al-Tilimsānī, *Sharḥ Ma'ālim uṣūl al-dīn*, 98–9.
27. It is worth noting that the Scottish "common sense" philosopher Thomas Reid (d.1796) also defended the view that causal "power" in the strict sense could only be attributed to a voluntary agent who can refrain from acting, leading him to deny that inanimate material objects have causal power. See Mander, *The Volitional Theory of Causation*, 73–86.
28. K 278–88. For brief and minimalistic definitions, see M 246–9.
29. Juwaynī, *al-Irshād*, 72–4; al-Salāljī, *al-'Aqīda al-Burhāniyya*, 27.
30. Audi, *Epistemology*, 57–8. Audi himself is skeptical whether blind-sight counts as "seeing."
31. Sanūsī argued for this extensively; see K 347–57 and W 329–40.
32. Ghazālī, *The Incoherence of the Philosophers*, 12–30, 134–43.
33. K 387–8. The relevant passage is in Ibn al-Tilimsānī, *Sharḥ Ma'ālim uṣūl al-dīn*, 240.
34. The Tunisian scholar al-Bakkī al-Kūmī (d.1510) wrote that the suggestion that God's attributes are contingent in themselves contravened the position of early Ash'arīs as well as later Ash'arīs in the Maghreb, whereas it found favor among later eastern Ash'arīs such as Fakhr al-Dīn al-Rāzī, al-Bayḍāwī, and al-Taftāzānī; see Bakkī al-Kūmī, *Taḥrīr al-maṭālib*, 159. He himself preferred to be agnostic on the issue. The sheer influence of Sanūsī ensured that the more conservative position remained prevalent in North Africa down to the modern period. Taftāzānī's acceptance of the claim that the divine attributes are "necessary by another" is noted in Wisnovsky, "One Aspect of the Avicennian Turn in Sunni Theology," 97–9.
35. The fact that Rāzī debated, read, and was influenced by Mu'tazilī scholars is well-established and noted, for example, in Schmidtke, "The Mu'tazilite Movement (III)," 174. On Rāzī's life and debates, see Griffel, "Fakhr al-Dīn al-Rāzī's Life and the Patronage He Received"; Kholeif, *A Study on Fakhr al-Dīn al-Rāzī and his Controversies in Transoxiana.*
36. al-Muqtaraḥ, *Sharh al-Irshād*, vol. 1, 623–4.
37. Pourjavady, "The Legacy of 'Aḍud al-Dīn al-Ījī," 340–2.
38. At the very least, it is clear that they read Avicenna's *Ishārāt* with the commentary of Ṭūsī, Ṭūsī's *Naqd al-Muḥaṣṣal*, and Ḥillī's commentary on Ṭūsī's *Tajrīd*.
39. Dawānī, *Sharḥ al-'Aqā'id al-'Aḍudiyya*, 42 (Ḥillī), 47 (Ibn Taymiyya).

Chapter 8

1. On Malebranche's and Edward's occasionalism, see Nadler, "Malebranche on Occasionalism" and Crisp and Strobel, *Jonathan Edwards*, 90–120. On occasionalism more generally, see Perler and Rudolph, *Occasionalismus* and Nadler, *Occasionalism*. A related view, advocated by, for example, George Berkeley (d.1753) and Thomas Reid (d.1796), is that all causation is volitional and that there is no such thing as inanimate physical or material causation, though such a view often acknowledges the individual human soul's causal powers. On this latter tradition, see Mander, *The Volitional Theory of Causation*.

2. For two classic articles that take occasionalism seriously and acknowledges that the standard medieval criticisms of the doctrine are not decisive, see Freddoso, "Medieval Aristotelianism and the Case Against Secondary Causation in Nature" and McCann and Kvanvig, "The Occasionalist Proselytizer."
3. Stearns, *Infectious Ideas*, 7–9; Huff, *The Rise of Early Modern Science: Islam, China, and the West*, 87–93.
4. For example: Frank, "The Structure of Created Causality According to al-Ashʿarī"; Rudolph, *Al-Māturīdī and the Development of Sunnī Theology in Samarqand*, 260; Griffel, *Al-Ghazali's Philosophical Theology*, 215–74.
5. Rudolph, "Occasionalism," 355.
6. Gimaret, *La doctrine d'al-Ashʿarī*, 75–120.
7. Muqtaraḥ, *al-Asrār al-ʿaqliyya*, 101–3; Ibn al-Tilimsānī, *Sharḥ Maʿālim uṣūl al-dīn*, 268–9.
8. Ibn Zakrī, *Bughyat al-ṭālib*, 255.
9. Dasūqī, *Ḥāshiya ʿalá Sharḥ Umm al-barāhīn*, 114; Sharqāwī, *Ḥāshiya ʿalá Sharḥ al-Hudhudī ʿalá l-Sanūsiyya*, 77; Bājūrī, *Ḥāshiya ʿalá l-Sanūsiyya*, 23.
10. In his *Commentary on the Shortened Short Creed*, Sanūsī mentioned in passing "the effectual attachment of God's Power and Will" (SS 182) that he identified with "the coming to be of beings" (*ṣudūr al-kāʾināt*). In his *Commentary on the Preliminaries*, he distinguished between the "apt" and "effectual" attachment of God's address (M 138), in the sense that the pre-eternal command of God, for example, pre-exists those to whom it is addressed and only becomes effective when its addressees come to be. Such passages may have encouraged later commentators to make use of the distinction more generally than Sanūsī himself did. It seems to me that one motivation for later commentators is the above-mentioned worry that if God's Will is pre-eternal, then the object/attachment of that Will should be pre-eternal as well. But it is not clear that the worry is justified if one is careful to avoid the presumption that God's Will is "in" time and temporally precedes the object of that Will.
11. Beebee, "Hume and the Problem of Causation"; Garrett, "Hume."
12. Nadler, *Occasionalism*, 165–88.
13. Gimaret, *Théories des l'acte humaine*, 120–8.
14. Gimaret, *Théories des l'acte humaine*, 134–53.
15. Gimaret, *Théories des l'acte humaine*, 132–4.
16. As noted in Gimaret, *Théories des l'acte humaine*, 168–70. Gimaret's pioneering analysis is based on Sanūsī's shorter theological writings, his *Commentary on the Short Creed* and *Commentary on the Preliminaries*. My discussion is primarily based on the more substantial *Commentary on the Long Creed*.
17. K 446-7; Ibn al-Tilimsānī, *Sharḥ Maʿālim uṣūl al-dīn*, 381.
18. Some medieval Latin theologians held that the sacraments do not themselves confer grace but are necessary (*sine qua non*) conditions for God's conferring grace; see Adams, "Powerless Causes"; Cross, *Duns Scotus*, 136–8; Perler and Rudolph, *Occasionalismus*, 189–201; Richardson, "Efficient Causation: From Ibn Sīnā to Ockham," 112–3.
19. Muqtaraḥ, *al-Asrār al-ʿaqliyya*, 129–41.
20. Juwaynī, *al-Irshād*, 190–1.
21. Juwaynī, *al-Irshād*, 217–8.
22. Juwaynī, *al-Irshād*, 195–200.
23. Stearns, *Infectious Ideas*, 125–30. Though I find Stearns's monograph illuminating as a whole, I believe his reading of Sanūsī as inconsistent and even hypocritical suffers from an imprecise notion of "secondary causation" and not being sufficiently alive to the fact that occasionalism is compatible with a Humean understanding of natural causation as regular conjunction.

24. Dorpmüller, *Religiöse Magie im "Buch der probaten Mittel,"* 195.
25. See the editors' introduction to Sanūsī, *Tafsīr mā taḍammanathu kalimāt khayr al-bariyya.*
26. I read *lā anna* rather than *li'anna* in the printed text.
27. I read *lā* not *illā* as in the printed text.
28. Sanūsī, *Mukammil Ikmāl al-Ikmāl*, vol. 6, 18–9. Sanūsī's commentary is mostly an abridgement of an earlier commentary by the Tunisian scholar al-Ubbī (d.1427 or 1428). But Ubbī's commentary does not have this particular discussion, which is Sanūsī's own intervention.
29. See the gloss by the Egyptian scholar Ismā'īl al-Ḥāmidī (d.1898) on the relevant passage in Ḥāmidī, *Ḥawāshin 'alá Sharḥ al-Kubrá*, 185. This also seems to be the upshot of the discussions in M 178–83 and MS 460–1.
30. Sanūsī, *Mukammil Ikmāl al-Ikmāl*, vol. 6, 19. The passage is also cited in K 276–7.
31. For recent overviews of the philosophy of causation and the distinction between Humean and non-Humean analyses, see Mumford and Anjum, *Causation* and Kutach, *Causation*. I adopt the phrase "causal oomph" from the latter source (ch. 2). For a sympathetic account of contemporary "regularity" theories of causation, see Psillos, "Regularity Theories."

Chapter 9

1. On this incident, see Nawas, *Al-Ma'mūn, the Inquisition, and the Quest for Caliphal Authority*; Madelung, "The Controversy on the Creation of the Koran"; Hurvitz, "Al-Ma'mūn (r.198/813–218/833) and the *Miḥna*"; Zaman, "Miḥna."
2. K 288–90. The argument from perfection is in Juwaynī, *al-Irshād*, 72–6 and in Ghazālī, *al-Iqtiṣād*, 182–3. It is criticized in Muqtaraḥ, *al-Asrār al-'aqliyya*, 107–10.
3. As was routinely explained in Islamic madrasa handbooks of logic, for example, in Sanūsī's *Epitome of Logic* (MM 13–6), a term is equivocal (*mushtarak*) if it is applied with different meanings (e.g., if "cool" is applied to new sunglasses and to weather), univocal (*muṭawāṭi'*) if applied with the same meaning (e.g., "animal" applied to cats and dogs), and analogical (*mushakkak*) if one application is prior, more fundamental, or more intense (e.g., "exists" applied to cause and effect).
4. M 256–7. I have not encountered this precise argument in earlier sources. Muqtaraḥ's student Abū Yaḥyá al-Sharīf proposed a variant: Every living being possibly speaks, God is living, so God possibly speaks, and everything that is possibly true of God is true of God, so God speaks; see Sharīf, *Abkār al-afkār al-'ulwiyya*, 223, 229. That argument is also in Ibn Zakrī, *Bughyat al-ṭālib*, 223. It is criticized in Āmidī, *Abkār al-afkār*, vol. 1, 370–1.
5. Juwaynī, *al-Irshād*, 107–8; Ghazālī, *al-Iqtiṣād*, 181–7; K 372–7.
6. The most detailed discussion of Mu'tazilī views on human and divine speech is Peters, *God's Created Speech*, esp. 1–37, 293–305, 308–12. A shorter but more recent discussion is in López-Farjeat, "'Abd al-Jabbār and al-Ghazālī on Divine Speech."
7. K 373–4. Sanūsī is closely following Ibn al-Tilimsānī, *Sharḥ Ma'ālim uṣūl al-dīn*, 302–4.
8. Jishumī, *al-Tahdhīb fī l-tafsīr*, vol. 3, 1828; Zamakhsharī, *al-Kashshāf*, vol. 1, 591. Sanūsī was familiar with the later work and quoted from it in an unrelated section of his *Commentary on the Long Creed* (K 360).

9. For helpful shorter surveys of the dispute, see Frank, "Moral Obligation in Classical Muslim Theology"; Shihadeh, "Theories of Ethical Value in Kalām"; McGinnis, "Islamic Ethics."
10. Ibn al-Malāḥimī, *al-Fā'iq fī uṣūl al-dīn*, 273–84.
11. Some of these epithets are mentioned (but not endorsed) in Hare, *God's Command*, 187 and Evans, *God & Moral Obligation*, 95. The "impious" charge is raised in Rachels, *The Elements of Moral Philosophy*, 50, the "less than human" charge in Paton, *The Modern Predicament*, 55.
12. In his *Commentary on the Short Creed*, Sanūsī wrote that God wills the unbelief of Abū Jahl, an enemy of the Prophet Muḥammad, "because He knows that it does not occur" (S 159). This misleadingly suggests that God simply brings about what He sempiternally knows to be the case, which would contradict other principles accepted by Sanūsī: that God is a voluntary agent; that God's Will is eternal and necessary and hence not caused or grounded (*mu'allal*); and that Knowledge is an ineffectual divine attribute (for on this account, Knowledge determines what God Wills). It also threatens to undermine the case for God having a Will at all, for it seems that God's Knowledge and God's Power would then be sufficient to determine why some possibilities are realized and others are not. Despite the formulation in the *Commentary on the Short Creed*, I think Sanūsī's considered position was that God's Will accords with God's Knowledge (and vice versa), and that God's Willing entails God's Knowledge. It is *not* that God's willing that Abū Jahl is an unbeliever is explained by—or a consequence of—God's Knowing that Abū Jahl is an unbeliever. The immediate context of the passage in the *Commentary on the Short Creed* is to show, against the Mu'tazilīs, that God wills Abū Jahl to be an unbeliever, and that we know this "because" God, by common agreement, Knows that Abū Jahl is an unbeliever.
13. Rudolph, *Al-Māturīdī and the Development of Sunnī Theology in Samarqand*, 296–300.
14. Ibn al-Malāḥimī, *al-Fā'iq fī uṣūl al-dīn*, 201–3.
15. Madelung, "Review: Sophia Vasalou, Moral Agents and Their Deserts," 564. For a sustained and sophisticated argument against identifying Mu'tazilism with "reason" and the Ash'arīs with obscurantism, see Farahat, *The Foundations of Norms in Islamic Jurisprudence and Theology*. Farahat's book is explicitly less concerned with historical reconstruction and more with appropriating medieval positions to address modern concerns in legal philosophy.
16. Vasalou, *Moral Agents and Their Deserts*, 12–37.
17. Ibn al-Malāḥimī, *al-Fā'iq fī uṣūl al-dīn*, 305, 552.
18. Shihadeh, "Theories of Ethical Value in Kalām," 396–404.
19. Ibn al-Tilimsānī, *Sharḥ Ma'ālim uṣūl al-dīn*, 409–18.
20. For an example of this line of thinking, see Al-Attar, *Islamic Ethics*.
21. For Kierkegaard's "teleological suspension of the ethical," see Carlisle, *Kierkegaard's Fear and Trembling*, 99–120. The question of whether Abraham's willingness to sacrifice his son is comparable to modern, religiously motivated terrorist actions is discussed on pages 75–7.
22. On Ibn Taymiyya's ethical thought, see Hoover, *Ibn Taymiyya's Theodicy of Perpetual Optimism*, esp. 34–9, 216–20, and Vasalou, *Ibn Taymiyya's Theological Ethics*, esp. chapter 4. He rejected Mu'tazilī/Shi'i ideas of God being obliged toward humans but also rejected Ash'arī divine voluntarism and emphasized that God acts for "wise" purposes.
23. Rachels, *The Elements of Moral Philosophy*, 48; Evans, *God & Moral Obligation*, 88–9; Zagzebski, *Philosophy of Religion*, 137.
24. Sanūsī, *Sharḥ al-asmā' al-ḥusná*, 38.

25. For a discussion, see Gert, "The Standard Meter by Any Name Is Still a Meter Long."
26. Rachels, *The Elements of Moral Philosophy*, 48; Evans, *God & Moral Obligation*, 92; Zagzebski, *Philosophy of Religion*, 136–7.
27. The objection is raised in Ibn al-Malāḥimī, *al-Fā'iq fī uṣūl al-dīn*, 122–3; Ḥillī, *Kashf al-murād*, 418; Suyūrī, *Irshād al-ṭālibīn*, 256.
28. I set out and discuss some of the arguments adduced by earlier Ash'arī theologians on this point in El-Rouayheb, "Must God Tell Us the Truth?"
29. Ījī, *al-Mawāqif*, 296.
30. Juwaynī, *al-Irshād*, 332–3.
31. J.L. Austin, *How to Do Things with Words*, esp. Lecture I.
32. The French philosopher Marin Mersenne (d.1648) raised this very point in his objections to Descartes's *Meditations*, writing, "Cannot God treat men as a doctor treats the sick, or a father his children? In both these cases there is frequent deception though it is always employed beneficially and with wisdom" (quoted in Baima and Paytas, "True in Word and Deed," 198.) For a modern philosophical-theological defense of the possibility of divine deception, see Wielenberg, "Divine Deception."

Chapter 10

1. See Wickens, *The Nasirean Ethics*.
2. A point brought out by Ayubi, *Gendered Morality*.
3. The commentary was written after *Sanūsī's Commentary on the Middle Creed*, which was completed in 1471 (see the citation in MS 251) and before Jazā'irī's death in 1479.
4. For the proper attribution of *Minhāj al-'ābidīn*, see Watt, "The Authenticity of the Works Attributed to al-Ghazālī," 37.
5. The classic study is Lovejoy, *The Great Chain of Being*. A convenient, shorter overview is Formigari, "Chain of Being." Lovejoy noted that what he called "extreme anti-rationalists," under which he included medieval Scotists and Ockhamists, rejected the basic idea of a *scala naturae* (pp. 69–70).
6. The two passages are regularly cited by the greatest of the Islamic panentheist mystics Ibn 'Arabī (d.1240); see the index of Quranic passages and hadith in William Chittick, *The Self-Disclosure of God*, 424–5, 427, 434. For "levels of existence" in the later Ibn 'Arabian tradition, with parallels drawn to Neoplatonism and Arthur Lovejoy's work on the "Great Chain of Being," see Morrissey, *Sufism and the Perfect Human*, 35–41.
7. Tha'ālibī, *al-Jawāhir al-ḥisān fī tafsīr al-Qur'ān*, vol. 4, 327.
8. Ubbī, *Ikmāl Ikmāl al-mu'lim*, vol. 7, 52–4.
9. MS 558. This passage is surprisingly critical if one assumes that Sanūsī was the author of the treatise *Nuṣrat al-faqīr*, mentioned in Chapter 2, which defends Sufis unqualifiedly and abusively rejects criticisms of them.
10. Further evidence for the recognition of the distinction is Sanūsī's discussion of the hoary question of the relation between correct reasoning and acquiring knowledge of the conclusion. He denied both that the relation is causal in the sense that correct reasoning causes knowledge of the conclusion *and* that it is merely customary in the sense that God habitually creates knowledge of the conclusion after correct reasoning but is free not to do so. Rather, Sanūsī preferred the view that the relation

is rationally necessary: Correct reasoning logically entails knowledge of the conclusion (K 127–8).

11. Kugle, *Rebel Between Spirit and Law*, 152–4.
12. See Bā'ūniyya, *The Principles of Sufism.*
13. The works most frequently cited are Qushayrī's *Risāla*, pseudo-Ghazālī's *Minhāj al-ʿābidīn*, and the following three works by Ibn ʿAṭā'ullāh: *al-Ṭarīq al-jādda ilá nayl al-saʿāda* (also known as *Tāj al-ʿarūs*), *al-Tanwīr fī isqāṭ al-tadbīr*, and *al-Ḥikam.* Also regularly cited is *al-Furūq*, a work on the principles of jurisprudence by the Egyptian-based Mālikī jurist and Ashʿarī theologian Shihāb al-Dīn al-Qarāfī (d.1285).
14. For the more sober and practically/ethically oriented trend within Sufism, represented by Qushayrī, Ghazālī, ʿAbd al-Qādir al-Jīlānī (d.1166), ʿUmar al-Suhrawardī (d.1235), and the early Shādhilīs, see Knysh, *Islamic Mysticism*, 169–71. For this "Ashʿarite Sufism," see also Meyer, "Theology and Sufism," 270–4.
15. Ghazālī, *Deliverance from Error*, 77–8.
16. Ibn Khaldūn, *The Requirements of the Sufi Path*, esp. 94–5.
17. See Jāmī, *The Precious Pearl.*
18. A similar interpretation of Sanūsī's Sufism is given in Andersson, "Sufism in al-Sanūsī's (d.895/1490) *al-Manhaj al-sadīd*," which was published and came to my attention after the present chapter was written and submitted for review.
19. On him, see Cornell, *Realm of the Saint*, 131–8. Later sources tried to link him to ʿAbd al-Qādir al-Jīlānī (d.1166) and Aḥmad al-Rifāʿī (d.1182), founders of the Qādirī and Rifāʿī orders, respectively. But the chains cited by Mallālī do not mention these figures, instead adducing as Abū Madyan's spiritual masters the Maghrebi Sufis Abū Yaʿizzá (d.1177) and Abū l-Ḥasan Ḥarāzim (d.1164), via whom he was linked to the Baghdad Sufis al-Saqaṭī (d.867) and al-Junayd (d.910).
20. On the spread of the Shādhilī order, see Knysh, *Islamic Mysticism*, 207–18; Cornell, *Realm of the Saint*, 144–54.
21. Knysh, *Islamic Mysticism*, 211.
22. Cornell, "Muḥammad ibn Sulaymān al-Jazūlī and the Place of *Dalā'il al-khayrāt* in Jazūlite Sufism"; Chih, "Prophetic Piety, Mysticism, and Authority in Premodern Arabic Devotional Literature."
23. Sāḥilī, *Bughyat al-sālik fī ashraf al-masālik.* According to Mallālī, Sanūsī wrote an epitome of Sāḥilī's work (MQ 364).
24. On *tajriba* in scientific methodology generally, see McGinnis, "Scientific Methodologies in Medieval Islam." On *tajriba* in medicine, see Pormann, "Avicenna on Medical Practice, Epistemology, and the Physiology of the Inner Senses"; Forcada, "Bronze and Gold: al-Fārābī on Medicine." On *tajriba* in the occult sciences, see Melvin-Koushki, "Is (Islamic) Occult Science Science?" and Langermann, "From My Notebooks: On Tajriba/Nissayon ('Experience')." The close connection between the occult sciences and "experiment" has been recognized since Lynn Thorndike's classic *A History of Magic and Experimental Science* (1923).
25. Lav, "Ash'arism, Causality, and the Cult of Saints." Lav's article is an important first step toward understanding the relationship between views of causality and the cult of saints in Islamic history. A fuller account should bring in Twelver Shi'i thinkers who accept both secondary causation and the cult of saints and shrines.
26. Three classic studies are: Dermenghem, *Le culte des saints dans l'Islam maghrébin*; Geertz, *Islam Observed*; and Eickelman, *Moroccan Islam.*
27. For an excellent study and edition, see Dorpmüller, *Religiöse Magie im "Buch der probaten Mittel."*

28. Compare MQ 541, 547, 549 and Dorpmüller, *Religiöse Magie im "Buch der probaten Mittel,"* 148, 191–2, 163. Of the four cases, only the last has the exact same wording in both sources, whereas in the first three cases the textual parallel is close but not exact. Mallālī stated that he was copying from Sanūsī's own handwriting, so the textual variations are probably due to the plastic transmission of *The Tried and Tested Means*, with later copyists feeling free to change or supplement the wording.
29. For a detailed breakdown of the advertised results of the various "tried and tested means," see Dorpmüller, *Religiöse Magie im "Buch der probaten Mittel,"* 43–50.
30. Dorpmüller, *Religiöse Magie im "Buch der probaten Mittel,"* 142–3, 156, 165–6.
31. Dorpmüller, *Religiöse Magie im "Buch der probaten Mittel,"* 23–38.
32. For a detailed text-critical study of manuscripts, see Dorpmüller, *Religiöse Magie im "Buch der probaten Mittel,"* 85–133. Dorpmüller also notes (on p. 51) that the lateness of the manuscripts and the plasticity of the textual transmission raises the possibility that the work is not by Sanūsī.
33. Stearns, *Revealed Sciences*, 82–98, 120–4.

Chapter 11

1. Ibn ʿAskar, *Dawḥat al-nāshir*, 122.
2. Ibn Zakrī, *Bughyat al-ṭālib*,141–2.
3. MQ 539.
4. Von Grünebaum and Abel, *Az-Zarnuji's Instruction of the Student*, 63; Ibn Jamaʿa, *Tadhkirat al-sāmiʿ wa-l-mutakallim*, 90, 105.
5. On Muḥammad ibn Abī Madyan, see Ibn Maryam, *al-Bustān*, 259; Ibn ʿAskar, *Dawḥat al-nāshir*, 134. On Bū l-Qāsim al-Zawāwī, see Ibn Maryam, *al-Bustān*, 71.
6. Mallālī completed his studies with Bū l-Qāsim al-Zawāwī (Ibn Maryam, *al-Bustān*, 71). His commentary has been published; see Mallālī, *Sharḥ Umm al-barāhīn*.
7. For his centrality in later chains of transmission of Sanūsī's works, see Kattānī, *Fihris al-fahāris*, 999 and Thaʿālibī, *Kanz al-ruwāt*, 184, 282. For a brief biographical entry, see Ibn ʿAskar, *Dawḥat al-nāshir*, 129. Ibn ʿAskar's statement that he died in the 920s of the Hijri era (1514–1523 CE) is inaccurate. Yassīthanī studied with him in Tlemcen in 1522 on the way to the East and then again in 1525 on his way back to Fes (Manjūr, *Fihris*, 31, 36).
8. Abun-Nasr, *A History of the Maghreb*, 170–2.
9. Manjūr, *Fihris*, 28–31.
10. Manjūr, *Fihris*, 78.
11. De Roche, De Castilla, and Tahali, *Les livres du sultan*, vol. 2, 214.
12. Ifrānī, *Ṣafwat man intashara*, 206–7. See also the editor's introduction to Suktānī, *Ḥāshiya ʿalá Sharḥ al-Ṣughrá*, 37–52.
13. Ifrānī, *Ṣafwat man intashara*, 202–3, 344–50.
14. Ibn Maryam, *al-Bustān*, 104–5. Ibn Maryam, writing around the year 1602, described him as alive at the time and as having been Mufti of Tlemcen for forty-five years. Sources written after his death mention that he was Mufti for sixty years, suggesting a death date around 1617 (Ifrānī, *Ṣafwat man intashara*, 101–2, Thaʿālibī, *Kanz al-ruwāt*, 81).
15. Ifrānī, *Ṣafwat man intashara*, 220, Thaʿālibī, *Kanz al-ruwāt* 1093–4.
16. Fierro and Molina, "al-Maqqarī." For a lively account of Maqqarī's teaching Sanūsī's *Short Creed* in Cairo and how his own creedal poem emerged out of this teaching, see ʿAyyāshī, *al-Riḥla al-ʿAyyāshiyya*, vol. 2, 410.

17. On this scholar, see Timbuktī, *Nayl al-ibtihāj*, 344–5. For an extant manuscript of his commentary, see Manūfī, *Sharḥ al-ʿAqīda al-Ṣughrá*.
18. Ibn Turkī, *Sharḥ al-manẓūma al-Jazāʾiriyya*.
19. Shaʿrānī, *al-Yawāqīt wa l-jawāhir*; Ibn Ḥajar al-Haytamī, *al-Taʿarruf fī l-aṣlayn wa l-taṣawwuf*. Sanūsī is not mentioned in the detailed discussion of whether imitation in creed is admissible in Ibn Qāsim al-ʿAbbādī, *al-Āyāt al-bayyināt*, vol. 4, 280–7.
20. Munāwī, *al-Kawākib al-durriyya*. Zakariyyā al-Anṣārī appears in vol. 3, 369–73 and Aḥmad Zarrūq in vol. 3, 166–72.
21. On the commentary tradition on Maqqarī's poem in Mauretania, see Graf, "ʿIlm al-kalām in Mauretanien."
22. On Ghunaymī and Raḥmānī, see Muḥibbī, *Khulāṣat al-athar*, vol. 1, 312–5 and vol. 2, 140. Kharashī's commentary has been printed; see Kharashī, *al-Farāʾid al-saniyya*.
23. On Shāwī, see Muḥibbī, *Khulāṣat al-athar*, vol. 4, 486–8. On the history of al-Azhar in the Ottoman period and the *riwāq* system, see Dodge, *Al-Azhar*, 77–91, 201–7.
24. Sharqāwī (d.1812), *Ḥāshiya ʿalá Sharḥ al-Hudhudī*; Dasūqī (d.1815), *Ḥāshiya ʿalá Sharḥ Umm al-barāhīn*; Bājūrī (d.1860), *Ḥāshiya ʿalá l-Sanūsiyya*; ʿIllaysh (d.1882), *Hidāyat al-murīd li-ʿAqīdat ahl al-tawḥīd*; Ḥāmidī (d.1898), *Ḥawāshin ʿalá Sharḥ al-Kubrá*.
25. Azra, *The Origins of Islamic Reformism in Southeast Asia*, 112–22.
26. Khūja, *al-Dhayl*, 55; Fakūn, *Manshūr al-hidāya*, 58–61.
27. Fakūn, *Manshūr al-hidāya*, 113–4.
28. Khūja, *al-Dhayl*, 94, 106–10, 132. The commentaries of Ibrāhīm al-Saraqusṭī on Sanūsī's *Muqaddimāt* and on the *Wusṭá* have been printed: see Saraqusṭī, *al-Mawāhib al-Rabbāniyya fī sharḥ al-Muqaddimāt al-Sanūsiyya* and *al-Hiba wa-l-ʿaṭāʾ fī sharḥ al-ʿAqīda al-Wusṭá*.
29. On the margins of Maqdīsh, *Ḥāshiya ʿalá Sharḥ al-Wusṭá* (1902) and separately as Sanūsī, *Sharḥ al-Wusṭá* (1909).
30. Jāmiʿ al-Zaytūna, *Tartīb al-durūs bi-Jāmiʿ al-Zaytūna*, 13, 15, 18, 19.
31. Brenner, "Kabbe"; Kane, *Beyond Timbuktu*, 88–9.
32. Timbuktī, *Nayl al-ibtihāj*, 602.
33. Timbuktī, *Nayl al-ibtihāj*, 563–72.
34. Hunwick and O'Fahey (eds.), *Arabic Literature of Africa*, vol. 4, 17–31 (work nr. 58); vol. 4, 15–7 (work nr. 5).
35. Hunwick and O'Fahey (eds.), *Arabic Literature of Africa*, vol. 4, 32–3. Two commentaries by Damascene scholars on this versification have been published: Nābulusī (d.1731), *al-Laṭāʾif al-unsiyya*, and Ḥasanī (d.1935), *al-Budūr al-jaliyya*.
36. Brenner, "Kabbe."
37. Dan Fodio, *Handbook on Islam*, 50–5.
38. Hunwick and O'Fahey (eds.), *Arabic Literature of Africa*, vol. 1, 18, 37–9, vol. 2, 34–7. Muḥammad al-Walī's commentary is discussed in van Dalen, *Doubt, Scholarship and Society in 17th Century Central Sudanic Africa*, ch. 5.
39. Hunwick and O'Fahey (eds.), *Arabic Literature of Africa*, vol. 1, 14–6.
40. Foudah, *A Refined Explanation of the Sanūsī Creed*.
41. Maqdīsh, *Ḥāshiya ʿalá Sharḥ al-Wusṭá*, 103. The passage is cited in the editor's introduction to Sanūsī, *Sharḥ Wāsiṭat al-sulūk*, 9.
42. The works of Sanūsī are, for example, prominent among the manuscripts on theology in the library of Aḥmad Pāshā al-Jazzār (d.1804), the ruler of northern Palestine; see Jarada, "Books on Islamic Theology (*tawḥīd*) and Sufism (*taṣawwuf*)," 316–7.
43. Kātib Çelebī, *Kashf al-ẓunūn*, vol. 1, 633.

44. On the broader trend of Ottoman "confessionalization" in the sixteenth and seventeenth centuries, see Krstić and Terzioğlu (eds.), *Entangled Confessionalizations?*
45. For example, (1) Manisa İl Halk Kütüphanesi MS 2960 (fols. 192ᵇ–196ᵃ, copied in 1089/1678); (2) Milli Kütüphanesi, MS Nevşehir Ürgüp Tahsin Ağa İlce Halk Kütüphanesi 85 (copied in 1116/1704–5), fols. 66ᵇ–72ᵃ; (3) Süleymaniye Kütüphanesi: MS Mehmet Taviloğlu 125 (copied in 1121/1709–10), fols. 12ᵇ–15ᵃ; (4) Bayezit Kütüphanesi, MS Veliyüddin Efendi 1343 (not dated), fols. 27ᵇ–31ᵃ. On the genre of *ʿilm-i ḥāl* more generally, see Terzioğlu, "Where *ʿİlm-i ḥāl* meets Catechism" and Krstić, "You must know your faith in detail."
46. He did not cite an incipit when mentioning the *Long Creed*, suggesting that he hadn't seen a copy, and he mistakenly thought that Sanūsī first wrote a commentary on this *Long Creed* and that the *Wusṭá* is an abridged commentary on the same creed (Kātib Çelebī, *Kashf al-ẓunūn*, vol. 5, 5–6), whereas in fact the *Wusṭá* is a separate creed. He mentioned Sanūsī's commentary on al-Jazāʾirī's creedal poem but again did not give the incipit (vol. 6, 80–1).
47. El-Rouayheb, *Islamic Intellectual History in the Seventeenth Century*, 230–1.
48. Zabīdī, *al-Muʿjam al-mukhtaṣṣ*, 431–2 (entry on ʿAbd al-Qādir al-Qusanṭīnī al-Atharī [d.1780]).
49. Vikør, *Sufi and Scholar on the Desert Edge*, 35–40.
50. For the attitude of Aḥmad al-Tījānī (d.1815), see Wright, *Realizing Islam*, 61–6. According to Wright, his attitude was lukewarm rather than hostile to Ashʿarī kalam.
51. Vikør, *Sufi and Scholar on the Desert Edge*, 203 (for the proposed curriculum of studies) and 218ff. (on Sanūsī's writings).
52. ʿAbduh, *Risālat al-tawḥīd*, 76–8.
53. The distinction between a "modernist" and "purist" trend in this period, confusingly both often described as "Salafi," is noted in Lauzière, *The Making of Salafism*, 4–10.
54. Von Kügelgen, *Averroes und die arabische Moderne*; Hildebrandt, *Neo-Muʿtazilismus?*
55. El Shamsy, *Rediscovering the Islamic Classics*, 182–91.
56. For some exceptions, dating to before the end of the First World War, and consisting of translations of Sanūsī's shorter creedal works, see Wolff, *El-Senusi's Begriffsentwicklung des muhammedanischen glaubensbekenntnisses*; Luciani, *Les prolégomènes théologiques de Senoussi*; and Horten, *Muhammedanische Glaubenslehre.* An English translation of the *Short Creed* is included in Watt, *Islamic Creeds*, 90–7, published in 1994.

Bibliography

Arabic

ʿAbduh, Muḥammad. *Risālat al-tawḥīd.* Edited by Bassam al-Jābī. Beirut & Limassol: Dār Ibn Hazm & al-Jaffān wa-l-Jābī, 2001.

Āmidī, Sayf al-Dīn. *Abkār al-afkār.* Edited by Aḥmad Muḥammad al-Mahdī. Cairo: Maktabat Dār al-Kutub, 2002.

ʿAyyāshī, ʿAbdullāh. *al-Riḥla al-ʿAyyāshiyya.* Edited by Saʿīd al-Fāḍilī & Sulaymān al-Qurashī. Abu Dhabi: Dār al-Suwaydi, 2006.

Baghdādī, ʿAbd al-Qādir. *Uṣūl al-dīn.* Istanbul: Matbaʿat al-Dawla, 1928.

Bājūrī, Ibrāhīm. *Ḥāshiya ʿalá l-Sanūsiyya.* Bulaq: Dār al-Ṭibāʿa, 1283/1866.

Bakkī al-Kūmī, Muḥammad. *Taḥrīr al-maṭālib li-mā taḍammanathu ʿaqīdat Ibn al-Ḥājib.* Edited by Nizār Ḥammādī. Beirut: Mu'assasat al-Maʿārif, n.d.

Balawī, Aḥmad al-Wādī'āshī.*Thabat.* Edited by ʿAbdullāh al-ʿImrānī. Beirut: Dār al-Gharb al-Islāmī, 1983.

Bāqillānī, Muḥammad b. al-Ṭayyib. *Tamhīd al-awā'il wa-talkhīṣ al-dalā'il.* Edited by ʿImād al-Dīn Aḥmad Ḥaydar. Beirut: Mu'assasat al-kutub al-thaqāfiyya, 1987.

Bayḍāwī, Nāṣir al-Dīn. *Ṭawāliʿ al-anwār min maṭāliʿ al-anẓār.* Edited by ʿAbbās Sulaymān. Beirut: Dār al-Jīl & Cairo: al-Maktaba al-Azhariyya, 1991.

Būqlī Ḥasan, Jamāl al-Dīn. *al-Imām ibn Yūsuf al-Sanūsī wa-ʿilm al-tawḥīd.* Algiers: al-Mu'assasa al-Waṭaniyya li-l-kitāb, 1985.

Dakhkhān, ʿAbd al-ʿAzīz. *al-Imām al-ʿallāma Muḥammad ibn Yūsuf al-Sanūsī al-Tilimsānī wa-juhūduhu fī khidmat al-ḥadīth al-nabawī al-sharīf.* Algiers: Dār Kardāda, 2011.

Dasūqī, Jalāl al-Dīn. *Ḥāshiya ʿalá Sharḥ Umm al-Barāhīn.* Būlāq: al-Maṭbaʿa al-ʿĀmira, 1297/1880.

Dawānī, Jalāl al-Dīn. *Risālat Ithbāt al-wājib al-jadīda.* In Aḥmad Tuysirkānī (ed.), *Sabʿ rasā'il,* 117–70. Tehran: Mīrāth-i Maktūb, 2002.

Dawānī, Jalāl al-Dīn. *Risālat Ithbāt al-wājib al-qadīma.* In Aḥmad Tuysirkānī (ed.), *Sabʿ rasā'il,* 69–114. Tehran: Mīrāth-i Maktūb, 2002.

Dawānī, Jalāl al-Dīn. *Risālat al-Zawrā'.* In Aḥmad Tuysirkānī (ed.), *Sabʿ rasā'il,* 173–84. Tehran: Mīrāth-i Maktūb, 2002.

Dawānī, Jalāl al-Dīn. *Sharḥ al-ʿAqā'id al-ʿAḍudiyya.* Edited by Sayyid Hādī Khusrawshāhī. Printed with the glosses of Muḥammad ʿAbduh in Jamāl al-Dīn al-Afghānī, *al-Āthār al-kāmila,* vol. 7, 39–147. Cairo: Maktabat al-Shurūq al-Duwaliyya, 2002.

Dawānī, Jalāl al-Dīn. *Shawākil al-ḥūr fī sharḥ Hayākil al-nūr.* Edited by Muḥammad Rajab ʿAlī Ḥasan. Amman: Dār al-Fatḥ, 2023.

Fakūn, ʿAbd al-Karīm. *Manshūr al-hidāya fī kashf ḥāl man iddaʿá l-ʿilm wa-l-wilāya.* Edited by Abū l-Qāsim Saʿdallāh. Bayrūt: Dār al-Gharb al-Islāmī, 1987.

Ghazālī, Abū Ḥāmid. *al-Iqtiṣād fī l-iʿtiqād*. Edited by Anas Muḥammad ʿAdnān al-Sharfāwī. Riyad: Dār al-Minhāj, 2012.

Ḥafīd al-Taftāzānī. *Sharḥ Tahdhīb al-manṭiq*. Edited by ʿAbd al-Ḥamīd al-Turkmānī. Amman: Dār al-Nūr al-mubīn, 2019.

Ḥāmidī, Ismāʿīl. *Ḥawāshin ʿalá Sharḥ al-Kubrá*. Cairo: Mustafa al-Babi al-Halabi, 1936.

Ḥasanī, Muḥammad Badr al-Dīn. *al-Budūr al-jaliyya fī sharḥ Naẓm al-Sanūsiyya*. Edited by ʿAbd al-Raḥmān ibn Diyāb Ṭaybah. Beirut: Dār al-Imām Yūsuf al-Nabhānī lil Nashr wa al-Tawzīʿ, 2023.

Ḥillī, Ibn Muṭahhar. *Kashf al-murād bi-sharḥ Tajrīd al-iʿtiqād*. Edited by Ḥasanzāde Āmulī. Qum: Muʾassasat al-Nashr al-Islāmī, 1433/2012.

Ibn al-ʿArabī. *al-Mutawassiṭ fī l-iʿtiqād wa-l-radd ʿalá man khālafa l-sunna min dhawī l-bidaʿ wa-l-ilḥād*. Edited by ʿAbdullāh al-Tawrātī. Tangier & Beirut: Dār al-Ḥadīth al-Kattāniyya, 2015.

Ibn ʿArafa. *al-Mukhtaṣar al-kalāmī*. Edited by Nizār Ḥammādī. Kuwait: Dār al-Ḍiyāʾ, 2014.

Ibn ʿAskar. *Dawḥat al-nāshir li-maḥāsin man kāna bi-l-Maghrib min mashāʾikh al-qarn al-ʿāshir*. Edited by Muḥammad Ḥajjī. Rabat: Dār al-Maghrib, 1976.

Ibn Ḥajar al-Haytamī. *al-Taʿarruf fī l-aṣlayn wa l-taṣawwuf*. Printed on the margins of Ibn ʿAllān al-Ṣiddīqī, *al-Talaṭṭuf fī l-wuṣūl ilá l-Taʿarruf*. Mecca & Cairo: Maktabat al-Taraqqi & Mustafa al-Babi al-Halabi, 1912–36.

Ibn Jamāʿa. *Tadhkirat al-sāmiʿ wa-l-mutakallim fī ādāb al-ʿālim wa-l-mutaʿallim*. Edited by Muḥammad al-ʿAjami. Beirut: Dār al-Bashāʾir al-Islāmiyya, 2008.

Ibn al-Malāḥimī. *al-Fāʾiq fī uṣūl al-dīn*. Edited by Wilferd Madelung & Martin McDermott. Tehran: Iranian Institute of Philosophy, 2007.

Ibn Maryam. *al-Bustān fī dhikr al-awliyāʾ wa-l-ʿulamāʾ bi-Tilimsān*. Algiers: al-Maṭbaʿa al-Thaʿālibiyya, 1908.

Ibn Qāsim al-ʿAbbādī. *al-Āyāt al-bayyināt*. Bulaq: Dār al-Ṭibāʿa al-ʿĀmira, 1289/1872.

Ibn Sīnā. *al-Shifāʾ: al-ʿIbāra*. Edited by M. el-Khodeiri & I. Madkour. Cairo: Dār al-Kitāb al-ʿArabī, 1970.

Ibn al-Tilimsānī. *Sharḥ Maʿālim uṣūl al-dīn*. Edited by Nizār Ḥammādī. Beirut: Muʾassasat al-Maʿārif, 2011.

Ibn Tūmart. *Aʿazz mā yuṭlab*. Edited by ʿAmmār Ṭālibī. Algiers: al-Muʾassasa al-Waṭaniyya li-l-kitāb, 1985.

Ibn Turkī. *Sharḥ al-manẓūma al-Jazāʾiriyya fī l-ʿaqāʾid*. Edited by Maḥmūd ʿAbd al-Ṣādiq al-Ḥassān. Kuwait: Dār al-Ḍiyāʾ, 2017.

Ibn Wāṣil. *Sharḥ al-Jumal: Commentary on the Jumal on Logic*. Edited by Khaled El-Rouayheb. Leiden: Brill, 2022.

Ibn Zakrī. *Bughyat al-ṭālib fī sharḥ ʿaqīdat Ibn al-Ḥājib*. Edited by ʿAbdullah ibn Yūsuf al-Shaykh Sīdī. Unpublished PhD Dissertation, Mohammad V University, Rabat, 1994.

Ifrānī, Muḥammad al-Ṣaghīr. *Ṣafwat man intashara min akhbār ṣulaḥāʾ al-qarn al-ḥādī ʿashar*. Edited by Abd al-Majīd Khayālī. Casablanca: Markaz al-Turāth al-Thaqāfī al-Maghribī, 2004.

Iḥnānah, Yūsuf. *Taṭawwur al-madhhab al-Ashʿarī fī l-gharb al-Islāmī*. Rabat: Manshūrāt Wizārat al-Awqāf, 2004.

Ījī, ʿAḍud al-Dīn. *Jawāhir al-kalām*. Edited by ʿAlī Nājiḥ ʿAbduh Azharī. Cairo: Dār al-Ṣāliḥ 2022.

Ījī, ʿAḍud al-Dīn. *al-Mawāqif*. Cairo: Maṭbaʿat al-ʿUlūm, 1357/1938.

ʿIllaysh, Muḥammad. *Hidāyat al-murīd li-ʿAqīdat ahl al-tawḥīd*. Cairo: Matbaʿat Muṣṭafá Efendī, 1306/1888.

Jāmiʿ al-Zaytūna. *Tartīb al-durūs bi-Jāmiʿ al-Zaytūna*. Tunis: al-Matbaʿa al-Rasmiyya al-ʿArabiyya, 1912.

Jishumī, al-Ḥākim. *al-Tahdhīb fī l-tafsīr*. Edited by Abd al-Raḥmān al-Sālimī. Cairo & Beirut: Dār al-Kitāb al-Miṣrī & Dār al-Kitāb al-Lubnānī, 2018–19.

Jurjānī, al-Sayyid al-Sharīf. *Sharḥ al-Mawāqif*. Istanbul: Maṭbaʿat al-Ḥājj Muḥarram al-Būsnawī, 1286/1869.

Juwaynī, Imām al-Ḥaramayn. *al-Irshād ilá qawāṭiʿ al-adilla fī uṣūl al-iʿtiqād*. Edited by Muḥammad Yūsuf Mūsá & ʿAlī ʿAbd al-Munʿim ʿAbd al-Ḥamīd. Cairo: Maktabat al-Khānjī, 1950.

Kātib Çelebī. *Kashf al-ẓunūn ʿan asmāʾ al-kutub wa-l-funūn*. Edited by Ekmeleddin Ihsanoğlu & Bashar Awad Marouf. London: Muʾassasat al-Furqān, 2021.

Kattānī, ʿAbd al-Ḥayy. *Fihris al-fahāris*. Beirut: Dār al-Gharb al-Islāmī, 1982.

Kharashī, Muḥammad. *al-Farāʾid al-saniyya fī sharh al-muqaddima al-Sanūsīyya*. Edited by Bashir Burman. Beirut: Dār al-Kutub al-ʿIlmiyya, 2015.

Khaṭṭāb, Muḥammad. *Fahāris al-Khizāna al-Ḥasaniyya bi-l-Qaṣr al-Malakī bi-l-Rabāṭ*. Rabat: no publisher indicated, 1985.

Khūja, Ḥusayn. *al-Dhayl li-kitāb Bashāʾir ahl al-īmān fī futūḥāt Āl ʿUthmān*. Tunis: al-Maṭbaʿa al-Rasmiyya al-ʿArabiyya, 1908.

Khūnajī, Afḍal al-Dīn. *Kashf al-asrār ʿan ghawāmiḍ al-afkār*. Edited by Khaled El-Rouayheb. Tehran: Iranian Institute of Philosophy, 2010.

Mallālī, Muḥammad. *Sharḥ Umm al-barāhīn*. Edited by Khālid Zahrī. Beirut: Dār al-kutub al-ʿilmiyya, 2003.

Manjūr, Aḥmad. *Fihris*. Edited by Muhammad al-Ḥajjī. Rabat: Dār al-Maghrib, 1976.

Manjūr, Aḥmad. *al-Ḥāshiya al-kubrá ʿalá Sharḥ Kubrá l-Sanūsī*. Edited by Idrīs al-Manjūr. Casablanca, 2012.

Manjūr, Aḥmad. *Mukhtaṣar Naẓm al-farāʾid wa-mubdī l-fawāʾid fī sharḥ Muḥaṣṣil al-maqāṣid*. Edited by ʿAbd al-Razzāq Daḥmūn. Beirut: Dār Ibn Ḥazm, 2014.

Manūfī, ʿAlī. *Sharḥ al-ʿAqīda al-Ṣughrá*. MS Süleymaniye Kütüphanesi, Istanbul: Yeni Cami 744, fols. 153^{a}–187^{a}.

Maqdīsh, Maḥmūd. *Ḥāshiya ʿalá Sharḥ al-Wusṭá*. Tunis: al-Matbaʿa al-Ḥajariyya, 1320/1902–3.

Maybudī, Qāḍī Mīr. *Sharḥ al-Shamsiyya*. Istanbul: no publisher indicated, 1289/1872.

Mīr Abū l-Fatḥ. *Ḥāshiya ʿalá Sharḥ al-Tahdhīb*. Istanbul: al-Ḥājj Muḥarram al-Būsnawī, 1305/1887.

Muḥibbī, Muḥammad Amīn. *Khulāṣat al-athar fī aʿyān al-qarn al-ḥādī ʿashar*. Cairo: al-Maṭbaʿa al-Wahbiyya, 1284/1867–8.

Munāwī, ʿAbd al-Raʾūf. *al-Kawākib al-durriyya fī tarājim al-sāda al-Ṣūfiyya*. Edited by Muḥammad Adīb al-Jādir. Beirut: Dār Sadir, 1999.

Muqtaraḥ, Taqī al-Dīn Muẓaffar. *al-Asrār al-ʿaqliyya fī l-kalimāt al-nabawiyya*. Edited by Nizār Ḥammādī. Beirut: Muʾassasat al-Maʿārif, 2009.

Muqtaraḥ, Taqī al-Dīn Muẓaffar. *Sharḥ al-Irshād*. Edited by Fatḥī Aḥmad 'Abd al-Razzāq. Kuwait: Dār al-Ḍiyā', 2021.

Nābulusī, 'Abd al-Ghanī. *al-Laṭā'if al-unsiyya 'alá l-manẓūma al-Sanūsiyya*. Edited by 'Umar al-Shaykhalī. Amman: Dār al-Nūr al-mubīn, 2015.

al-Qāḍī 'Iyāḍ. *al-I'lām bi-ḥudūd wa-qawā'id al-islām*. Edited by Muḥammad Ṣadīq al-Minshāwī al-Sūhājī & Maḥmūd 'Abd al-Raḥmān 'Abd al-Mun'im. Cairo: Dār al-Faḍīla, 1995.

Qalṣādī, 'Alī. *Riḥlat al-Qalṣādī*. Edited by Muḥammad Abū l-Ajfān. Tunis: al-Sharika al-Tūnisiyya li-l-Tawzī', 1978.

Qalshānī, Aḥmad. *Taḥrīr al-maqāla fī sharḥ al-Risāla*. Edited by al-Ḥabīb ibn Ṭāhir & Muḥammad al-Madanīnī. Beirut: Mu'assasat al-Ma'ārif, 2008.

Qurashī, Muḥyī al-Dīn. *al-Jawāhir al-muḍiyya fī ṭabaqāt al-ḥanafiyya*. Edited by 'Abd al-Fattāḥ al-Ḥilū. Cairo: Dār Iḥyā' al-Kutub al-'Arabiyya, 1978.

Rāzī, Quṭb al-Dīn. *Lawāmi' al-asrār bi-Sharḥ Maṭāli' al-anwār*. Edited by Abū l-Qāsim Raḥmānī. Tehran: Mu'assasah-i Pizhūhishī-yi Ḥikmat va Falsafah-i Īrān, 2014.

Rāzī, Quṭb al-Dīn. *Sharḥ al-Shamsiyya*. Istanbul: Ahmed Efendi Matbaası, 1325/1907.

Sāḥilī, Muḥammad. *Bughyat al-sālik fī ashraf al-masālik*. Edited by 'Abd al-Raḥīm al-'Alamī. Rabat: Wizārat al-Awqāf wa-al-Shu'ūn al-Islāmīyah, 2003.

Salāljī, 'Uthmān. *al-'Aqīda al-burhāniyya wa-l-fuṣūl al-īmāniyya*. Edited by Nizār Ḥammādī. Beirut: Mu'assasat al-Ma'ārif, 2008.

Sanūsī, Muḥammad b. Yūsuf. *al-'Aqīda al-Ṣughrá*. Manuscripts of Turkish translation: (i) Manisa İl Halk Kütüphanesi, Manisa. MS 2960 (fols. 192^{b}–196^{a}, copied in 1089/1678); (ii) Milli Kütüphanesi, Ankara. MS Nevşehir Ürgüp Tahsin Ağa İlce Halk Kütüphanesi 85 (copied in 1116/1704–5), fols. 66^{b}–72^{a}; (iii) Süleymaniye Kütüphanesi, Istanbul. MS Mehmet Taviloğlu 125 (copied in 1121/1709–10), fols. 12^{b}–15^{a}; (iv) Bayezit Kütüphanesi, MS Veliyüddin Efendi 1343 (n.d.), fols. 27^{b}–31^{a}.

Sanūsī, Muḥammad b. Yūsuf. *Mukammil Ikmāl al-Ikmāl*. Printed with Ubbī, *Ikmāl Ikmāl al-Mu'lim*. Cairo: Maṭba'at al-Sa'āda, 1327/1909–1328/1910.

Sanūsī, Muḥammad b. Yūsuf [?]. *Nuṣrat al-fuqayyir fī l-radd 'alá Abī l-Ḥasan al-Ṣughayyir*. Edited by Ḥasan Ḥāfiẓī 'Alawī. *Da'wat al-ḥaqq* 9(2002): 4–129.

Sanūsī, Muḥammad b. Yūsuf. *Sharḥ al-asmā' al-ḥusná*. Edited by Nizār Ḥammādī. Beirut: Mu'assasat al-Ma'ārif, 2008.

Sanūsī, Muḥammad b. Yūsuf. *Sharḥ Mukhtaṣar Ibn 'Arafa*. Manuscript: Süleymaniye Library, Istanbul: Ragıp Paşa 904.

Sanūsī, Muḥammad b. Yūsuf. *Sharḥ Muqaddimat Īsāghūjī*. Manuscript: Princeton University Library, Islamic Manuscripts, Garrett Y2802.

Sanūsī, Muḥammad b. Yūsuf. *Sharḥ Wāsiṭat al-sulūk*. Edited by Nizār Ḥammādī. Damascus: Dār al-Taqwá & Tunis: Dār al-Imām Ibn 'Arafa, 2019.

Sanusi, Muḥammad b. Yūsuf. *Sharḥ al-Wusṭá*. Tunis: Maṭba'at al-Taqaddum al-Waṭaniyya, 1327/1909.

Sanūsī, Muḥammad b. Yūsuf [?]. *Tafsīr mā taḍammanathu kalimāt khayr al-bariyya min ghāmiḍ asrār al-ṣinā'a al-ṭibbiyya*. Edited by Hayā Muḥammad al-Dawsarī & 'Abd al-Qādir Aḥmad 'Abd al-Qādir. Kuwait: Dār Ibn al-Nadīm, 1999.

Saraqusṭī, Ibrāhīm. *al-Hiba wa-l-ʿaṭāʾ fī sharḥ al-ʿAqīda al-Wusṭá*. Tūnis: al-Maṭbaʿa al-Tūnisiyya, 1345/1926–7.

Saraqusṭī, Ibrāhīm. *al-Mawāhib al-rabbāniyya fī sharḥ al-Muqaddimāt al-Sanūsiyya*. Beirut: Dār al-Muqtabas, 2015.

Shahrastānī, ʿAbd al-Karīm. *Kitāb al-Milal wa l-niḥal*. Edited by William Cureton. London: Society for the Publication of Oriental Texts, 1842–6.

Shaʿrānī, ʿAbd al-Wahhāb. *al-Yawāqīt wa l-jawāhir fī bayān ʿaqāʾid al-akābir*. Cairo: Muṣṭafá al-Bābī al-Ḥalabī, 1959.

Sharīf, Abū Yaḥyá. *Abkār al-afkār al-ʿulwiyya fī sharḥ al-Asrār al-ʿaqliyya*. Edited by Nizār Ḥammādī. Beirut: Muʾassasat al-Maʿārif, 2011.

Sharqāwī, ʿAbdullāh. *Ḥāshiya ʿalá Sharḥ al-Hudhudī ʿalá l-Sanūsiyya*. Bulaq: Dār al-Ṭibāʿa, 1289/1872.

Subkī, Tāj al-Dīn. *Ṭabaqāt al-shāfiʿiyya al-kubrá*. Edited by Maḥmūd al-Ṭanāḥī & ʿAbd al-Fattāḥ al-Ḥilū. Cairo: ʿĪsá l-Bābī l-Ḥalabī, 1964–76.

Suktānī, ʿĪsá. *Ḥāshiya ʿalá Sharḥ al-Ṣughrá*. Edited by Aḥmad ʿĀrif bin Dhī Kafal. Cairo: Dār al-Ṣāliḥ, 2021.

Suktānī, ʿĪsá. *al-Tuḥfa al-mufīda fī sharḥ al-ʿaqīda al-Ḥafīda*. Edited by Nizār Ḥammādī & Fatḥī Aḥmad ʿAbd al-Razzāq. Kuwait: Dār al-Ḍiyāʾ, 2012.

Suyūrī, Miqdād. *Irshād al-ṭālibīn ilá Nahj al-mustarshidīn*. Edited by Mahdī al-Rajāʾī & Maḥmūd al-Marʿashī. Qum: Maktabat Āyatullāh al-Marʿashī al-ʿĀmma, 1405/1984–5.

Taftāzānī, Saʿd al-Dīn. *Sharḥ al-ʿAqāʾid al-Nasafiyya*. Printed with the glosses of Kestelī and Hayālī and the superglosses of Bihishtī. Istanbul: Şirket-i Sahafiye-i Osmaniye Matbaasi, 1326/1908.

Taftāzānī, Saʿd al-Dīn. *Sharḥ al-Maqāṣid*. Istanbul: Maṭbaʿat al-Ḥājj Muḥarram al-Būsnawī, 1305/1888.

Taftāzānī, Saʿd al-Dīn. *Sharḥ al-Shamsiyya*. Lithograph. Lucknow: al-Maṭbaʿ al-Yūsufī, 1317/1899.

Thaʿālibī, ʿAbd al-Raḥmān. *al-Jawāhir al-ḥisān fī tafsīr al-Qurʾān*. Edited by ʿAlī Muḥammad Muʿawwaḍ, ʿĀdil Aḥmad ʿAbd al-Mawjūd, & ʿAbd al-Fattāḥ Abū Sinna. Beirut: Dār Iḥyāʾ al-turāth al-ʿarabī, 1997.

Thaʿālibī, ʿĪsá. *Kanz al-ruwāt al-majmūʿ min durar al-majāz wa-yawāqīt al-masmūʿ*. Edited by ʿAbd al-ʿAzīz Dakhkhān. Sharjah: Jāmiʿat al-Shārjah, 2020.

Timbuktī, Aḥmad Bābā. *Nayl al-ibtihāj bi-taṭrīz al-Dībāj*. Edited by ʿAbd al-Hamid al-Harrāma. Tripoli: Dār al-Kātib, 2000.

Ubbī, Muḥammad. *Ikmāl Ikmāl al-Muʿlim*. Cairo: Maṭbaʿat al-Saʿāda, 1327/1909–1328/1910.

Zabīdī, Muḥammad Murtaḍá. *al-Muʿjam al-mukhtaṣṣ*. Edited by Niẓām Muḥammad Ṣāliḥ Yaʿqūbī & Muḥammad ibn Nāṣir al-ʿAjamī. Beirut: Dāral-Bashaʾir al-Islamiyya, 2006.

Zahrī, Khālid. *al-Maṣādir al-Maghribiyya li-l-ʿaqīda al-Ashʿariyya: bibliyūghrāfiyā wa-dirāsa bibliyūmitriyya*. Tetouan: Markaz Abī l-Ḥasan al-Ashʿarī l-il-Dirāsāt wa-l-Buḥūth, 2017.

Zamakhsharī, Jārullāh Maḥmūd. *al-Kashshāf ʿan ḥaqāʾiq ghawāmiḍ al-tanzīl*. Beirut: Dār al-Kitāb al-ʿArabī, 1947.

Zarrūq, Aḥmad. *Ightinām al-fawāʾid fī sharḥ Qawāʿid al-ʿaqāʾid*. Edited by Nizār Ḥammādī. Kuwait: Dār al-Ḍiyāʾ, 2022.

Western Languages

Abrahamov, B. "Scripturalist and Traditionalist Theology." In Sabine Schmidtke (ed.), *The Oxford Handbook of Islamic Theology*, 263–79. New York & Oxford: Oxford University Press, 2016.

Abun-Nasr, J. *A History of the Maghreb*. Cambridge: Cambridge University Press, 1971.

Adams, M.M. "Powerless Causes: The Case of Sacramental Causality." In P. Machamer & G. Wolters (eds.), *Thinking About Causes: From Greek Philosophy to Modern Physics*, 47–76. Pittsburgh: University of Pittsburgh Press, 2007.

Adamson, P. *Philosophy in the Islamic World: A Very Short Introduction*. Oxford: Oxford University Press, 2015.

Adamson, P. *Ibn Sina (Avicenna): A Very Short Introduction*. Oxford: Oxford University Press, 2023.

Ahmed, S. "Satanic Verses." In J.D. McAuliffe (ed.), *Encyclopedia of the Qur'an*, vol. 5, 531–6. Leiden: Brill, 2001.

Ahmed, S. *What Is Islam? The Importance of Being Islamic*. Princeton: Princeton University Press, 2015.

Amharar, I. "Autour d'un commentaire de la Muršida attribué à al-Sanūsī (m. 895/1490): discussion de la thèse de Ġurāb et tentative d'identification." *al-Qantara* 43(2022): 2–18.

Andersson, T. "Sufism in al-Sanūsī's (d. 895/1490) *al-Manhaj al-sadīd fī sharḥ kifāyat al-murīd*." *Journal of Sufi Studies* 14(2025): 50–68.

Al-Attar, M. *Islamic Ethics: Divine Command Theory in Arabo-Islamic Thought*. New York & London: Routledge, 2010.

Audi, R. *Epistemology: A Contemporary Introduction to the Theory of Knowledge*. New York & London: Routledge, 2011.

Austin, J.L. *How to Do Things with Words*. Edited by J. Urmson & M. Sbisa. 2nd edition. Cambridge: Harvard University Press, 1975.

Avicenna. *The Physics of The Healing*. Edited and translated by Jon McGinnis. Provo, Utah: Brigham Young University Press, 2009.

Ayubi, Z. *Gendered Morality: Classical Islamic Ethics of the Self, Family, and Society*. New York: Columbia University Press, 2019.

Azra, A. *The Origins of Islamic Reformism in Southeast Asia*. Hawaii: University of Hawaii Press, 2004.

Baima N.R. & T. Paytas. "True in Word and Deed: Plato on the Impossibility of Divine Deception." *Journal of the History of Philosophy* 58(2020): 193–214.

Bā'ūniyya, 'Ā'isha. *The Principles of Sufism*. Edited and translated by Th. Emil Homerin. New York: New York University Press, 2014.

Bdaiwi, Ahab. "Philosophia Ottomanica: Jalal al-Din Davani on Establishing the Necessary Being." In Hani Khafipour (ed.), *The Empires of the Near East and India: Source Studies of the Ottoman, Safavid, and Mughal Literate Communities*, 319–33. New York: Columbia University Press, 2019.

Beebee, H. "Hume and the Problem of Causation." In Paul Russell (ed.), *The Oxford Companion to Hume*, 228–48. New York: Oxford University Press, 2014.

Belo, C. "Averroes (d.1198), The Decisive Treatise." In K. El-Rouayheb & S. Schmidtke (eds.), *The Oxford Handbook of Islamic Philosophy*, 278–95. Oxford & New York: Oxford University Press, 2017.

Bencheneb, H. "al-Sanūsī, Muḥammad b. Yūsuf." In P. Bearman (ed.), *Encyclopedia of Islam,* 2nd edition, vol. 9, 20–2. Leiden: Brill 1960–2002.

Benevich, F. "The Classical Ash'ari Theory of Aḥwāl: al-Juwaynī and His Opponents." *Journal of Islamic Studies* 27(2016): 136–75.

Bennett, D. "The Mu'tazilite Movement (II): The Early Mu'tazilites." In Sabine Schmidtke (ed.), *The Oxford Handbook of Islamic Theology*, 142–58. New York & Oxford: Oxford University Press, 2016.

Bennison, A. *The Almoravid and Almohad Empires*. Edinburgh: Edinburgh University Press, 2016.

Bertolacci, A. "Ibn Sīnā (d. 428/1037): Metaphysics of the Shifā'." In Khaled El-Rouayheb & Sabine Schmidtke (eds.), *The Oxford Handbook of Islamic Philosophy*, 143–68. New York & Oxford: Oxford University Press, 2017.

Bireley, R. *The Refashioning of Catholicism, 1450–1700*. Washington, DC: The Catholic University of America Press, 1999.

Brenner, L. "Kabbe." In V.Y. Mudimbe & K. Kavwahirehi (eds.), *Encyclopedia of African Religions and Philosophy*, 357–8. Dordrecht: Springer, 2021.

Brown, J.A.C. *Hadith: Muḥammad's Legacy in the Medieval and Modern World*. Oxford: Oneworld, 2009.

Brunschvig, R. *Deux récits de voyage inédits en Afrique du Nord au XVe siècle*. Paris: Larose Éditeurs, 1936.

Burhanuddin, J. "The Popularizing of Sunni Doctrine in Southeast Asia: *Sifat dua puluh* in Malay Kitab Jawi in the 19th century." *Afkār* 24(2022): 275–314.

Calverley, E.E. "Al-Abharī's Īsāghūjī fī l-manṭiq." In W.G. Shellabear (ed.), *The Macdonald Presentation Volume*, 75–85. Princeton: Princeton University Press, 1933.

Cantwell Smith, W. *The Meaning and End of Religion*. New York: Macmillan, 1962.

Cantwell Smith, W. *On Understanding Islam: Selected Studies*. The Hague & New York: Mouton Press, 1981.

Carlisle, C. *Kierkegaard's Fear and Trembling: A Reader's Guide*. London & New York: Continuum, 2010.

Chatti, S. *Arabic Logic from al-Farabi to Averroes: A Study of the Early Arabic Categorical, Modal, and Hypothetical Syllogistics*. Cham: Birkhäuser, 2019.

Chih, R. "Prophetic Piety, Mysticism, and Authority in Premodern Arabic Devotional Literature: al-Jazuli's *Dala'il al-Khayrat* (15th Century)." *International Journal of Middle East Studies* 54(2022): 462–83.

Chittick, W. *The Self-Disclosure of God: Principles of Ibn 'Arabī's Cosmology*. New York: State University of New York Press, 1998.

Cornell, V. *Realm of the Saint: Power and Authority in Moroccan Sufism*. Austin: University of Texas Press, 1998.

Cornell, V. "Muḥammad ibn Sulaymān al-Jazūlī and the Place of *Dalā'il al-khayrāt* in Jazūlite Sufism." *Journal of Islamic Manuscripts* 12(2021): 235–64.

Craig, W.L. *The Kalam Cosmological Argument*. New York: Barnes & Noble, 1979.

Craig W.L. & J.D. Sinclair. "The Kalam Cosmological Argument." In Willian Lane Craig & J.P. Moreland (eds.), *The Blackwell Companion to Natural Theology*, 101–201. Chichester, UK & Malden, MA: Wiley-Blackwell, 2012.

Crisp O. & K. Strobel. *Jonathan Edwards: An Introduction to His Thought*. Grand Rapids, MI: William B. Eerdsmans, 2018.

Cross, R. *Duns Scotus*. New York & Oxford: Oxford University Press, 1999.

Dan Fodio, U. *Handbook on Islam*. Translated by Aisha Bewley. Bradford: Diwan Press, 2017.

Davidson, H.A. *Proofs for Eternity, Creation and the Existence of God in Medieval Islamic and Jewish Philosophy*. New York & Oxford: Oxford University Press, 1987.

Davidson, H.A. *Alfarabi, Avicenna, & Averroes on Intellect: Their Cosmologies, Theories of the Active Intellect, & Theories of Human Intellect*. New York & Oxford: Oxford University Press, 1992.

Davies, B. *Thomas Aquinas's Summa Contra Gentiles: A Guide and Commentary*. New York & Oxford: Oxford University Press, 2016.

Dermenghem, É. *Le culte des saints dans l'Islam maghrébin*. Paris: Gallimard, 1954.

De Roche, F., N. De Castilla, & L. Tahali. *Les livres du sultan: Materiaux pour une histoire du livre et de la vie intellectuelle du Maroc saadien (XVIe siècle)*. Paris: Memoires de l'academie des inscriptions et belles-lettres, 2022.

Despois, J., A. Raynal, & S. Chaker. "Beni Snous." In S. Chaker (ed.), *Encyclopédie Berbère*, vol. X, 1468–70. Paris: Edisud, 1991.

Dodge, B. *Al-Azhar: A Millennium of Muslim Learning*. Washington, DC: Middle East Institute, 1961.

Dorpmüller, S. *Religiöse Magie im "Buch der probaten Mittel": Analyse, kritische Edition und Übersetzung des Kitāb al-Muǧarrabāt von Muḥammad ibn Yūsuf as-Sanūsī (gest. um 895/1490)*. Wiesbaden: Harrassowitz, 2005.

Effingham, N. *An Introduction to Ontology*. Cambridge, UK & Malden, MA: Polity, 2013.

Eickelman, D. *Moroccan Islam: Tradition and Society in a Pilgrimage Center*. Austin: University of Texas Press, 1976.

Eire, C. *Reformations: The Early Modern World, 1450–1650*. New Haven: Yale University Press, 2016.

El-Omari, R. "The Muʿtazilite Movement (I): The Origins of the Muʿtazila." In Sabine Schmidtke (ed.), *The Oxford Handbook of Islamic Theology*, 130–41. New York & Oxford: Oxford University Press, 2016.

El-Rouayheb, K. "From Ibn Ḥajar al-Haytamī (d. 1566) to Khayr al-Dīn al-Ālūsī (d. 1899): Changing Views of Ibn Taymiyya Among Non-Ḥanbalī Sunnī Scholars." In Shahab Ahmed & Yossef Rapoport (eds.), *Ibn Taymiyya and His Times*, 269–318. Karachi & Oxford: Oxford University Press, 2010.

El-Rouayheb. K. *Islamic Intellectual History in the Seventeenth Century: Scholarly Currents in the Ottoman Empire and the Maghreb*. Cambridge: Cambridge University Press, 2015.

El-Rouayheb, K. "Must God Tell Us the Truth? A Problem in Ashʿari Theology." In Behnam Sadeghi, Asad Ahmed, Adam Silverstein, & Robert Hoyland (eds.), *Islamic Cultures, Islamic Contexts: Essays in Honour of Professor Patricia Crone*, 411–29. Leiden: Brill, 2015.

El-Rouayheb, K. "Arabic Logic After Avicenna." In Catarina Novaes-Dutilh & Stephen Read (eds.), *The Cambridge Companion to Medieval Logic*, 69–93. Cambridge: Cambridge University Press, 2016.

El-Rouayheb, K. *The Development of Arabic Logic (1200–1800)*. Basel: Schwabe Verlag, 2019.

El-Rouayheb, K. "The Argument of Superposition (*burhān al-taṭbīq*) and Its Critics in the Medieval Islamic World." In Urs Gösken, Patric Schaerer, Roman Seidel, James Weaver, & Thomas Würz (eds.), *Mobilität des Denkens: Festschrift für Ulrich Rudolph*, 165–92. Leiden: Brill, 2025.

El Shamsy, A. *Rediscovering the Islamic Classics*. Princeton: Princeton University Press, 2020.

Evans, C.S. *God & Moral Obligation*. Oxford & New York: Oxford University Press, 2013.

Farahat, O. *The Foundations of Norms in Islamic Jurisprudence and Theology*. Cambridge: Cambridge University Press, 2019.

Fierro, M. *'Abd al-Mu'min: Mahdism and Caliphate in the Islamic West*. Oxford: Oneworld, 2021.

Fierro M. & L. Molina. "al-Maqqarī." In D. Stewart & J. Lowry (eds.), *Essays in Arabic Literary Biography, 1350–1850*, 273–83. Wiesbaden: Harrassowitz, 2009.

Forcada, M. "Bronze and Gold: al-Fārābī on Medicine." *Oriens* 48(2020): 367–415.

Formigari, L. "Chain of Being." In Philip Wiener (ed.), *Dictionary of the History of Ideas*, vol. 1, 325–35. New York: Scribner, 1973.

Foudah, S. *A Refined Explanation of the Sanūsī Creed*. Translated by Suraqah Abdul Aziz. Rotterdam: Sunni Publications, 2013.

Frank, R.M. "The Structure of Created Causality According to al-Ash'arī: An Analysis of the Kitāb al-Luma'." §§ 82–164. *Studia Islamica* 25(1966): 13–75.

Frank, R.M. "Attribute, Attribution, and Being: Three Islamic Views." In Parviz Morewedge (ed.), *Philosophies of Existence: Ancient and Medieval*, 258–78. New York: Fordham University Press, 1982.

Frank, R.M. "Moral Obligation in Classical Muslim Theology." *Journal of Religious Ethics* 11(1983): 204–23.

Frank, R.M. "Knowledge and Taqlīd: The Foundation of Religious Belief in Classical Ash'arism." *Journal of the American Oriental Society* 109(1989): 37–62.

Frank, R.M. "Al-Ustādh Abū Isḥāḳ: An *'Aḳīda* Together with Selected Fragments." *Mélanges de l'Institut Dominicain d'Études Orientales* 19(1989): 129–202.

Frank, R.M. "The Ash'arite Ontology I: Primary Entities." *Arabic Sciences and Philosophy* 9(1999): 163–231.

Freddoso, A.J. "Medieval Aristotelianism and the Case Against Secondary Causation in Nature." In T.V. Morris (ed.), *Divine & Human Action: Essays in the Metaphysics of Theism*, 74–118. Ithaca & London: Cornell University Press, 1988.

Fromherz, A.J. *The Almohads: The Rise of an Islamic Empire*. London: I.B. Tauris, 2010.

Gardet, L. & G. Anawati. *Introduction à la théologie musulmane: essai de théologie compare*. Paris: J. Vrin, 1948.

Garrett, D. "Hume." In H. Beebee, C. Hitchcock, & P. Menzies (eds.), *The Oxford Handbook of Causation*, 73–91. Oxford: Oxford University Press, 2009.

Garson, J. *Modal Logic for Philosophers*. Cambridge: Cambridge University Press, 2013.

Geertz, C. *Islam Observed: Religious Development in Morocco and Indonesia*. Chicago: University of Chicago Press, 1971.

Gert, H. "The Standard Meter by Any Name Is Still a Meter Long." *Philosophy and Phenomenological Research* 65(2002): 50–68.

Ghazālī. *Deliverance from Error.* Translated by Richard McCarthy. Louisville, Kentucky: Fons Vitae, 2000.

Ghazālī. *The Incoherence of the Philosophers.* Edited and translated by Michael Marmura. Provo, Utah: Brigham Young University Press, 2000.

Gimaret, D. *Théories des l'acte humaine en théologie musulmane.* Paris: Vrin, 1980.

Gimaret, D. *La doctrine d'al-Ash'arī.* Paris: Cerf, 1990.

Graf, G. "'Ilm al-kalām in Mauretanien anhand maurischer Kommentare zur Iḍā'at ad-duǧunna fī i'tiqād ahl as-sunna von al-Maqqarī (st. 1041/1632)." *Asiatische Studien* 72(2018): 751–94.

Griffel, F. *Apostasie und Toleranz im Islam: die Entwicklung zu al-Ġazālīs Urteil gegen die Philosophie und die Reaktionen der Philosophen.* Leiden: Brill, 2000.

Griffel, F. "Ibn Tūmart's Rational Proof for God's Existence and Unity and His Connection to the Niẓāmiyya *Madrasa* in Baghdad." In P. Cressier, M. Fierro, & L. Molina (eds.), *Los almohades: problemas y perspectivas*, 753–813. Madrid: Consejo Superior de Investigaciones Científicas, 2005.

Griffel, F. "Fakhr al-Dīn al-Rāzī's Life and the Patronage He Received." *Journal of Islamic Studies* 18(2007): 313–44.

Griffel, F. *Al-Ghazali's Philosophical Theology.* New York & Oxford: Oxford University Press, 2009.

Griffel, F. "Al-Ghazali at His Most Rationalist: The Universal Rule for Allegorically Interpreting Revelation." In Georges Tamer (ed.), *Islam and Rationality: The Impact of al-Ghazali. Papers Collected on His 900th Anniversary*, 89–120. Leiden: Brill, 2015.

Hare, J. *God's Command.* Oxford & New York: Oxford University Press, 2015.

Hildebrandt, T. *Neo-Mu'tazilismus? Intention und Kontext im modernen arabischen Umgang mit dem rationalistischen Erbe des Islam.* Leiden: Brill, 2007.

Hoover, J. *Ibn Taymiyya's Theodicy of Perpetual Optimism.* Leiden: Brill, 2007.

Hoover, J. "Ḥanbalī Theology." In Sabine Schmidtke (ed.), *The Oxford Handbook of Islamic Theology*, 625–46. New York & Oxford: Oxford University Press, 2016.

Horten, M. *Muhammedanische Glaubenslehre: Die Katechismen des Fudali und des Sanusi.* Bonn: Marcus & Weber, 1916.

Huff, T. *The Rise of Early Modern Science: Islam, China, and the West.* Cambridge: Cambridge University Press, 2017.

Hunwick, J.O. & R.S. O'Fahey. *Arabic Literature of Africa.* Leiden: Brill, 1994.

Hurvitz, N. "Al-Ma'mūn (r. 198/813–218/833) and the *Miḥna*." In Sabine Schmidtke (ed.), *The Oxford Handbook of Islamic Theology*, 649–59. New York & Oxford: Oxford University Press, 2016.

Ibn Khaldūn. *The Requirements of the Sufi Path: A Defense of the Mystical Tradition.* Edited and translated by Carolyn Baugh. New York: New York University Press, 2022.

Jāmī, 'Abd al-Raḥmān. *The Precious Pearl.* Translated and annotated by Nicholas Heer. Albany: State University of New York Press, 1979.

Jarada, H. "Books on Islamic Theology (*tawḥīd*) and Sufism (*taṣawwuf*): Rational Verification and Experiential Learning in Ottoman Palestine." In S. Aljoumani,

G. Burak, & K. Hirschler (eds.), *The Library of Aḥmad Pasha al-Jazzār: Book Culture in Late Ottoman Palestine*, 315–40. Leiden: Brill, 2025.
Jusoh, C. R. *The Malay Exposition of al-Sanusi's Umm al-barahin*. Batu Caves, Selangor: Islamic and Strategic Studies Institute, 2016.
Kane, O. *Beyond Timbuktu: An Intellectual History of Muslim West Africa*. Cambridge, MA: Harvard University Press, 2016.
Kholeif, F. *A Study on Fakhr al-Dīn al-Rāzī and His Controversies in Transoxiana*. Beirut: Dārel-Machreq, 1966.
Knysh, A. *Ibn 'Arabi in the Later Islamic Tradition: The Making of a Polemical Image in Medieval Islam*. Albany: State University of New York Press, 1999.
Knysh, A. *Islamic Mysticism: A Short History*. Leiden: Brill, 2000.
Krstić, T. "You Must Know Your Faith in Detail: Redefinition of the Role of Knowledge and Boundaries of Belief in Ottoman Catechisms (*'ilm-i ḥāls*)." In Tijana Krstić & Derin Terzioğlu (eds.), *Historicizing Sunni Islam in the Ottoman Empire*, 155–95. Leiden: Brill, 2021.
Krstić, T. & D. Terzioğlu. (eds.) *Entangled Confessionalizations? Dialogic Perspectives on the Politics of Piety and Community Building in the Ottoman Empire, 15th–18th Centuries*. Piscataway, NJ: Gorgias Press, 2022.
Kugle, S. *Rebel Between Spirit and Law: Aḥmad Zarrūq, Sainthood, and Authority in Islam*. Bloomington: Indiana University Press, 2006.
Kutach, D. *Causation*. Cambridge & Malden, MA: Polity, 2014.
Lammer, A. "Time and Mind-Dependence in Sayf al-Dīn al-Āmidī's Abkār al-afkār." In Dag Hasse & Amos Bertolacci (eds.), *Arabic, Hebrew and Latin Reception of Avicenna's Physics and Cosmology*, 101–62. Berlin, Boston: De Gruyter, 2018.
Langermann, Y. T. "From My Notebooks: On Tajriba/Nissayon ('Experience'): Texts in Hebrew, Judeo-Arabic, and Arabic." *ALEPH: Historical Studies in Science and Judaism* 14(2014): 147–76.
Lauzière, H. *The Making of Salafism: Islamic Reform in the Twentieth Century*. New York: Columbia University Press, 2016.
Lav, D. "Ash'arism, Causality, and the Cult of Saints." *Jerusalem Studies in Arabic and Islam* 50(2021): 255–312.
Lawless, R. "Tlemcen, Capital City of the 'Abd al-Wadids: A Study of the Functions of a Medieval Islamic City." *Islamic Quarterly* 18(1974): 14–20.
Lawless, R. & G. Blake. *Tlemcen: Continuity and Change in an Algerian Islamic Town*. London & New York: Bowker, 1976.
Leo Africanus. *The History and Description of Africa*. London: Haklyut Society, 1896.
López-Farjeat, L.X. "'Abd al-Jabbār and al-Ghazālī on Divine Speech and Their Theories of Language." *The Muslim World (Hartford)* 111(2021): 444–65.
López-Farjeat, L.X. *Classical Islamic Philosophy: A Thematic Introduction*. Routledge: New York, 2022.
Lovejoy, A. *The Great Chain of Being: A Study of the History of an Idea*. Cambridge, MA: Harvard University Press, 1936.
Luciani, J.-D. *Les prolégomènes théologiques de Senoussi*. Algiers: Fontana, 1908.
Macdonald, D.B. *Development of Muslim Theology, Jurisprudence and Constitutional Theory*. New York: Charles Scribner's, 1903.

Madelung, W. "The Origins of the Controversy Concerning the Creation of the Koran." In J. Barral (ed.), *Orientalia hispanica sive studia F.M. Pareja octogenario dictata*, 504–25. Leiden: Brill, 1974.

Madelung, W. "Review: Sophia Vasalou, Moral Agents and Their Deserts: The Character of Muʿtazilite Ethics." *Bulletin of the School of Oriental and African Studies* 73(2009): 564–5.

Makdisi, G. "Law and Traditionalism in the Institutions of Learning of Medieval Islam." In Gustav von Grunebaum (ed.), *Theology and Law in Islam*, 75–88. Wiesbaden: Otto Harrassowitz, 1971.

Mander, W.J. *The Volitional Theory of Causation: From Berkeley to the Twentieth Century*. Oxford University Press, 2023.

Marcais, W. *Les monuments arabes de Tlemcen*. Paris: A. Fontemoing, 1903.

McCann, H.J & J.L. Kvanvig. "The Occasionalist Proselytizer: A Modified Catechism." *Philosophical Perspectives* 5(1991): 587–615.

McGinnis, J. "Scientific Methodologies in Medieval Islam." *Journal of the History of Philosophy* 41(2003): 307–27.

McGinnis, J. *Avicenna*. New York & Oxford: Oxford University Press, 2010.

McGinnis, J. "Creation and Eternity in Medieval Philosophy." In Heather Dyke & Adrian Bardon (eds.), *A Companion to the Philosophy of Time*, 73–86. Malden, MA, Wiley-Blackwell, 2013.

McGinnis, J. "Islamic Ethics." In Thomas Williams (ed.), *The Cambridge Companion to Medieval Ethics*, 77–100. Cambridge: Cambridge University Press, 2019.

McGinnis, J. "Simple Is as Simple Does: Plantinga and al-Ghazali on Divine Simplicity." *Religious Studies* 58(2022): 97–109.

Melvin-Koushki, M. "Is (Islamic) Occult Science Science?" *Theology and Science* 18(2020): 303–24.

Meyer, T. "Theology and Sufism." In Tim Winter (ed.), *The Cambridge Companion to Islamic Theology*, 258–87. Cambridge: Cambridge University Press, 2008.

Morrissey, F. *Sufism and the Perfect Human: From Ibn ʿArabī to al-Jīlī*. Abingdon & New York: Routledge, 2020.

Muhtaroğlu, N. "Plantinga and Ashʿarites on Divine Simplicity." *Kader* 18(2020): 488–99.

Mumford, S. & R.L Anjum. *Causation: A Very Short Introduction*. Oxford: Oxford University Press, 2013.

Nadler, S. "Malebranche on Occasionalism." In Steven Nadler (ed.), *The Cambridge Companion to Malebranche*, 112–38. Cambridge: Cambridge University Press, 2000.

Nadler, S. *Occasionalism: Causation Among the Cartesians*. Oxford & New York: Oxford University Press, 2011.

Nagel, T. *The History of Islamic Theology from Muhammad to the Present*. Princeton: Markus Wiener Publishers, 2000.

Nawas, J. *Al-Ma'mūn, the Inquisition, and the Quest for Caliphal Authority*. Atlanta: Lockwood Press, 2015.

Olson, C. "Beyond the Avicennian Turn: The Creeds of Muḥammad b. Yūsuf al-Sanūsī." *Studia Islamica* 115(2020): 101–40.

Olson, C. "The Magian Position: Legal Consequences for Creedal Ignorance in the Far Maghrib, 8th/14th–11th/17th century." *Islamic Law and Society* 31(2024): 145–93.

Osler, M. *Reconfiguring the World: Nature, God, and Human Understanding from the Middle Ages to Early Modern Europe.* Baltimore: Johns Hopkins University Press, 2010.

Paton, H.J. *The Modern Predicament: A Study in the Philosophy of Religion.* London: George Allen and Unwin & New York: Macmillan, 1955.

Perler, D. & U. Rudolph. *Occasionalismus: Theorien der Kausalität im arabisch-islamischen und im europäischen Denken.* Göttingen: Vandenhoeck & Ruprecht, 2000.

Peters, J.R.T.M. *God's Created Speech: A Study in the Speculative Theology of the Mu'tazilî Qâdî l-Qudât Abûl-Hasan 'Abd al-Jabbâr bn Ahmad al-Hamadânî.* Leiden: Brill, 1976.

Pormann, P. "Avicenna on Medical Practice, Epistemology, and the Physiology of the Inner Senses." In Peter Adamson (ed.), *Interpreting Avicenna*, 91–108. Cambridge: Cambridge University Press, 2013.

Pourjavady, R. *Philosophy in Early Safavid Iran Najm al-Dīn al-Nayrīzī and His Writings.* Leiden: Brill, 2011.

Pourjavady, R. "The Legacy of 'Aḍud al-Dīn al-Ījī: His Works and His Students." In Ayman Shihadeh & Jan Thiele (eds.), *Philosophical Theology in Islam: Later Ash'arism, East and West*, 337–70. Leiden: Brill, 2020.

Powers, D. *Law, Society, and Culture in the Maghrib, 1300–1500.* Cambridge: Cambridge University Press, 2002.

Priest, G. *An Introduction to Non-Classical Logic: From If to Is.* Cambridge: Cambridge University Press, 2008.

Provenzali, F. *El-Bostan, ou, Jardin des biographies des saints et savants de Tlemcen par Ibn Maryem ech-Cherif el-Meliti.* Algiers: Fonata Frères, 1910.

Pruss, A. *Infinity, Causation & Paradox.* Oxford: Oxford University Press, 2018.

Psillos, S. "Regularity Theories." In Helen Beebee, Christopher Hitchcock, & Peter Menzies (eds.), *The Oxford Handbook of Causation*, 131–57. Oxford & New York: Oxford University Press, 2009.

Rachels, J. *The Elements of Moral Philosophy.* 2nd edition. New York: McGraw-Hill, 1993.

Rescher, N. *The Development of Arabic Logic.* Pittsburgh: University of Pittsburgh Press, 1964.

Rescher, N. *Temporal Modalities in Arabic Logic.* Dordrecht: D. Reidel, 1967.

Rescher N. & A. vander Nat. "The Theory of Modal Syllogistic in Medieval Arabic Logic." In Nicholas Rescher (ed.), *Studies in Modality*, 17–56. Oxford: Basil Blackwell, 1974.

Richardson, K. "Avicenna and the Principle of Sufficient Reason." *The Review of Metaphysics* 67(2014): 743–68.

Richardson, K. "Efficient Causation: From Ibn Sīnā to Ockham." In T. Schmaltz (ed.), *Efficient Causation: A History*, 105–31. Oxford & New York: Oxford University Press, 2014.

Rosenthal, F. *The Muqaddimah of Ibn Khaldūn.* New York, Pantheon, 1958.

Rudolph, U. *Al-Māturīdī and the Development of Sunnī Theology in Samarqand.* Translated by Rodrigo Adem. Leiden: Brill, 2010.

Rudolph, U. "Ḥanafī Theological Tradition and Māturīdism." In Sabine Schmidtke (ed.), *The Oxford Handbook of Islamic Theology*, 280–96. New York & Oxford: Oxford University Press, 2016.

Rudolph, U. "Occasionalism." In Sabine Schmidtke (ed.), *The Oxford Companion to Islamic Theology*, 347–63. New York & Oxford: Oxford University Press, 2016.

Russell, R.M. (ed.) *The Oxford Handbook of Natural Theology.* New York & Oxford: Oxford University Press, 2013.

Schmidtke, S. "The Muʿtazilite Movement (III): The Scholastic Phase." In Sabine Schmidtke (ed.), *The Oxford Handbook of Islamic Theology*, 159–80. New York & Oxford: Oxford University Press, 2016.

Shihadeh, A. "The Existence of God." In T. Winter (ed.), *The Cambridge Companion to Islamic Theology*, 197–217. Cambridge: Cambridge University Press, 2008.

Shihadeh, A. "Classical Ashʿarī Anthropology: Body, Life and Spirit." *The Muslim World (Hartford)* 102(2012): 433–77.

Shihadeh, A. "Theories of Ethical Value in Kalām." In Sabine Schmidtke (ed.), *The Oxford Handbook of Islamic Theology*, 384–407. New York & Oxford: Oxford University Press, 2016.

Sorabji, R. *Time, Creation and the Continuum: Theories in Antiquity and the Early Middle Ages.* Chicago: University of Chicago Press, 1983.

Stearns, J. *Infectious Ideas: Contagion in Premodern Islamic and Christian Thought in the Western Mediterranean.* Baltimore: Johns Hopkins University Press, 2011.

Stearns, J. *Revealed Sciences: The Natural Sciences in Seventeenth-Century Morocco.* Cambridge: Cambridge University Press, 2021.

Street, T. "Toward a History of Syllogistic After Avicenna: Notes on Rescher's Studies on Arabic Modal Logic." *Journal of Islamic Studies* 11(2000): 209–28.

Street, T. "An Outline of Avicenna's Syllogistic." *Archiv für Geschichte der Philosophie* 84(2002): 129–60.

Street, T. "Arabic Logic." In D.M. Gabbay & J. Woods (eds.), *Greek, Indian and Arabic Logic.* Vol. 1 of *Handbook of the History of Logic*, 523–96. Amsterdam: Elsevier, 2004.

Street, T. "Suhrawardī on Modal Syllogisms." In A. Akasoy & W. Raven (eds.), *Islamic Thought in the Middle Ages*, 163–78. Leiden: Brill, 2008.

Street, T. "Medieval and Modern Interpretations of Avicenna's Modal Syllogistic." In F. Opwis & D. Reisman (eds.), *Islamic Philosophy, Science, Culture, and Religion: Essays in Honor of Dimitri Gutas*, 232–56. Leiden: Brill, 2012.

Street, T. "Afḍal al-Dīn al-Khūnajī (d. 1248) on the Conversion of Modal Propositions." *Oriens* 42(2014): 454–513.

Street, T. "Al-ʿAllāma al-Ḥillī (d.1325) and the Early Reception of Kātibī's *Shamsiyya*: Notes Towards a Study of the Dynamics of Post-Avicennan Logical Commentary." *Oriens* 44(2016): 267–300.

Street, T. "Kātibī (d. 1277), Taḥtānī (d. 1365), and the Shamsiyya." In K. El-Rouayheb & S. Schmidtke (eds.), *The Oxford Handbook of Islamic Philosophy*, 348–74. New York: Oxford University Press, 2016.

Street, T. (ed. & trans.) *Najm al-Dīn al-Kātibī: The Rules of Logic.* New York: New York University Press, 2024.

Strobino R. "Per Se, Inseparability, Containment and Implication: Bridging the Gap Between Avicenna's Theory of Demonstration and Logic of the Predicables." *Oriens* 44(2016): 181–266.

Strobino, R. "Ibn Sina's Logic." *The Stanford Encyclopedia of Philosophy* (Fall 2018 Edition), Edward N. Zalta (ed.), URL = <https://plato.stanford.edu/archives/fall2018/entries/ibn-sina-logic/>.

Strobino R. & P. Thom. "The Logic of Modality." In C. Dutilh-Novaes & S. Read (eds.), *The Cambridge Companion to Medieval Logic,* 342–69. Cambridge: Cambridge University Press, 2016.

Stump, E. *Aquinas.* London & New York: Routledge, 2003.

Syndicat d'initiative de Tlemcen. *Tlemcen et sa région: Livret guide publié par le syndicat d'initiative de Tlemcen.* Toulouse: A. Thiriat, 1921.

Taliaferro, C. "The Project of Natural Theology." In William Lane Crag & J.P. Moreland (eds.), *The Blackwell Companion to Natural Theology,* 1–23. Malden, MA & Chichester, UK: Wiley Blackwell, 2012.

Taylor, R.C. "Averroes: Religious Dialectic and Aristotelian Philosophical Thought." In P. Adamson & R.C. Taylor (eds.), *Cambridge Companion to Arabic Philosophy,* 180–200. Cambridge: Cambridge University Press, 2005.

Terzioğlu, D. "Where *ʿİlm-i ḥāl* Meets Catechism: Islamic Manuals of Religious Instruction in the Ottoman Empire in the Age of Confessionalization." *Past & Present* 220(2013): 79–114.

Thiele, J. "Abū Hāshim al-Jubbāʾī's (d. 321/933) Theory of 'States' (*aḥwāl*) and Its Adoption by Ashʿarite Theologians." In Sabine Schmidtke (ed.), *The Oxford Handbook of Islamic Theology,* 364–83. New York & Oxford: Oxford University Press, 2016.

Thiele, J. "Between Cordoba and Nīsābūr: The Emergence and Consolidation of Ashʿarism (Fourth–Fifth/Tenth–Eleventh Century)." In Sabine Schmidtke (ed.), *The Oxford Handbook of Islamic Theology,* 225–41. New York & Oxford: Oxford University Press, 2016.

Thiele, J. "Facing the Mahdi's True Belief: Abū ʿAmr al-Salālijī's Ashʿarite Creed and the Almohads' Claim to Religious Authority." *al-ʿUṣūr al-Wusṭā* 26(2018): 96–112.

Thiele, J. "Ashʿarism in the Hafsid Era." In A. Shihadeh & J. Thiele (eds.), *Philosophical Theology in Islam: Later Ashʿarism East and West,* 298–336. Leiden: Brill, 2020.

Thom, P. "Logic and Metaphysics in Avicenna's Modal Syllogistic." In Sh. Rahman, T. Street, & H. Tahiri (eds.), *The Unity of Sciences in the Arabic Tradition: Metaphysics, Logic and Epistemology and Their Interactions,* 361–76. Dordrecht: Springer, 2008.

Thorndike, L. *A History of Magic and Experimental Science.* London: Macmillan, 1923.

Trieger, A. "Origins of Kalām." In Sabine Schmidtke (ed.), *The Oxford Handbook of Islamic Theology,* 27–43. New York & Oxford: Oxford University Press, 2016.

Tritton, A.S. *Muslim Theology.* London: Luzac, 1947.

Vallicella, W.F. "Divine Simplicity." *The Stanford Encyclopedia of Philosophy* (Winter 2023 Edition), Edward N. Zalta & Uri Nodelman (eds.). URL = <https://plato.stanford.edu/archives/win2023/entries/divine-simplicity/>.

Van Dalen, D. *Doubt, Scholarship and Society in 17th Century Central Sudanic Africa.* Leiden: Brill, 2016.

Van den Boogert, N. *The Berber Literary Tradition of the Sous: With an Edition and Translation of "The Ocean of Tears" by Muḥammad Awzal (d.1749).* Leiden: Nederlands Instituut voor het Nabije Oosten, 1997.

Van Ess, J. "The Logical Structure of Islamic Theology." In G.E. von Grünebaum (ed.), *Logic in Classical Islamic Culture,* 21–50. Wiesbaden: Otto Harrassowitz, 1970.

Van Ess, J. *The Flowering of Muslim Theology.* Cambridge, MA: Harvard University Press, 2006.

Vasalou, S. *Moral Agents and Their Deserts: The Character of Mu'tazilite Ethics.* Princeton: Princeton University Press, 2008.

Vasalou, S. *Ibn Taymiyya's Theological Ethics.* Oxford & New York: Oxford University Press, 2016.

Vikør, K. *Sufi and Scholar on the Desert Edge: Muḥammad b. 'Alī al-Sanūsī and His Brotherhood.* Evanston, IL: Northwestern University Press, 1995.

Von Grünebaum, G. & T.M. Abel. *Az-Zarnuji's Instruction of the Student: The Method of Learning.* New York: King's Crown Press, 1947.

Von Kügelgen, A. *Averroes und die arabische Moderne: Ansätze zu einer Neubegründung des Rationalismus im Islam.* Leiden: Brill, 1994.

Watt, W.M. "The Authenticity of the Works Attributed to al-Ghazālī." *Journal of the Royal Asiatic Society* 84(1952): 24–45.

Watt, W.M. *Islamic Philosophy and Theology.* Edinburgh: Edinburgh University Press, 1962.

Watt, W.M. *Islamic Philosophy and Theology: An Extended Survey.* Edinburgh: Edinburgh University Press, 1985.

Watt, W.M. *Islamic Creeds: A Selection.* Edinburgh: Edinburgh University Press, 1994.

Wickens, G.M. *The Nasirean Ethics.* London: George Allen & Unwin, 1964.

Wielenberg, E.J. "Divine Deception." In Trent Dougherty & Justin P. McBrayer (eds.), *Skeptical Theism: New Essays,* 236–49. Oxford: Oxford University Press, 2014.

Wilson, C. *Epicureanism at the Origins of Modernity.* Oxford: Oxford University Press, 2008.

Wisnovsky, R. "The Nature and Scope of Arabic Philosophical Commentary in Post-Classical (ca.1100–1900) Islamic Intellectual History: Some Preliminary Observations." In P. Adamson, H. Balthussen, & M.W.F. Stone (eds.), *Philosophy, Science and Exegesis in Greek, Arabic and Latin Commentaries,* vol. 2, 149–91. London: Institute of Advanced Studies, 2004.

Wisnovsky, R. "One Aspect of the Avicennian Turn in Sunni Theology." *Arabic Sciences and Philosophy* 14(2004): 65–100.

Wisnovsky, R. "Avicenna." In Peter Adamson & Richard Tayler (eds.), *The Cambridge Companion to Arabic Philosophy,* 92–136. Cambridge: Cambridge University Press, 2005.

Wisnovsky, R. "Avicennism and Exegetical Practice in the Early Commentaries on the Ishārāt." *Oriens* 41(2013): 349–78.
Wolff, M. *El-Senusi's Begriffsentwicklung des muhammedanischen glaubensbekenntnisses.* Leipzig: F.C.W. Vogel, 1848.
Wright, Z.V. *Realizing Islam: The Tijaniyya in North Africa and the Eighteenth-Century Muslim World.* Chapel Hill: University of North Carolina Press, 2020.
Zagzebski, L. *Philosophy of Religion: An Historical Introduction.* Malden, MA: Blackwell, 2007.
Zaman, M.Q. "Miḥna." In Richard C. Martin (ed.), *Encyclopedia of Islam and the Muslim World*, vol. 2, 448–50. New York: Macmillan, 2004.
Zarepour, M.S. "Avicenna on Mathematical Infinity." *Archiv für Geschichte der Philosophie* 102(2020): 379–425.
Zuppolini, B. "Aristotle on Per Se Accidents." *Ancient Philosophy* 38(2018): 113–35.
Zysow, A. "Karrāmiyya." In Sabine Schmidtke (ed.), *The Oxford Handbook of Islamic Theology*, 252–62. New York & Oxford: Oxford University Press, 2016.

Index

For the benefit of digital users, indexed terms that span two pages (e.g., 52–53) may, on occasion, appear on only one of those pages.

'Abduh, Muḥammad, 257–58
Abū 'Abbās Aḥmad I, 6–7, 245–46
Abū 'Abdallāh Muḥammad IV, 6–7, 233, 243, 245–46
Abū Madyan, 6, 236–37
Africa. *See* Aḥmad Bābā al-Timbuktī; Dan Fodio; *Kabbe*; Sanūsī, reception in sub-Saharan Africa
Aḥmad Bābā al-Timbuktī, 252–53
Almohads, 23, 24, 25–26
  See also Ibn Tūmart
Āmidī, Sayf al-Dīn, 134, 273n.4
anthropomorphism, 18–20, 21, 22–24, 47, 51–52, 53, 65, 82–83, 141, 161, 162–63, 199
Ash'arī, Abū l-Ḥasan, 20, 22, 36, 169–70, 171–72
Ash'arism
  on anthropomorphism, 23, 47, 51–52, 65, 141, 146–47, 162–63, 199
  core principles of, 21–22
  differences between Eastern and North African, 26–30, 117–18, 139–40, 142, 157–58
  on imitation in creed, 32–40
  on natural and occult sciences, 189–94, 236–44
  spread in North Africa, 22–26
  and Sufism, 235–36
  See also divine command morality; occasionalism
Averroes, 31–32, 133, 156–57
Avicenna
  didactic poem on medicine, 16
  on divine simplicity, 155–57
  on incipients without beginning, 133
  logic, 86, 97–98, 104, 107, 110, 112
  mapping argument, 135–36
  on necessary existence, 145
  proofs for the existence of God, 116–17, 139–40

Baghdādī, 'Abd al-Qāhir, 36, 125, 138–39
Bakkī al-Kūmī, Muḥammad, 35, 40, 43, 50, 51
Balawī, Aḥmad al-Wādī'āshī, 6–7, 8, 10, 245–46
Bāqillānī, Abū Bakr, 44, 125, 138–39
Bayḍāwī, al-Qāḍī, 26–27, 28–29, 117–18, 166–67

causation
  Humean theories of, 182–83, 193–94
  secondary causation, 126, 127, 128, 133, 169–70, 192–93, 229, 239
  sine qua non causes, 187
  See also creation of human acts; occasionalism
Christians
  Sanūsī on, 13, 47–48, 141, 145–46, 200–1
  theology, 31, 82–83
  trinity, 150
  views of Jesus, 78–79, 200
conditionals, logic of, 107–12
creation of human acts, 179–87
  See also occasionalism

Dan Fodio, Usman, 253
Dawānī, Jalāl al-Dīn, 29–30, 95–96, 140, 167, 220–21
divine command ethics, 22, 29–30, 183–84, 206–19
divine deception, 215–19

divine simplicity. *See* Avicenna; God's attributes; Mu'tazilism

essentialist/externalist propositions, 98–101

free will. *See* Creation of human acts

Ghazālī, Abū Ḥāmid
  against anthropomorphism, 23, 162
  Deliverance from Error, 235–36
  on imitation, 35
  on kalam theology, 31–32
  on logic, 84–85, 140
  on miracles, 69
  against the philosophers, 27, 82–83
  Revival of the Religious Sciences, 11–12, 79
  the 'rule of interpretation', 148
  Trails of the Worshippers (falsely attributed), 225
God
  Avicenna's proofs for the existence of, 116–17, 139–40
  as just, 18–19, 23–24, 214–15
  Juwaynī's proofs for the existence of, 125–27, 132
  Sanūsī's proofs for the existence of, 61–63, 125–40
  as timeless, 129–30, 144–45
God's attributes
  attributes of acts (*afʿāl*), 69–70
  entitative (*maʿānī*) attributes, 60, 67–69, 149–55
  as eternal and immutable, 163–65
  as necessary of existence, 145, 157–59
  negative (*salbiyya*) attributes, 60, 64–67, 143–49
  per se (*nafsiyya*) attributes, 59–60, 122–23, 141–43
  seven core attributes, 159–63
  twenty attributes, 58–59
  See also anthropomorphism; *ḥāl*
great chain of being, 227–28

ḥāl, 60–61, 150–51, 153–54, 269n.3
Ḥanbalism, 19–20, 21, 65, 82–83, 146, 148–49, 161, 167, 195, 196–97, 200, 202–3

Ibn Abī Zayd al-Qayrawānī, 22–23, 24–25, 79, 256–57
Ibn al-'Arabī, Abū Bakr, 25–27, 37–38, 188
Ibn 'Arabī, Muḥyī al-Dīn, 25–26, 29–30, 82–83, 235–36
Ibn 'Arafa, 15, 85–86, 106, 111, 134–35
Ibn 'Aṭā'ullāh al-Iskandarī, 11–12, 235–36
Ibn Dihāq, 25–27, 166, 192–93
Ibn Ḥanbal, 19–20, 196
Ibn Khaldūn, 24, 31–32, 235–36
Ibn Rushd. *See* Averroes
Ibn Sīnā. *See* Avicenna
Ibn Taymiyya, 2–3, 147–48, 167, 213–14, 257–58
Ibn al-Tilimsānī, 25–28, 133–34, 136, 139–40, 157, 164, 166, 173, 188, 212, 220
Ibn Tūmart, 23–26, 79
Ibn Wāṣil, 104, 106, 107
Ibn Zakrī, 10–11, 35, 43, 51, 54–55, 245–46
Ījī, 'Aḍud al-Dīn, 16, 26–27, 29, 166–67, 217
'ilm-i ḥāl, 254–55

Jazūlī, Aḥmad, 236–37
Jesus, 78–79, 200–1
Juwaynī, Imām al-Ḥaramayn
  against anthropomorphism 23, 162
  on the creation of human acts, 185, 188–89
  on existence not being an attribute 142–43
  on proofs for God's existence 125–27, 132
  on the "state" (*ḥāl*), 150–51
  The Guidance, 25–26, 32–34, 77, 131–32, 139, 142–43, 150–51, 162, 166, 188, 192–93, 197–98, 217–18

Kabbe, 14, 252–53
Kadizadelis, 254–55
Kasb. *See* creation of human acts
Kātib Çelebī, 254–55
Khūnajī, Afḍal al-Dīn, 16, 86–88, 106–7

Leo Africanus, 7–8

magic, 177, 241–43, 244
Mallālī, Muḥammad, 8–17, 29, 53–54, 190–91, 193–94, 236–38, 241–42, 243, 245–46, 247–48
Manjūr, Aḥmad, 55, 248–49
Māturīdism, 20, 70–71, 91, 150–51, 167, 169–70, 195, 196–97, 208, 213–14, 255
miḥna, 196–97
  See also Quran
miracles, 23–24, 68–69, 72–73, 176–77, 198, 217–19
modal logic, 101–7
Muqtaraḥ, Taqī al-Dīn
  argument against incipients without beginning, 137–38
  commentary on Juwaynī's *Guidance*, 25–26, 77, 166, 197–98
  debates Christians in Egypt, 166
  on imitation, 33–34
  on the possibility of women prophets, 77
  Secrets of Reason, 25–26, 166, 173, 188
Mu'tazilis
  declared unbelievers by Ibn Dihāq, 192–93
  declared their opponents unbelievers, 82–83, 196–97, 270n.15
  on God's attributes, 18–19, 149–51, 153–55
  on God's Speech, 201–4
  Ḥanafīs and, 18–19, 82–83
  on the impossibility of women prophets, 77, 211
  and the Miḥna, 196–97
  on moral values, 18–19, 206, 211

necessary existence, 145

occasionalism
  and ethics, 221–24, 229–30
  and monotheism, 78, 176–77, 192–93
  and natural and occult sciences, 189–94, 238–44
  rooted in God's Power and Will, 66–67, 179–80, 188
  and the veneration of saints, 239
  See also causation; creation of human acts
orthodoxy and orthopraxy, 31–32, 82–83
Ottomans. *See 'ilm-i ḥāl*; Kātib Çelebī; Sanūsī, reception in Ottoman Turkey

Philoponus, 131–32

Qāḍī 'Iyāḍ, 79
Quran
  creation of, 18
  figurative and literal interpretation of, 18, 47, 65, 146–47, 148, 162–63, 199
  See also anthropomorphism; God's Attributes; miḥna; miracles
Qushayrī, 36–37, 225, 231–32, 235–36

Rāzī, Fakhr al-Dīn
  on the creation of human acts, 185
  debates theological opponents, 167
  and the development of Arabic logic, 86
  and the development of Islamic theology, 25–29
  on the divine attributes, 157–58
  Landmarks of the Principles of Religion, 25–26, 27–28, 117–18, 121, 133–34, 139–40, 157, 166, 173, 212
  on proofs for the existence of God, 117–18, 119, 121, 133–34
  on reason and moral values, 212

Sāḥilī al-Mālaqī, Muḥammad, 237, 240
Salafism, 19–20, 147–48, 213–14, 258
Salāljī, 'Uthmān, 25–27, 162, 188
Sanūsī
  against anthropomorphism, 47, 51–52, 65, 141, 146–47
  contemporary opponents of, 10–11, 54–55
  on divine command morality, 183–85, 207–13
  on divine deception, 216–18
  on divine justice, 214–15

Sanūsī (*cont.*)
reception in Egypt, 250–51
reception in Maghreb, 247–49, 251–52
reception in Malay Archipelago, 14, 55–56, 250–51, 254–55
reception in Ottoman Turkey, 254–55
reception in sub-Saharan Africa, 14, 252–54
as saint, 11–13, 245–47
on the "state" (*ḥāl*), 60–61, 150–51, 153–54, 269n.3
students of, 247–48
studied by commoners, 6, 50, 54–55, 80–81
as Sufi, 222–25, 231–33, 235–39
teachers of, 9–11
translations of, 1, 80–81, 252–53
versifications of, 89, 250–51, 252–53
works of, 14–16
works questionably attributed to, 17, 190–91, 241–43
Sanūsiyya Sufi order, 256–57
Shādhilī, Abū l-Ḥasan, 236–37
Shahrastānī, Muḥammad, 185, 187, 270n.16
Sharīf, Abū Yaḥyá, 25–27, 134–35, 166, 188, 220, 273n.4
Shi'ism, 18–19, 29–30, 75–76, 91, 167, 195, 213–14, 235–36
Sufism
and Ash'arism, 235–36
neo-Sufism, 256–57
panentheism, 29–30, 82–83, 235–36
and popular religion, 241–42
See also Ibn 'Arabī; Ibn 'Aṭā'ullāh; Jazūlī; Qushayrī; Sāḥilī; Sanūsī as Sufi; Shādhilī; Zarrūq
Suyūṭī, Jalāl al-Dīn, 255–56

Taftāzānī, Sa'd al-Dīn, 87–88, 90–91, 166–67
Tha'ālibī, 'Abd al-Raḥmān, 9, 221, 228
Time. *See* God, as timeless
Ṭūsī, Naṣīr al-Dīn, 166–67, 220–21

Ubbī, Muḥammad, 15–16, 228

women
and male-oriented philosophical ethics, 220–21
on the possibility of women prophets, 77, 211
required by Sanūsī to learn the creed, 45–46, 53–54

Zabīdī, Muḥammad Murtaḍá, 255–56
Zamakhsharī, Jārullāh Maḥmūd, 204, 266n.20
See also Mu'tazilīs
Zarrūq, Aḥmad, 38–39, 43, 50, 51, 79, 235–37, 250
Zayyānid dynasty, 6–7, 233, 243, 245–46
See also Abū 'Abbās Aḥmad I; Abū 'Abdallāh Muḥammad IV